SSSP

Springer
Series in
Social
Psychology

SSSP

Kelly G. Shaver

The Attribution of Blame
Causality, Responsibility,
and Blameworthiness

Springer-Verlag
New York Berlin Heidelberg Tokyo

Kelly G. Shaver
Department of Psychology
College of William and Mary
Williamsburg, Virginia 23185
U.S.A.

With 12 Figures

Library of Congress Cataloging in Publication Data
Shaver, Kelly G.,
    The attribution of blame.
    (Springer series in social psychology)
    Bibliography: p.
    Includes index.
    1. Attribution (Social psychology)   I. Title.
II. Series.
HM291.S45   1985   302   85-2688

Media conversion by Ampersand Publisher Services, Inc., Rutland, Vermont.
Printed and bound by R.R. Donnelley & Sons, Harrisonburg, Virginia.
Printed in the United States of America.

9 8 7 6 5 4 3 2 1

ISBN 0-387-96120-8 Springer-Verlag New York Berlin Heidelberg Tokyo
ISBN 3-540-96120-8 Springer-Verlag Berlin Heidelberg New York Tokyo

Once again, to Carole

Preface

How can we identify the causes of events? What does it mean to assert that someone is responsible for a moral affront? Under what circumstances should we blame others for wrongdoing? The related, but conceptually distinct, issues of causality, responsibility, and blameworthiness that are the subject of this book play a critical role in our everyday social encounters. As very young children we learn to assert that "it wasn't *my* fault," or that "I didn't *mean* to do it." Responsibility and blame follow us into adulthood, as personal or organizational failings require explanation.

Although judgments of moral accountability are quickly made and adamantly defended, the process leading to those judgments is not as simple as it might seem. Psychological research on causality and responsibility has not taken complete advantage of a long tradition of philosophical analysis of these concepts. Philosophical discussions, for their part, have not been sufficiently aware of the psychological realities. An assignment of blame is a social explanation. It is the outcome of a process that begins with an event having negative consequences, involves judgments about causality, personal responsibility, and possible mitigation. The result can be an assertion, or a denial, of individual blameworthiness. The purpose of this book is to develop a comprehensive theory of *how* people assign blame.

This theory traces the course of the process through which a rational perceiver would assign blame for a moral offense, while recognizing that errors can, and do, occur. The theory considers both philosophical investigation of "causality" and "responsibility" and the more recent social psychological study of what these terms mean to ordinary people. What is the cause? Is anyone responsible? Who is to blame? The book suggests how the answers to these questions should be combined into a single process that constitutes the attribution of blame.

Any scholarly endeavor necessarily builds both on intellectual tradition and on exchange with students and colleagues, and this work is no exception. The book has been a long time in the making: I was first introduced to the analysis of intention in an undergraduate course in the philosophy of mind over twenty years ago, and soon thereafter my conception of the attribution process was shaped by Edward E. Jones and the ideas of Fritz Heider and Harold H. Kelley. More recently I have drawn on the knowledge of a colleague in Philosophy, David Jones, and the expertise of a colleague in Psychology, Cynthia H. Null. Over the years my views on causality, responsibility, and blameworthiness have been influenced in discussions with numerous students, particularly Matthew S. Davis, Charles W. Huff, and Frances G. Slocumb.

I am particularly grateful to the staff at Springer-Verlag for their encouragement to undertake this project, and for their help during its completion. I am also grateful to the Anheuser-Busch Corporation, whose Faculty Research Fellowship to the College of William and Mary supported the initial work on the book. Thanks are due to Edward Sankowski for his comments on philosophical portions of the book, and especially to Daniel M. Wegner for his thorough and perceptive review of the entire manuscript. Their suggestions have contributed substantially to the final product.

Williamsburg, VA   KELLY G. SHAVER

Contents

Preface   vii

1. **Events and Accountability**   1

   Explaining Negative Events   3
   Attribution in Social Judgment   6
   Toward a Theory of Blame   8

2. **Causes and Explanations**   11

   The Psychological-Context View of Scienific Explanation   12
   The Nature of Causality   16
   Causality and the Theory of Blame   30

3. **The Attribution of Causality**   35

   Personal and Impersonal Causality   36
   The Naive Analysis of Action   38
   Multiple Events: An Individual Differences View   39
   Multiple Antecedents of Effects or Actions   45
   Perception of Multiple Causes   50
   Attribution of Causality   59

4. **Dimensions of Responsibility**   63

   Senses of Responsibility   64
   Moral Responsibility Versus Legal Responsibility   67
   Causality: A Precondition for Responsibility?   70
   Standards for Moral Evaluation   72
   The Dilemma of Determinism   74
   Characteristics of Voluntary Action   78
   Some Warnings About Excuses   81

Responses to an Accusation 83
Dimensions of Responsibility 84

5. **Attributions of Responsibility** **87**

Levels of Responsibility 88
The Origins of Intention 96
Dimensions of Responsibility and Attribution 101

6. **Rationality and Bias: Intentions, Reasons, and Motives** **115**

Definitions of Intention 115
Reasons as Causes 122
Motivation of Perceivers 129

7. **Attributions of Causality and Responsibility:**
    Discovered or Imposed? **137**

What Sorts of Causes? 138
Dimensions of Responsibility 143

8. **A Theory of Blame** **155**

Metatheory for the Attribution of Blame 156
A Theory of Blame Assignment 162
The Assignment of Blame 165
Conclusions 173

References **177**

Author Index **185**

Subject Index **189**

Chapter 1
Events and Accountability

What was the cause? Is anyone responsible? Who is to blame? These are the first questions asked after a misfortune or a moral affront. The event itself could be as privately experienced as a lovers' quarrel or as public as technological failure at a nuclear power generating plant; it could could have been produced carelessly or after careful premeditation; its consequences could be as ephemeral as momentary chagrin or as terrible as widespread destruction and loss of life. Whatever their other features, negative events demand explanation, a demand frequently satisfied by finding someone who is *answerable* for the occurrence. How that search proceeds is the topic of this book.

At first it might appear that the straightforward questions about causality, responsibility, and culpability would have an equally direct answer: People are accountable for the events they bring about. But is this always, or even usually, the case? Most probably not, and some of the complications can be illustrated by an incident that occurs in M. C. Smith's (1981) novel *Gorky Park*, a thriller that chronicles a Moscow homicide investigator's attempt to unravel the mystery surrounding a murder of three people in one of the city's parks. The story blends personal courage and betrayal with political intrigue, painting a picture of a criminal justice system in which judgments of personal responsibility for wrongdoing are heavily influenced by ideology.

At one point the investigator hears a lecture given to the staff of the prosecutor's office by an anonymous doctor from the "Serbsky Institute":

> It is a finding of the institute that criminals suffer from a psychological disturbance we term pathoheterodoxy.... In an unjust society a man may violate laws for valid social or economic reasons. In a just society there are no valid reasons except mental illness.... Recognizing this fact ... affords the violator an opportunity to be quarantined until his illness can be expertly treated.... It is our duty to spare society from injury and to save a sick man from the consequences of his acts. (Smith, 1981, p. 187)

In short, if a society treats its people equitably, the only presumed cause of criminal activity is mental illness, which cause absolves the individual of any responsibility for offenses against the law. The lecture was not a central element of the story, but it does identify three general perspectives from which the issue of blameworthiness might be examined.

First, the judgments of causality, responsibility, and culpability made in a particular case are affected by more widely held cultural values. A society that shared the doctor's opinion would have empty jails and overflowing mental hospitals. In the context of the novel, and assuming the worst about Soviet justice, the position that all crime is caused by mental illness does sound quite sinister. Fairness requires noting that involuntary civil commitment in the United States has also been characterized as a means of controlling deviance (Szasz, 1974), and that the recent "guilty but mentally ill" verdict in criminal trials is a more limited version of what the physician in M. C. Smith's novel (1981) has proposed. The task of this chapter, however, is neither to examine the values inherent in the Western cultural tradition nor to document the rules of a democratic society. Those values and rules will remain in the background, receiving attention indirectly through discussion of Western philosophical thought regarding causality and responsibility. Especially in the definition of causality as including human agency, and in my position on the issue of free will versus determinism, the larger cultural perspective will be represented in a psychological analysis of blame.

A second general perspective on blame that is illustrated by the example is that of the perceiver's own motives in the situation. Quite apart from the societal purposes that might also be served, confining a criminal offender in a mental institution allows the imprisoning agent to assume the role of "healer" rather than "avenger." In an even more cynical view, the discovery by the fictitious doctor of a condition of "pathoheterodoxy" will enhance still further his status as one trained to heal the sufferers from this antisocial behavior pattern. Again, these ulterior motives are easy to imagine in the context provided by the novel.

To argue that personal motives may influence the assignment of blame is not, however, to claim that the motivation is always negative. For example, in Western legal tradition there are circumstances in which blame will be assigned to a particular person not because of an event that person has actually caused, but because of the necessity to compensate an identified victim. Such compensation is, in reality, an error in attribution, but it is one committed in the service of a positive goal.

Nor is it always the case that the perceiver will be aware of his or her motives for attributing blame. For example, if people subscribe to the belief that the world is a relatively stable and predictable place, in which suffering is the just consequence either of incorrect action or unworthy character, they may unwittingly blame innocent victims of misfortune. Drawing examples from law, education, and social problems, Ryan (1976) argues that although the true cause of the problem is usually inherent in the structure of society, blame is often placed on a victim. Unemployment, for instance, can be seen not as the consequence of general economic conditions, but as the product of individual laziness. In a narrower sense, experimental research on people's need to believe in a just world (Lerner & Miller, 1978) has identified situational factors that will lead perceivers to blame demonstrably "innocent" victims of suffering. Especially in the latter circumstances, where the socially desirable response would be a mixture of understanding and sympathy, it is highly unlikely that perceivers are consciously aware of how their motives are influencing their assignments of responsibility and blame. Some of the reasons why an individual perceiver might blame one person while exonerating another are considered in Chapter 6, as part of the the discussion of the potential for distortion in the attribution of responsibility and the assignment of blame.

The third general perspective on blame inherent in the example has to do not with the values of the larger society or with the motives of individual perceivers, but with the *process* of blame assignment through which those values and motives can be applied. The fictitious doctor's explanation includes an identified cause of criminal activity—the troublesome "pathoheterodoxy"—a notion that the offender's actions produce consequences that are distasteful to the society, and a proposal for "treatment" of the offender that depends fundamentally on this conception of the process. The doctor's ascription of all criminal behavior to mental illness is a logical, though extreme, extension of the *Hadfield* (1800), *M'Naghten* (1843), *Durham v. United States* (1954), and *United States v. Brawner* (1972) rules for the criminal plea of not guilty by reason of insanity. If we are willing to excuse the criminal activity that we believe was the consequence of a mental disease, the product of an irresistible impulse, or the result of a diminished capacity to distinguish right from wrong, we are asserting that the action was not under the personal, volitional control of the offender. This assertion, like the fictitious doctor's view of criminal activity, presumes the existence of a particular constellation of cause, intention, and volition that *would* lead to an assignment of blame and to which the "insane" person's actions are an exception.

In short, cultural values and individual motives are part of the "why" people blame others, but whatever the value or motive there ought to be a common description of "how" blame is assigned. So, although in Chapter 4 it is shown that the assignment of criminal responsibility is not a perfect model for the assignment of blame for a moral offense, both judgments rely on a similar process through which a "rational perceiver" might proceed. Charting the course of that process is the goal of this book.

Explaining Negative Events

To begin by belaboring the obvious—people are never blamed for doing good. The events of interest to a psychological analysis of blame therefore will be those social occurrences or changes in physical states that lead to negative consequences. Note that by this definition neither a physical object nor a person would be included in the class of events, although changes in the state of the object, or various actions of the person, would constitute events. Neither would it be likely that an "event" would be a physical happening outside the realm of experience of persons (the metaphorical tree falling in the forest with no one to hear it would not, by this criterion, be an event). Pleasant features of the physical environment and positive social behavior would also be outside the class of events of interest to a psychological theory of blame.

In other words, anything negative that initiated what Kruglanski, Hamel, Maides, and Schwartz (1978) have called the *epistemic search* would be included in the category of events to be accounted for through a process of blame assignment. The definition rightly emphasizes the role of the perceiver, by limiting the domain to those *perceived* events *thought* to have negative consequences. Not all perceivers will notice events to the same degree, and not all will agree on the magnitude (or even presence) of the negative consequences presumed to flow from the event. The definition avoids becoming tautological by excluding physical events not ordinarily accessible to the senses (such as neurochemical changes in the brain) and by excluding objects and people not presently undergoing some change that leads to negative consequences. Neither a mountain range nor a sociopath is an event, although an avalanche and a specific action of the sociopath would be events for which causes would be sought, responsibility would be determined, and blame would be assigned.

An assignment of blame is, therefore, a particular sort of social explanation. It is the outcome of a process that begins with an event having negative consequences, involves judgments about causality, personal responsibility, and possible mitigation. The result can be a denial, or an assertion, of individual blameworthiness. But the process is by no means as simple as it would seem.

Consider the assertion "He caused the harm." For this assertion to be meaningful, there must be a consensual definition of precisely what constitutes a "cause" of any occurrence, positive or negative. In contrast to the way the term is frequently employed in the physical sciences, the accepted definition of cause must permit human actions to serve as the causes of events. Finally, the assertion assumes that perceivers can in theory isolate the causal contribution made by a person from other conditions that might have been involved in the production of the occurrence. Philosophers have been trying to explicate the concept of causality for centuries, and the debate continues today, so it cannot be taken for granted that the term's meaning is unequivocal. Careful construction of the foundation for a theory of blame assignment will, therefore, require discussion of the major philosophical positions on causation.

Even if it is possible to arrive at a logically defensible definition of a "cause," only half the necessary work on the subject of causality will have been accomplished. Philosophical analysis of the concept of causality represents the rules of language and thought as they have been reflected on by experts. To some degree, then, this kind of analysis provides a prescription for how a rational perceiver *should* conceive of causality. Whether or not that conception is inherent in the causal judgments made by ordinary perceivers (without philosophical reflection) is a question that can be answered only by examining social psychological research. It is the task of this volume to develop a psychological model of blame assignment, and that requires study of the perception of social causality (as distinct from the perception of physical causality represented in the work of Michotte, 1963).

What is true for causality is true for other elements of the process as well. Moral philosophy suggests what factors ought to be involved in judgments of responsibility, and social psychological research has identified some of the factors that naive perceivers believe are involved. Linguistic analysis can describe the features of mitigation, and social psychology can show what excuses will be accepted for misbehavior. In an important sense, philosophical discussions of causality, responsibility, and culpability can be regarded as archival data, while the data from social psychological research are primarily experimental. Neither source of concepts is sufficient by itself: Only a synthesis of the two can produce a comprehensive psychological model of blame assignment.

Describing philosophical analysis as a source of archival data about blame assignment illustrates the uniquely *social* nature of the judgments involved. Philosophers can differentiate one sort of cause from another and in the abstract can provide a rational account of the relationship between cause and effect. Scientists can examine repeated instances of the occurrence of phenomena and offer their own "objective" view of causality. Each discipline, however, has its limits. Philosophers do not always agree on either the descriptions of events or the causal statements implied by those events. Asking a dozen philosophers whether human agents have free will is likely to produce a dozen different answers. For their part, scientists are limited by the state of the art of their instruments, the methods of analysis available to them, and the fact that their descriptions, like the philosophers' prescriptions, carry theoretical baggage that cannot be left behind on the platform. Indeed, showing the degree to which scientific endeavor is affected by the prevailing *Weltanschauung* of practicing scientists has been one of the principal contributions of recent work in the history of science (e.g., Kuhn, 1962).

The logical consequence of this line of reasoning is that the "Truth" about causality, responsibility, and culpability cannot be known apart from the intellectual tradition in which the questions have been asked. This conclusion has quite different implications for an analysis of blame, depending on whether the theory of blame to be constructed is a philosophical or a psychological theory. For philosophical purposes the prevailing intellectual tradition is an obstacle to understanding, an obstacle that can never be overcome. The absence of a theory-free criterion is undoubtedly one of the major reasons that philosophical debate about the nature of causality still rages on, centuries after it began. For psychological purposes, however, the prevailing intellectual tradition, particularly as expressed in philosophy, *is* the criterion. An individual perceiver's judgments will be considered rational if they conform to the standards identified through conceptual analysis. So, while it is essential for a theory of blame to specify in detail the intellectual foundation on which it rests, it is not necessary to show that this foundation, in turn, reflects "the truth."

That conclusions will necessarily be theory laden has differential implications not only for discovery of "the truth," but also for tolerance for "error." In a philosophical approach to the assignment of blame, error in reasoning is to be excluded at all costs. By constrast, in a psychology of blame, "error" (defined as a discrepancy between the conceptually based ideal of what rational perceivers ought to do in the abstract and what a specified perceiver actually does) is an aspect of judgment to be included. Indeed, one of the objectives of a psychological theory of blame is to suggest situational factors that might lead to errors in judgment and to identify points in the process where such errors would be most likely to occur. The overall psychological model will be a rational one, but it will not be exclusively so. Thus, the resulting model is a special case of attribution theory, a body of work in social psychology that attempts to account for the social explanations offered by "naive perceivers."

Attribution in Social Judgment

To blame someone for the occurrence of a negative event is, as already noted, to make a uniquely social judgment. But the judgment itself is not unique. Rather, it is much like the inferences individuals make to explain other aspects of their social worlds. In the attempts to understand why people act the way they do, or to identify significant elements of people's personalities, we engage in *attribution processes*: cognitive processes directed toward identification of the invariant properties of people and features of the social environment.

Attribution theories outline the conditions that will presumably lead a perceiver to decide that a behavior or event of interest was produced by a *dispositional property* of the person involved, not by factors in the external environment. Contemporary theory is founded on the comprehensive and fruitful work of Heider (1958), who systematically examined everyday language in order to formalize the ways in which any layman might interpret the actions of another. Not everyone has access to the principles of scientific psychology, or to its explanations for human action. Yet, everyone does attribute responsibility for events, describe people as if they had enduring personality characteristics, and assess the relative contributions of skill, motivation, and luck to the completion of tasks. What questions these "naive psychologists" ask will be reflected in language.

According to Heider's (1958) theory, the ordinary perceiver's analysis of action distinguishes dispositional aspects of personal force—ability, power, intention—from dispositional aspects of environmental force—task difficulty, opportunity, or luck. To complete a task, a person's ability must exceed the task difficulty, the person must have the intention to perform the task, and there must be exertion in the direction specified by the intention. Whether the event to be explained is task performance or not, an actor's personal responsibility is thought to increase as the ratio of personal force to environmental force increases. The present work owes a substantial intellectual debt to Heider's perceptive analysis of the everyday interpretations of events, and his ideas are discussed in greater detail in Chapter 5.

Suppose that a perceiver has determined that an action was intentionally produced. Does that intentional action inform the perceiver about the personal dispositions of the actor, or merely reflect strong pressures exerted by the social environment? This question states the problem addressed by correspondent inference theory (Jones & Davis, 1965; Jones & McGillis, 1976), a specific attributional model designed to make some of Heider's ideas more precisely testable. Perceivers often infer an actor's motives and dispositions from actions they have not personally witnessed (judgments rendered by juries are but one prominent example), and correspondent inference theory suggests a way that this can be accomplished. The theory first presumes that the actor had some foreknowledge of the consequences of his or her behavior, that there was an intention to bring about some of these known consequences, and that the actor had sufficient ability to translate the intention into a successful performance. Every action is conceived of as a *choice*, even if the choice is only between action and inaction.

If behavior can be considered the product of choices between two, or among multiple, possible courses of action, then the alternatives can be examined to enumerate the effects that would follow each choice. Whether they have witnessed the behavior or not, perceivers can use their own experience to reconstruct what effects would be likely, to identify the effects that would be common to all choices, and to isolate those effects unique to the course of action chosen. If these "noncommon" effects are few in number and low in assumed desirability, the perceiver can be certain that the action taken reflected a personal disposition. This correspondence between the action and the underlying disposition presumed to have produced it is, of course, greater for socially undesirable effects, so the model has obvious implications for an attributional analysis of blame. Correspondent inference theory, like Heider's naive analysis of action, receives more attention in Chapter 5.

Until this point in the outline of attribution theory, it might appear that attribution processes concentrate on the determination of responsibility once issues of causality have been settled, but that is not the case. Heider's work also bears on the perceiver's decisions about the causes of events, as does a more recent formulation of attribution theory by Kelley (1967, 1972, 1973). This body of theory assumes that there are two very different sets of circumstances in which causal inferences must be made: those in which repeated observations are possible and those in which there is only a single observation of the event of interest. When we look for the causes of our own internal states of pleasure or pain, we have a very long history of experience on which to draw, and the same lengthy acquaintance will characterize our interactions with close friends or family. So dispositional properties can be inferred with good reliability from repeated observations. By contrast, in many social situations, and especially in the case of the misfortunes and moral offenses that are the object of explanation by a psychology of blame, there is only a single instance.

When repeated observations are possible, Kelley's theory builds on Heider's suggestion that perceivers employ a variant of the logical Method of Difference (Mill, 1888): An effect should be attributed to that potential cause that is present when the effect is present, but absent when the effect is absent. If a perceiver observes an effect occurring distinctively in the presence of a particular actor, if that effect is consistently produced across different circumstances, and if other perceivers have also noticed the conjunction, then the perceiver can rather confidently attribute the effect to the actor involved.

If repeated observations, or comparisons with others, are not possible, the theory argues that the perceiver will rely on any one of several relatively stable cognitive structures called *schemata* to "fill in" for the missing data. For example, the law establishes penalties for various criminal activities on the assumption that for rational actors the penalties will serve as obstacles to prohibited behavior. Offenders who violate the laws in full knowledge of the penalties are judged more harshly than offenders who are unaware of the penalties, notwithstanding the notion that "Ignorance of the law is no excuse" (Holmes, 1881, p. 47). This sort of judgment reflects an attributional principle called *augmentation*, which holds that a presumed cause is endowed with greater force if it appears to have overcome an obstacle against the action performed. Kelley's (1967, 1973) attribution theory has served as a stimulus for a burgeoning social psychological literature on the attribution of causes for events, and it is considered more thoroughly in Chapter 3.

Toward a Theory of Blame

The attribution approach to social judgment lays an excellent foundation for the development of a theory of blame, but a complete account of the psychological process involved in inferences of causality, responsibility, and blameworthiness requires more. Attribution researchers have too frequently concentrated on the processes *specified in their own theories*, overlooking alternative explanations provided by the philosophy of mind, and virtually excluding from consideration personal motives that are inconsistent with the model of human beings as rational problem solvers. These cases in which the reach of attribution theory has exceeded its grasp are by no means limited to the attribution of causality and responsibility, but the problem must be addressed in any theory of blame.

Explorations of the meanings of causality and responsibility are, of course, as old as ancient philosophy. Discussions of the concepts of causality in the philosophy of science begin with Aristotle's (1952) theory of causes. His *formal* cause (the archetype or form for an entity) and *material* cause (the substrate out of which the entity comes to exist) are primarily descriptive of physical objects. But his notion of an *efficient* cause (the "primary source of the change or coming to rest") and his idea of a *final* cause (the "that for the sake of which" an action is performed or an entity is created) much more clearly pertain to human actions. Antecedents of the philosophy of mind and of the notion of responsibility can be seen still earlier, in Plato's *Dialogues* (1952). In the Phaedo, for example, Socrates asserts that the soul rules and governs the body, expressing his disappointment with the position that human action might be nothing other than bodily movement without internal direction.

The later development of the ideas of cause and responsibility has occupied a great deal of philosophical discourse, and debate on these issues continues today in the literature of action theory and moral philosophy. A selective review of philosophical treatments of causality appears in Chapter 2 in order to specify the conceptual foundation for the way in which the theory of blame will use the term. A similar selective review of moral philosophy and the notion of responsibility is the substance of Chapter 4, again to identify dimensions of responsibility that will be used here. It should be emphasized that neither of these chapters attempts to contribute to philosophical discourse on the topics of causality or responsibility. Rather, each reviews some of the fundamentals required for attributional discussions of causality (Chapter 3) and responsibility (Chapter 5).

The remaining chapters represent an attempt to deal with some of the other limitations in contempoary attribution theory. Chapter 6 discusses intention, reasons for acting, and the perceiver's motives in attributing responsibility and blame. It is concluded that notwithstanding some recent arguments to the contrary, an actor's reasons can serve as the causes of his or her behavior, and that a perceiver's motives may distort attributions of causality and responsibility. Chapter 7 presents research on causality and responsibility to make a general point about the relationship between theory and the attributional behavior that theory purports to describe. The first study reported suggests that the traditional distinction between "internal" and "external" causes may need to be supplemented by a third category of superphysical causality. The second study reports the outcome of a multidimensional scaling of responsibility-related words, finding support for one of the principal dimensions of responsibility, but including a caution to keep the theoretical structure in better touch with the "naive perceivers," whose judgments that structure seeks to explain.

The final chapter discusses excuses and mitigation and presents a theory of the assignment of blame. This theory incorporates both the philosophical distinctions and the psychological distinctions that have been discussed previously. It traces the course of the process through which a rational perceiver should assign blame for a negative occurrence, while recognizing that errors can and do occur. The theory suggests how answers to the questions "What is the cause?" "Is anyone responsible?" and "Who is to blame?" should be combined into a single process that constitutes the attribution of blame.

Chapter 2
Causes and Explanations

In the late afternoon of January 13, 1982, during a blinding snowstorm, Air Florida Flight 90 from Washington, D.C. to Tampa and Fort Lauderdale crashed into the Fourteenth Street Bridge just seconds after taking off from National Airport. The airplane had undergone de-icing procedures 45 minutes before take-off, but lumbered down the airport's 6,870-foot runway, failed to gain altitude, struck the bridge crowded with rush-hour traffic, and plunged into the iced-over waters of the Potomac River. Upon impact the tail section of the plane separated from the main portion of the fuselage, and this forward part of the aircraft quickly sank into the river. Only five of the 79 people aboard the plane were rescued; an additional four people were killed who had been traveling across the bridge at the time of impact.

The first set of questions raised by this tragic event is specific to the occurrence. Was the de-icing procedure performed too long before the actual take-off? Apart from its timing, was the de-icing performed skillfully? Did the pilots, unaccustomed to winter flying conditions, underestimate the magnitude of the problems they faced? Or were they more concerned with regaining the time lost on the schedule or taking off before the airport was closed than with the weather conditions? Should the airport officials have closed the runways and cancelled the flight as well as others scheduled for later in the day? Should the supervisors in the tower have noticed an ice build-up on the plane's wings during the time it spent waiting for permission to take off? Is the flight path—which is dictated by noise-abatement regulations that require an immediate turn in order to follow the river—inherently unsafe? Is the runway at National Airport just too short? (One of the other local airports has runways over 10,000 feet long.) How do the internal de-icing systems of the plane, a Boeing 737, compare with those of other aircraft? Were all of the other flight systems of the plane working properly? These and other specific questions are the ones that an individual perceiver might ask in attempting to understand the cause of the crash, and they are the sort of questions that the National

Transportation Safety Board might have asked in its search for the causes of the accident.

There is, however, a second set of questions raised by this occurrence, or by any other significant event. What does it mean to say that something is a cause and something else is an effect? Does the identification of a cause in one set of circumstances tell us anything about the likelihood that the same cause will produce the identical (or a similar) effect in the future? How can "the cause" of an event be distinguished from other factors in the situation that are merely "conditions" for the occurrence but not the true cause? Perhaps most importantly for our present purposes, how well do the descriptions of causality provided by traditional philosophy (both philosophy of science and metaphysics) correspond to the descriptions that might be given by ordinary people not trained in the language of philosophy? This second set of questions constitutes the subject matter of the present chapter, although the specific incident will be used to illustrate the principles involved. The causal analysis described here is necessarily selective, so a few words are in order about the reasons for the choices that have been made.

The Psychological-Context View of Scientific Explanation

As noted in Chapter 1, the present theory of blame relies on the insights provided by philosophical and psychological analyses of human knowledge and action. Within philosophy, epistemology (philosophical inquiry into human knowledge) and action theory (philosophical study of human behavior) provide a conceptual foundation for the study of causality, responsibility, and blameworthiness. Within psychology, the principles of attribution theory can be used to describe the inference process that leads to blame assignment. In none of these disciplines is there an unequivocal assertion of just what it is that people are doing when they are identifying the causes of events, or for that matter, determining which human agents, if any, should be held accountable for the occurrence of the events in question.

This problem can be illustrated by considering philosophical treatment of the notion of causality. Aristotle's (1952) theory of four causes was the most thoroughly specified ancient analysis of causality, with the final cause and efficient cause most closely approximating the contemporary meaning of "cause." General philosophical issues of causality can be seen throughout Western philosophy, as in Russell's (1945) history. A comprehensive study of the notion of causality in philosophy of science has more recently been completed in two volumes by Wallace (1972, 1974). Arguments about the nature of causation have typically been scholarly, but occasionally have been polemical. The current range of philosophical opinion includes the following views of Brand (1976):

> Causal phenomena are a constant factor in our lives; they are part of the
> ordinary furnishings of the universe. Understanding the nature of causation,

moreover, is a prerequisite for understanding free will, human action, time, laws of nature, empirical knowledge—indeed, almost every area of philosophical inquiry. (p. ii)

The other end of the spectrum is represented by modern proponents of Russell's (1925) remark that

The law of causality, I believe, like much that passes muster among philosophers, is a relic of a bygone age, surviving, like the [British] monarchy, only because it is erroneously supposed to do no harm. (p. 180)

Psychology in general, and social psychology in particular, have not devoted a comparable level of energy to questions about the nature of causality. But examples of equally vehement disagreement within psychological science spring readily to mind. Proponents of Freudian theory would argue that unconscious processes play an important role in human action, while subscribers to Skinnerian behaviorism would believe them to play no part whatsoever. Are there inherited racial differences in intelligence, and if so, would those differences have any implications for social policy? Obviously, the mere presence of controversy in a discipline is not a sufficient reason to dismiss the contributions that the discipline might make to a theory of blame assignment. At the same time, however, it is important to identify in conceptual terms the sources of potential disagreement. Such an identification can be accomplished through what I shall call the *psychological-context* view of scientific explanation.

The accumulation of scientific knowledge is often characterized in the popular press and even in textbooks on methodology as the orderly and gradual advancement of understanding, a continuous growth produced through the efforts of highly skilled but personally disinterested seekers after truth—steady, but dull. Recent analyses of the history of science, however, have begun to dispute both of these stereotypes.

First, in contrast to the view of science as continuous and gradual progress, Kuhn (1962), for one, has argued that real advancement in scientific understanding is characterized by infrequent but dramatic shifts in world view. Ideas such as Copernicus's heliocentric theory of the solar system and Einstein's general theory of relativity are considered truly revolutionary, that is, they are discontinuous changes in human thought that made it impossible to continue to believe a substantial portion of previous scientific knowledge. These occasional revolutionary ideas then constitute the working assumptions for subsequent generations of scientists, until the experiments and observations that form the core of what Kuhn calls "normal science" identify too many exceptions to the prevailing view.

Enough of these exceptions, or even of a few very critical ones, will force another dramatic reorganization of the conceptual landscape. As Wallace (1974) has noted, neither classical philosophers of science nor classical methodologists (some of whose work is now adduced as evidence for the view of science as discontinuous) would have subscribed to Kuhn's position. It must be emphasized that either view is making a statement about the psychological reality of practicing scientists. Even in a dramatic paradigm shift, what is changed is not the natural phenomena being studied, but the *psychological context* within which research is being carried out.

Second, just as Kuhn (1962) has suggested an alternative to the traditional view of the scientific enterprise as the steady accumulation of knowledge, so Holton (1973) has suggested a formal alternative to the view that the individual scientist is a passionless investigator driven only by a devotion to precision in method. Holton acknowledges that the published scientific literature is properly "dry-cleaned of the personal elements" (1973, p. 20), but points out that this antiseptic result does not do justice to the "personal struggle" of the individual scientist. The pursuit of knowledge is a creative process that involves conjecture, intuition, and a host of preconceptions, some of which would, no doubt, arise from the individual scientist's personal version of the prevailing paradigm.

This analysis is much more than a reiteration of the idea that science cannot be truly value free. It is a dimensional system that locates every scientific statement in what Holton calls a "proposition space." The x axis of this space represents the *purely empirical* content of any scientific statement, content that will "ultimately boil down to meter readings" (Holton, 1973, p. 21). The y axis of the space is perpendicular to the x axis and represents the *purely theoretical* content of the scientific statement, those "propositions concerning logic and mathematics" (1973, p. 21) that express relationships among elements of any theoretical structure. To qualify as a scientific statement, a proposition must not only fall on the plane described by these two axes, it must also have a value greater than zero on each dimension. Thus, to say that "20% of the public approves of the President's performance in his job" is to make an empirical statement, but not a scientific one. In a similar fashion, to claim that "God created the universe in seven days" is to make a theoretical statement, not a scientific one.

In Holton's (1973) view the published scientific literature falls on this plane of discourse, including both those theoretically relevant empirical propositions whose truth value can be verified through observation or experimentation and those empirically based theoretical propositions whose truth value and internal consistency can be established through logic and mathematics. What the plane does *not* include are what Holton calls the *thematic* aspects of science, either on the institutional level or on the level of the individual investigator. Examination of the discourse on the plane reveals "neither how the individual scientific mind arrives at the products that later can be fitted into the contingent plane, nor how science as an historical enterprise grows and changes" (1973, p. 23).

To take both the prevailing scientific world view and the individual investigator's preconceptions into account in the analysis, Holton (1973) suggests addition of a third dimension orthogonal to the first two. This z axis, which can be thought of as extending out from the flat page, contains both the *themata* of historical importance in science and the presuppositions of the individual researcher. Specification of the third dimension makes it immediately apparent that many of the significant scientific disagreements revolve around themata, not data or theory.

Consider the familiar argument about reductionism, the assertion that the theoretical formulations of one area can be reduced to the less molar terms of a different approach without any loss of meaning. For example, can the behavioral description of paranoia be reduced to a discussion of neurochemistry? This, of course, is the crux of the argument between the "behavioral model" and the "medical model" of emotional disorder. Adherents to the behavioral model do not dispute the empirical fact that various pharmacotherapeutic agents are differentially effective depending on the kind of emotional disorder involved (the x axis). Nor would the proponents of the behavioral model dispute the theoretical claims made (the y axis) on the basis of these pharmacologic findings. Rather, the argument centers on whether neurochemical events *alone* will ever account completely for the observed variations in symptoms and responses to medication. Thus the controversy is a thematic one, occurring on the z axis.

It is important to notice that investigators can disagree about one thematic element while agreeing about others, and that the themata themselves can change through time. Supporters of both the medical and behavioral models would certainly agree that emotional disorder *has* a cause, and they would agree that scientific methods are appropriate for discovering that cause (e.g., each would reject the "possession by demons" thema prevalent in the earliest days of the study of psychopathology). In his analysis Holton (1973) describes how some themata might remain quite stable through time, while others would wax and wane over the years.

This possibility for change through time is what interests the historian of science, and Wallace (1974) has actually suggested that change over time be represented as yet another dimension of the model, a t axis best thought of as a progression along a time line of the entire $x-y-z$ proposition space. Regardless of the number of dimensions in the model, what is critical in my view is that the themata, like the empirical observations and the theoretical propositions, are influential only because they are represented in the consciousness of individual historians of science, individual philosophers of science, and individual practicing researchers. What is a cause? What constitutes an adequate scientific explanation? These specific themata, like the more general *Weltanschauung* provided by the prevailing paradigm, form the psychological context for research and theory.

The psychological context is an implicit component of any scientific endeavor, but in the present circumstances it needs to be made explicit for two very different reasons. First, psychological study of blame has its roots in behavioral science, not in physical science, and the themata for the two are likely to be different. For example, in a standard work on the philosophy of science, Bunge (1959) equates explanation with prediction: "A theory can predict to the extent which it can describe and explain" (p. 307). But this particular thematic element is not shared by life or behavioral scientists. As Mayr (1965), a biologist, has noted in response, "It is evident that Bunge is a physicist; no biologist would have made such a statement. The theory of natural selection can describe and explain phenomena with considerable precision, but it cannot make reliable predictions . . . " (p. 43).

Very few psychological theories—even those with substantial explanatory power—can make detailed predictions on the level of individual behavior. The need to distinguish the themata of behavioral science from those of physical science is an important feature of the opening discussion of causality and explanation in Cook and Campbell's (1979) work on quasi-experimental designs, and in the future, making the distinction is likely to be the rule rather than the exception.

The second reason for thorough specification of themata guiding the study of blame assignment, especially themata involving causality and explanation, is simply that questions about causality constitute a major portion of the raw material in the psychology of blame. Not only the investigators but also the *subjects* are concerned with the causes of events. It will be important to maintain a distinction between the "scientific status" of a perceiver's naive view of the causes of an event and the scientific status of the theory invoked to account for that perceiver's view. In the attribution literature, for example, it has been argued that perceivers behave like "scientists" in their attempts to attribute causality (Kelley, 1973). Whether or not this analysis will prove correct will be determined in large measure by the criteria used to describe the behavior of scientists, where that behavior is specified not only in terms of methods employed and theories proposed, but also in terms of themata that may govern the scientific enterprise.

The Nature of Causality

The attributional analysis of blame attempts to describe how ordinary perceivers answer questions about causality, responsibility, and blame-worthiness. In so doing, it cannot help but be affected by its own theoretical assumptions regarding these issues. So before asking how perceivers use the terms, and especially before establishing "standards" against which the judgments of perceivers are to be compared, the theory's *own* treatment of causality and responsibility must be identified and shown to be internally consistent. Like other theories in the behavioral sciences, a psychological theory of blame rests on a foundation provided by philosophical investigations of causation and accountability. These foundations are identified in the present chapter (for causality) and in Chapter 4 (for responsibility). In neither case is the objective to conduct a philosophical investigation of the topic. Rather, the purpose is to provide the philosophical underpinning for a conception of causality and responsibility that will ultimately make *psychological* sense.

At the outset it is important to note a feature of the upcoming discussion that may be unexpected for readers accustomed to dealing with data. There is no "truth" to a philosophical treatment of causality (or of responsibility) apart from that treatment's ability to persuade. "The correct" philosophical description of causality or responsibility cannot simply be presented. The various *alternative* positions need to be described and judged against the criteria of internal consistency and agreement with commonsense experience. If Russell (1945) is correct in his assertion that "No one has yet succeeded in inventing a philosophy at once credible and self-consistent" (p. 613), then our choice will be to select those philosophical themata regarding causality and responsibility that will be the most credible.

Although Descartes (e.g., 1641/1952) is usually credited with narrowing philosophical analysis of causality from Aristotle's (1952) four possibilities to efficient causality alone, modern philosophical treatments of causality are usually traced to the British empiricists, Locke, Berkeley, and particularly Hume (Wallace, 1974). Empiricism is the philosophical doctrine that all knowledge, with the possible exceptions of logic and mathematics, is derived from experience. Locke is regarded as the founder of empiricism (Wallace, 1974); but the most extreme empiricist position was Berkeley's (1710/1952) doctrine, *esse est percipi*: matter does not really exist apart from our perceptions of its existence. Only because Berkeley believed that God was always perceiving the universe was it possible for him to argue that material objects did not disappear completely during the time that no human was looking at them. Hume's conception of material objects was not as radically empiricist as Berkeley's, but his analysis of causation did express a similar skepticism about the logical necessity of cause and effect.

Regularity Theory

Hume's analysis of causation first appeared in Book I of his *Treatise of Human Nature* and was later recast with omissions into the philosophical essays that have come to be known as the *Enquiry Concerning Human Understanding* (1748/1952). The argument begins with a division of all of the perceptions of the mind into two classes. *Ideas* are reflections, memories, and constructions, while *impressions* are the more forceful and vivid perceptions that occur "when we hear, or see, or feel, or love, or hate, or desire, or will" (Hume, 1748/1952, p. 455). All of the contents of mind or imagination are constructed out of sense impressions, including even nonexistent entities such as a "golden mountain" or a "virtuous horse," which have been compounded out of ideas derived from sense impressions. Part of the proof of this contribution of sense impressions is based on the assertion that individuals who lack a sensory capability, or who have not had experience with a particular impression, can have no idea built on the impression. A person blind from birth will have no idea of color, a "man of mild manners can form no idea of inveterate revenge or cruelty . . . " (Hume, 1748/1952, p. 456).

Ideas are associated with one another in one of only three ways. The first means of association is resemblance, exemplified by our thought of the original object upon seeing a picture of it. The second is contiguity in space or time, exemplified by a thought of the remainder of a building upon hearing a discussion of one apartment. The third is *cause* or *effect*, and this relation alone allows us to make inferences about "matters of fact," such as the conclusion drawn by an explorer who discovers parts of a machine in the sand that a desert island was previously inhabited.

To this point the argument hardly seems controversial. Examining our own experience, we can easily distinguish vivid impressions from less forceful ideas, and we may be able to identify people whose dispositions are so tolerant that we suspect they might really be incapable of an idea of cruelty. Perhaps other relations among ideas could be proposed, but Hume's three can be made to sound like an exhaustive set. Having led us to drop our defenses, Hume makes the argument that subsequent generations of philosophers have attempted to refute, *"that causes and effects are discoverable, not by reason but by experience . . . "* (Hume, 1748/1952, p. 459, emphasis in original). If, in our experience, two events are contiguous in space and time and have been *constantly conjoined* such that one event always precedes another, we will conclude that the preceding event is the cause of the succeeding event. It is only our experience, however, not any intellectual examination of the presumed cause *prior to* experience with that cause, that gives rise to the relation of cause and effect. A number of mechanical examples (e.g., two smooth marble slabs that can be slid apart horizontally but not separated vertically, the action of one billiard ball hitting another, the fact that a stone released from the grasp falls down rather than up) are adduced to support the argument that the effect cannot be found *in* the cause, even through the "most accurate scrutiny and examination" (Hume, p. 459).

With very few exceptions, (e.g., Brand, 1976), philosophers of science include in their definitions of cause and effect the requirement that the presumed cause must precede the presumed effect in time. In more precise terms the cause is a process "the *last* instant of which is also the *first* instant of the segment of the time series occupied by the process which is the effect . . . " (Ducasse, 1969, p. 48, emphasis in original). Hume's analysis therefore is like others in assuming that causes precede effects. His position is distinctive in the radical empiricist notion that causality is nothing more than an experienced set of constant conjunctions between events. Although there is an exception that we shall consider in a moment, the major import of Hume's work is that there must be repeated observations of the constant conjunction in order to infer causes, "Even after one instance or experiment where we have observed a particular event to follow upon another, we are not entitled to form a general rule, or foretell what will happen in like cases . . . " (Hume, 1748/1952, p. 476).

Because of this insistence on repeated instances, Hume's analysis has come to be known as the *regularity* theory of causality.

Just as perceptions of causality in physical systems are dependent on regularity of a constant conjunction between presumed cause and presumed effect, perceptions of causality in social behavior are also dependent upon repeated observations: "The most irregular and unexpected resolutions of men may frequently be accounted for by those who know every particular circumstance of their character and situation" (Hume, 1748/1952, p. 481). Not surprisingly, this assertion sounds like the philosophical foundation for the behaviorist view that an individual's current activities can be understood and predicted fully, provided that there is complete knowledge of the individual's past history and current reinforcement contingencies. The modern philosophy of science that led to behaviorism can, upon careful reading of a history like Wallace's (1974), be traced directly back to Hume. The fundamental principle of regularity theory—acquisition of knowledge through observation of constant conjunctions—also serves as the philosophical idea behind Kelley's (1967, 1973) theory about the *attribution* of causality, as shown in the next chapter.

The regularity theory is as important for what it denies as for what it asserts. Specifically, it first denies that there are any contents of mind other than perceptions (these divided into impressions and ideas). Next, it denies that there is some independently specifiable *relation* between cause and effect. In other words, there are not two kinds of events that give rise to impressions: cause–events, the meaning of which can be understood only if they are necessarily followed by effects, and effect–events, the meaning of which can be understood only if we conceive of them as necessarily preceded by causes. There is only one category of event, and through experience (not through the application of reason) we come to learn that some elements of the category consistently follow others, while different elements of the category constantly precede others. There is, in short, no relation of *necessity* between a presumed cause and a presumed effect.

Recognizing that in this space it is impossible to do full justice to the complexity of Hume's (1748/1952) analysis (or, for that matter, to any of the philosophical positions to be considered), what are the implications of regularity theory for a perceiver attempting to understand why Flight 90 crashed shortly after take-off? Like other philosophical analyses of causality, regularity theory would direct our attention to an event that (1) preceded the crash, and (2) was contiguous with the crash in space and time. What are some of the possibilities? As noted earlier, the list is a lengthy one: the snowstorm, failure of the de-icing procedures, the long wait after de-icing, faulty equipment in the aircraft, too short a runway, the presence of a bridge, inexperience or bad judgment on the part of the pilots, failure of the air controllers to recognize the possible effects of the frightful weather conditions, or still some other potential cause. All of these factors meet the tests of preceding the crash and being contiguous with it in space and time. Are these characteristics of the environment, aspects of mechanical devices, and human actions (or inactions) *together* the cause of the mishap, or does the regularity theory allow us to rule out some of the possibilities?

Because the theory denies a principle of causal necessity, all it can do is direct us to look for constant conjunctions of events. But there is only *one* mishap to explain, and, indeed, if a few of the conditions are specified in detail, this particular crash can be made to be unique in everyone's experience. It was the only crash at National Airport that has ever involved a snowstorm, a flight crew with little winter experience, and a 45-minute delay between de-icing and take-off.

One of the difficulties attendant on the formulation of a principle of causality using simple mechanical examples is that social events, which are dramatically more complex than mechanical events, can be defined in a fashion that makes each unique. At the very least, the participants in a social interaction are not exactly the same people at time $t + 1$ that they were at time t, because of the interaction that they have had during the intervening moments. This may appear to be a philosophical quibble, but suppose that the interactants were a husband and wife, and between the two points in time the wife had said, "Darling, I want a divorce." Few people would be prepared to argue that either participant is now the "same person" as before the words were spoken.

In fairness to Hume it should be pointed out that in the *Treatise* (but not in the *Enquiry*, 1748/1952), Hume asserted that "We may attain the knowledge of a particular case merely by one experiment, provided it be made with judgment, and after a careful removal of all foreign and superfluous circumstances" (cited in Ducasse, 1969, p. 10). This assertion, of course, is the major exception noted earlier to Hume's empiricist insistence on knowledge derived only from multiple constant conjunctions, and is logically inconsistent with the fundamental principle of regularity theory. In Wallace's (1974) view, both the possibility of a single definitive experiment and the rules that Hume proposed in the *Treatise* for distinguishing causes from effects reflect Hume's admiration for the methodological advances made by Newton and other contemporary scientists. The first three of Hume's eight "rules" involve contiguity of cause and effect, temporal priority of the cause, and constant conjunction—aspects of causal judgment that we have already considered. The other five rules are best regarded as principles for making inferences from induction. For present purposes, suffice it to say that they offer no clear solution to the problem.

Suppose the event to be explained were not defined in a manner that makes it unique. Could the regularity theory then provide a method for distinguishing which of the many possible causes actually produced the crash? What if we included in our experience all of the accumulated knowledge about aviation in winter? Airports do not typically close down in snowstorms, and even when they do, landings are stopped before take-offs are prohibited. It is unlikely that we would find a "constant conjunction" of snowstorms and accidents. The runways at National Airport does not vary in length from day to day; the particular make of airport makes thousands of flights a month; the pilots involved had not had accidents before. No matter what the causal event, the widest possible "constant conjunction" would show a very small fraction of the cases in which that potential cause was connected to a crash. This line of reasoning leads to the unacceptable conclusion that not only will we be unable to ascertain which of the potential causes actually produced the crash, we will also be unable to find *any* cause whatsover. No causal event has participated in enough constant conjunctions to yield a certain judgment of causality. Regardless of its philosophical merits, regularity theory is deficient as an explanation either for this crash or for social events, so alternatives need to be considered.

Necessity Theory

Perhaps the best known criticism of Hume's view of causation is contained in Kant's (1781/1952) *Critique of Pure Reason*. By his own admission Kant's purpose was to engage in a "critical inquiry into the faculty of reason, with reference to the cognition which it strives to attain *without the aid of experience* . . . " (p. 2, emphasis in original). The argument begins with a distinction between knowledge gained as a consequence of experience (empirical knowledge) and knowledge that is absolutely independent of all experience (knowledge *a priori*). *A priori* ideas can be differentiated from empirical ideas on the basis of two related criteria, necessity and universality. A judgment will involve necessity and universality if it admits of no exceptions, indeed, if the very meaning of the words involved requires the idea to be as it is. The battle if joined early, as Kant (1781/1952) chooses the idea of causality to serve as an example of necessity and universality:

> The conception of a cause so plainly involves of a necessity of connection with an effect, and of a strict universality of the law, that the very notion of a cause would entirely disappear, where we to derive it, like Hume, from a frequent association of what happens with that which precedes. . . . (p. 15)

The concept of cause and effect is also one of the three *relations* included in the table of the categories of understanding, an elementary *a priori* relation used in the cognitive work necessary to build a thorough understanding of experience. In short, what Hume held to be an inference built up through constant conjunction, Kant held to be a fundamental and innate property of all human cognition.

Up to this point in the argument, Kant's criticism has taken only the form of presupposition and definition, not demonstration (Ducasse, 1969). To prove to us that causality is an *a priori* judgment, Kant must show, not merely presuppose, that the principle of necessity exists and that causation is one form of judgment that entails such a principle. Although Beck (1967) points out that there is still scholarly disagreement regarding just what portion of the

Critique constitutes Kant's answer to Hume, most writers believe that the reply, including what Kant thought was the requisite proof, is contained in a section entitled the "Second Analogy of Experience" (Beauchamp, 1974; Ducasse, 1969; Suchting, 1967).

In this "Second Analogy," Kant distinguished between the *objective* order of phenomena in the world and the *subjective* order of perception or introspection. When we reflect on our internal perceptions of an external entity, our conscious reflection must necessarily pass from one part of the external object to another in succession. Kant's example involved the perceptions that accompany attainment of a full understanding of a house, as opposed to the understanding of a passing ship. Standing outside a house, we might begin at the roof and look at the second story, then the first story, and then the foundation. But that succession in perception could easily be reversed, because the phenomenon being perceived (the house) consists of stationary parts that coexist at the same time. There is no succession in the object that determines a particular succession in perception. By contrast, Kant describes the internal order of perception that accompanies our viewing a ship passing before us as it floats downstream. As the ship goes by, we see its bow, its deck amidships, and its stern. There is an order in our subjective perception, but at the same time there is an objective order to the phenomenon that prevents our reversing the subjective order.

The conclusion to be drawn from the comparison of these two examples is that our *knowledge* that the subjective order is reversible in the one case but not reversible in the other requires an *a priori* understanding of necessity, and employment of a principle of causality that involves succession in time. What is important here is not the particular content of one perception as compared with the other, but rather the fact that we can recognize the two cases to *be* different. Thus Kant agrees with Hume that the external world is represented in our perceptions, but Kant's argument leads to the conclusion that our very ability to recognize the necessary sequences in constantly conjoined events implies the existence of a purely cognitive—not experiential—principle of causality.

How might the necessity theory help to identify a cause of the fatal crash of Flight 90? It has already been shown that a cause must be contiguous in either space or time with the effect and that the cause must precede the effect. Is there anything about the notion of causal necessity that permits choice among the potentially causal events that were conjoined with the effect? One contribution that Kant's "Second Analogy of Experience" (1781/1952) suggests is that we should attend very closely to the time order involved in the phenomenon. The snowstorm preceded the de-icing procedure, which was followed by a 45-minute wait prior to take-off. At the point of take-off the tower clearance preceded the pilots' decision to begin rolling; this decision was immediately followed by operation of the various mechanical systems of the aircraft; and at some point along the runway, the pilots needed to decide whether to continue or abort the take-off. After the plane left the runway, its mechanical systems and airfoils failed to produce sufficient lift, and the plane crashed.

Once the time order has been specified carefully, the idea of necessity permits choice among possible causes, which is not possible using the notion of constant conjunction alone. For example, if the snowstorm were *necessarily* a cause of the crash, then every plane taking off during the storm ought to have crashed (which did not happen). Indeed, if every step in the sequence is examined by itself, the de-icing, the wait, the tower clearance, and the relatively permanent features of the setting, all appear to lose causal force. What remains is that part of the causal sequence beginning with the decision by the pilots to start the take-off roll. That decision possesses a degree of causal necessity not inherent in preceding elements of the sequence: Without that decision, all of the earlier features of the circumstances would have made no causal difference.

Thus, the necessity theory rules out some of the possibilities while identifying at least one specific cause of the crash. But is the answer entirely satisfactory? No. Regardless of their logical status, features of the situation such as the snowstorm and the possibly faulty de-icing procedure would certainly seem *psychologically* important in the eventual outcome. To say that the pilots' decision to take off was *the* cause would leave our perceiver wondering whether the outcome would have been the same if the decision had been made in the brilliant sunshine of a late summer afternoon. Of course it would not. So the other features of the situation need to be included in the causal equation in some limited degree, and the notion of necessity alone does not accomplish this.

A second difficulty with the necessity theory is that there are aspects of the causal sequence that *follow* the pilots' decision to begin the take-off that seem to have the same necessary quality seen in the decision. Working backward from the crash, if the mechanical systems of the aircraft had been able to maintain sufficient lift, then nothing previous would have mattered. If the pilots had aborted the take-off, nothing prior to that decision would have mattered. If during the roll the plane had generated sufficient speed and lift, then nothing previous would have mattered. If all of these factors possess the same degree of causal necessity, is our perceiver to regard them as equally important? Or will there be an attempt to claim that one (or more, but not all) of the factors is more crucial than the others? If such a claim is to be made, on what basis will it be justified? Necessity theory alone does not provide an answer to any of these questions, so one additional alternative to Hume's constant conjunction needs to be examined.

Activity Theory

Modern proponents of regularity and necessity theories might, at this point in the discussion, cry "Foul!" The explanatory task set forth here is not the one for which either theory was initially constructed. Both Hume and Kant thought they were engaged in the practice of *metaphysics*—the study of things transcending nature, such as "the concepts of existence, thing, property, event; the distinctions between particulars and universals, individuals and classes; the nature of relations, change, causation; and the nature of mind, matter, space, and time" (Hancock, 1967, pp. 289–290). So the relations between cause and effect that Hume and Kant considered were presumed to obtain in physical systems, not in human action (despite Hume's generalization of the constant conjunction to human affairs). It is not just that most of their examples involved changes in physical systems, it is also that the significant questions they hoped to settle dealt with instances of causality in which human agency was not an issue.

For this reason every particular example of causality discovered either through the constant conjunction or through the application of the criteria of necessity and universality was thought to be merely a "singular" representation of a general law, a universal principle known as the "uniformity of nature." Discovering that a single stone will fall with an acceleration of 32 feet/second (for necessity theory) or that there is a constant conjunction of such accelerations across numerous trials (for regularity theory) is informative about a causal law of gravity, at least to the extent that the singular instance can be generalized through application of the principle of uniformity of nature.

The notion that every true instance of causality is a representation of a universal law of nature has two consequences that should be noted here. First, because of the nature of the inferences involved, much of the philosophical disagreement (especially modern arguments between proponents of regularity and necessity theories, as illustrated in a volume edited by Beauchamp, 1974) concerns technical matters involved in the generalization. How to determine the truth value of a "counterfactual conditional" (a contrary-to-fact subjunctive, conditional statement such as "If the moon were a planet, it would move in an elliptical orbit") is a matter important to recent philosophy, but not to a *psychological* theory of blame.

Second, to apply the uniformity of nature principle to intentional action by human agents would be difficult at best. The difficulty arises from two sources noted earlier, complexity and change. Human behavior is so complex that a detailed description of the actions involved can make each event seem unique. In such a case it would be a contradiction in terms to claim that the event was really the singular representation of a universal causal law. Even if the complexity can be dealt with, the change cannot. Universal laws must apply not only in all conditions, but through all time. To argue that a human action was an instance of a universal causal law would require that the action be independent of the passage of time. Even the strongest advocates of the position that human actions are regular and replicable would not argue that the regularity *must* exist by virtue of a universal principle of uniformity of nature. Thus, partly because of the problems connected with application of regularity and necessity theories to human action and partly because of each theory's inclusion of a principle of uniformity of nature, neither theory is able to give a complete account of precisely the kind of causal event of interest to a psychology of blame: A specific cause–effect sequence initiated by a human agent.

One philosophical theory that more closely approximates psychological theory is the general position that has become known as *activity* theory, because it regards human agency as the paradigmatic instance of causality. Roots of the activity theory can be found in Reid's (1863a, 1863b) "common sense" critique of Hume's view of causation as constant conjunction. Reid's philosophy has been collected in two volumes (1863a, 1863b), and his views on causation are often most succinctly summarized in his letters:

> In physics the word *cause* has another meaning, which, though I think it an improper one, yet is distinct, and, therefore, may be reasoned upon. When a phenomenon is produced according to a certain law of nature, we call the law of nature the cause of that phenomenon; and to the laws of nature we accordingly ascribe power, agency, efficiency. The whole business of physics is to discover, by observation and experiment, the laws of nature, . . . this we call discovering the causes of things. But this, however common, is an improper sense of the world *cause*. (Letter to Dr. James Gregory, 1863a, p. 66, emphasis in orginal)

The sense of "cause" that Reid prefers is a version of the Aristotelian efficient cause that limits such production of effects to the actions of human beings. Where Hume had argued that our experience with the world provides us with nothing but knowledge of the constant conjunction of cause and effect, Reid (1863b) believed that our own *inner* experience provides a more fundamental notion of causality:

> It is very probable that the very conception or idea of active power, and of efficient causes, is derived from our voluntary exertions in producing effects; and that, if we were not conscious of such exertion, we should have no conception at all of a cause, or of active power, and consequently no conviction of the necessity of a cause of every change which we observe in nature. (p. 604)

The exercise of will, therefore, is not only the sole source of our notion of cause and effect, it is also the source of the *a priori* idea that cause and effect are necessarily connected. Referring to his chapter on the ambiguities involved in descriptions of causality, Reid (1863a) concluded that "nothing can be an efficient cause, in the proper sense, but an intelligent being" (p. 65).

Despite Reid's use of human introspection as the source of his understanding of causality and despite his claim that the exercise of human will is the paradigmatic case of causation, his version of activity theory did not limit the possibility of agency to human beings. On the contrary, Reid (1863b) claimed that the activity seen in inert matter—the physical causes that were the subject of regularity and necessity theories—reflected the actions of an intelligent God:

> The *physical laws of nature* are the rules according to which the Deity commonly acts in his natural government of the world.... Neither miraculous events, which are contrary to the physical laws of nature, nor such ordinary acts of the Divine administration as are without their sphere, are impossible, nor are they *effects without a cause*. God is the cause of them, and to him only are they to be imputed. (p. 628, emphasis in original)

Reid's (1863b) imputation of the laws of nature and exceptions to those laws to God is a position quite similar to that espoused by Descartes, Newton, and Berkeley (Wallace, 1974), and it is obviously a thematic component of his philosophy of science. Although in modern philosophy and social psychology it is fashionable to leave deities out of formal theory, in Chapter 7 it is argued that perceivers have not quite so thoroughly abandoned superphysical explanations for events.

Social psychologists will recognize in Reid's (1863a, 1863b) ideas the sort of analysis of common sense found in Heider's (1958) explanation of the way that a psychologically untrained perceiver might explain the causes of action. The parallel includes both subject matter and method of understanding. As discussed in Chapter 3, Heider describes human actions in terms of power, ability, intention, and exertion—terms that are the modern equivalents of the concepts employed by Reid. As for the similarities in style, a great deal of Heider's analysis depends on his own introspection into human capacities and motives. This similarity is especially interesting because Heider's justification of the examination of common sense does not refer to Reid, but does include a rationale provided by Ryle (1949), who would have disagreed most strenuously with Reid's views.

Emphasis on human agency leads activity theory to search, not for universal laws of nature that might be revealed by singular instances of cause and effect, but for *the* cause of any particular happening. The approach is exemplified in work by Collingwood (1940), who first distinguishes among three senses of the word "cause." The third sense corresponds to the singular instance of a universal law, so it is not important for present purposes. The other two senses, however, contain the idea of human agency as a central ingredient.

The first of Collingwood's (1940) senses is *historical* sense; what is caused is a "free and deliberate act of a conscious and responsible agent, and 'causing' him to do it means affording him a motive for doing it" (p. 285). Although this sense describes the use of "causality" in history, it also represents a kind of *psychological* usage. If I provide you with the motive to commit a crime, then I have caused you to engage in the offense. Even though you freely and deliberately committed the crime, I should share the responsibility. Collingwood's view of the psychological component of historical causality is limited to the idea of shared responsibility; for the purposes of this discussion, however, another aspect of historical causality should also be noted. When a perceiver attempts to explain a social event, the explanation may ultimately depend on the perceiver's beliefs about the actor's motives, regardless of the source of those motives. In the terms used later in this volume (Chapter 6), the act of affording a person a motive would be a cause, but the motive, once acquired, would be the actor's *reason* for acting, itself a cause of the actor's subsequent behavior.

Second is Collingwood's (1940) *practical science* sense of causality; what is caused is an event in nature rather than the deliberate act of a person, but the role of a human agent is not diminished. "Cause" in this sense is an event or state of things that, when produced or prevented by the actions of a person who intervenes in the process, will produce or prevent the occurrence of the effect. This definition is a bit cumbersome, but the central idea is the *controllability* of the cause (leading some to call the causal theory involved "manipulability," rather than "activity"). Collingwood's examples of the disciplines that employ this sense of the word "cause" are engineering and medicine, but he explicitly denies "applied science" as a synonym for "practical science." The definition of "practical science" is a contingent one, or "in Aristotle's terminology 'what admits of being otherwise'" (Collingwood, 1940, p. 297). By contrast, applied science involves the use of theoretical propositions in attempts to solve practical problems, but with no advance guarantee that the desired solutions will result. Applied science knowledge may be power, but practical science knowledge *is* power, and the immediate consequences of its application are known in advance.

The example of a practical science cause is the change in position of an electric light switch that produces illumination of a darkened room. Turning a light switch to the "on" position "is our 'means' of producing a further state of things, viz. incandescence . . . in a certain filament. What is immediately produced (the position of the switch) is the 'cause' . . . " in the practical science sense (Collingwood, 1940, p. 297).

Two aspects of this definition deserve comment. First, although what is defined to be "the cause" is a state of nature, it is not the initial step in the temporal order of succession, but is immediately preceded by human intervention. Such causes exist because people have previously created them (or in an example like the cause of polio, discovered them), and they await human intervention. This is, as Collingwood notes, an "anthropocentric idea that man looks at nature from his own point of view . . . anxious to find out how he can manipulate nature for achieving his own ends" (p. 310). Second, whether the cause is being produced (in the case of a light switch's being turned on), or prevented (in the case of a polio vaccination's being administered), the human intervention is much like that observed in the historical sense of causality. In Collingwood's words the second sense rests on the "anthropomorphic idea that man's manipulation of nature resembles one man's manipulation of another man . . . " (pp. 310–311).

The activity theory thus holds that our understanding of the term "cause" initially arises from introspective observation of the exercise of our own will, and it further argues that the consequences of such human activity can be seen both in the actions of other people and in changes in states of nature. What does this view of human agency contribute to our perceiver's attempt to explain the causes of the crash of Flight 90? The temporal sequence had been narrowed by necessity theory to those events beginning with the pilots' decision to start the take-off roll: the human intervention designed to increase the speed of the plane, the failure of the mechanical systems to respond appropriately, the human decision not to abort the take-off, and the failure of the mechanical systems to maintain sufficient lift. The principle of necessity alone cannot single any one of these out as *the* cause, because in an important "but for" sense each can be regarded as necessary.

Activity theory, however, focuses our attention not on the physical states of nature (the mechanical systems of the aircraft), but on the human actions that might have prevented failures in those physical states from eventuating in the crash. In short, although a failure to maintain lift might be a significant part of the problem, fault for the occurrence would have to rest with the pilots, because their actions did not prevent this factor from affecting the outcome. This certainly brings us closer to a full explanation of the event, but the account is still not completely satisfying. Somehow we believe that the weather conditions, the de-icing procedures, and the 45-minute wait ought to be endowed with some minimal degree of causal efficacy, and so far they have not been. Analysis of such additional conditions was included in Collingwood's ideas about causation, but because conditions have also been discussed by philosophers not identified with activity theory, causes and conditions will be treated in a separate section.

Causes and Conditions

Modern philosophical accounts of causes and conditions are traced to Mill's (1888) discussion of the law of causation in his *System of Logic*. There Mill asserts that to "adopt a distinction familiar in the writings of the Scotch metaphysicians, and especially of Reid, the causes with which I concern myself are not *efficient*, but *physical*, causes" (1888, p. 236, emphasis in original). What Mill does not say at this point is that he proposes to use the sense of cause that Reid considered *improper* (although Mill's arguments against activity theory in a later section leave little doubt about his position). Knowledge of the physical causes of interest can be obtained, Mill argues, entirely from experience. Thus, Mill's version of causality is a variant of regularity theory, with two significant exceptions. The first exception is that the cause–effect sequences to be identified through experience are *invariable*, a stronger statement than Hume's notion of constant conjunction. Not only has the cause always preceded the effect, it will of necessity always do so in the future.

The second exception, of greater interest to us, is that this invariable sequence seldom involves a single antecedent and a single consequent. "It is usually between a consequent and the sum of several antecedents; the concurrence of all of them being requisite to produce, that is, to be certain of being followed by, the consequent" (Mill, 1888, p. 237). Mill argues that although it is common to refer to one of the antecedents as "the cause" (usually the antecedent in closest temporal proximity to the effect), while other antecedents are regarded as mere conditions, this differentiation among antecedents is an error. "All the conditions were equally indispensable to the production of the consequent; and the statement of cause is incomplete, unless in some shape or other we introduce them all" (Mill, 1888, pp. 237–238). So, while Mill has referred to the distinction between causes and conditions, he believes it to be an empty distinction and ultimately does away with it.

The first major critic of Mill's view was Ducasse (1969), who disagreed with Mill's claims that *any* condition might be called *the* cause, and so a choice to elevate one condition to the status of "cause" was "capricious." According to Ducasse, Mill

> . . . is wrong. There is no capriciousness about it. His believing this is, in fact, due to the obsession under which he labors all along, namely that inquiry into causation is inquiry into laws. The truth is on the contrary that it is directly and primarily an inquiry concerning *single, individual events*. (Ducasse, 1969, p. 19, emphasis in original)

In Collingwood's terms, Mill is talking about the natural science sense of causality, while Ducasse is talking about the practical science sense. Indeed, Ducasse uses an example of his automobile engine's ceasing to run, which Collingwood also employs. When your engine stops, your question "Why?" is not a request for a universal law of nature. It is a request for identification of "the single *difference* between the circumstances of the engine at the moment when it was running, and at the moment when it was not" (Ducasse, 1969, p. 19). Just as the cause is the single difference from the one moment to the next, the *conditions* are the circumstances that remained constant across the two moments.

In more formal terms Ducasse considered causes, conditions, and effects all to be changes or states. So it would be possible to identify both the cause of an automobile's continuing to run (a state) and the cause of its stopping (a change). The distinction between a cause and a condition would then be drawn on the basis of whether one particular antecedent of the effect was necessary for the production of the effect or sufficient for production of the effect. A change or state would be a *cause* if it were sufficient for production of the change or state that was the effect. In contrast, an antecedent that was necessary but not sufficient for production of the effect would be a *condition*. As is the usual case with the technical meanings of "necessary" and "sufficient," the former means "cannot occur in the absence of," while the latter means "can produce." More is said about the relationship among causes and conditions in Chapter 3. For now it is sufficient to note that in terms of the example of Flight 90's crash, the snowstorm, the de-icing procedure, and the wait for departure would, for Ducasse, be conditions.

In arguing against Mill's assertion that there is no basis for selecting one of the antecedents in preference to any others, Ducasse established a logical rationale involving change versus constancy, and sufficiency versus necessity. In the next significant argument against Mill's position, Collingwood (1940) described what is best thought of as a psychological rationale. Collingwood's argument was part of his comparison among the three senses of the word "cause," and not surprisingly his conclusion was that the choice of a particular antecedent as *the* cause would depend on which antecedent(s) could be produced or prevented by human action. Only the antecedent(s) susceptible to alteration through such human intervention will be selected as *the* cause. Within that limited set of possibilities, the choice will follow a principle Collingwood called "relativity of causes." A person is most likely to select as "the cause" that antecedent over which he or she, personally, has the most control. So for the supervisor of the de-icing procedures at the airport, the cause of the crash would have been faulty de-icing. For the tower personnel the cause would have been the 45-minute wait in the storm. For the aircraft manufacturer the cause would have been inadequate on-board de-icing systems.

The principle of relativity of causes certainly anticipates the more general psychological idea that a perceiver's own viewpoint will affect his or her judgments of causality. But as "psychological" as it sounds, the principle is probably psychologically naive. Especially in a modern industrialized (and litigious) country, it seems unlikely that each participant–observer will be arguing that the mishap was really *his* or *her* fault. On the contrary, a psychological version of the principle would suggest a two-stage alternative. In the first stage the kind of familiarity with possible causes implied by relativity would lead the observer to identify as "most probable" the cause(s) with which he or she has the most experience in producing or preventing. But the course of the second stage of the judgment would be determined by the valence of the effect to be explained. The relativity principle would apply as originally stated only for positively valued effects. For negatively valued effects there would be a thorough search of why one's most probable cause was really *not* the sufficient factor. Similar self-protective principles applying to moral affronts are described in Chapter 6.

Causality and the Theory of Blame

Discussion of causes and conditions concludes the historical review of causation. It should be noted, however, that numerous critical issues are still being debated in contemporary philosophy. Indeed, in a detailed analysis of the concept of causation, Brand (1976) was able to find logical difficulties or problems of application in regularity theory, necessity theory, activity theory, and the manner by which causes are to be distinguished from conditions. Brand's purpose was constructive—to suggest the most promising avenues for further philosophical analysis of causation. His criticisms of earlier formulations, however, show that the analysis of causality remains an active area of inquiry.

It is precisely because of the continuing philosophical arguments regarding causation that any discipline's fundamental position on causality should be regarded as a *thematic* component of the psychological context shared by investigators in the area. Moreover, each discipline should build on whichever thematic position (1) has withstood the test of time and (2) is most appropriate for its own purposes. Proposals that have not been convincingly refuted in the last hundred years are unlikely to be dispatched in the near future, so appropriateness will be the more important of these two criteria. By that criterion the physical sciences would find the most comfort in regularity theory, in a search for universal laws rather than in an attempt to explain singular events in Collingwood's natural science sense of causality and in Mill's position on causes and conditions. On the other hand, behavioral science in general and attributional theory of blame in particular require the possibility of human agency inherent in activity theory, attempt to account for people's explanations of singular events, would resonate to Collingwood's historical and practical science senses of causality, and are concerned with distinctions between causes and conditions. This concluding section of the chapter, therefore, makes explicit the causal themata that contribute to the psychological context for the present theory.

Causation Must Include Human Agency

The principle of causation to be adopted by an attributional analysis of blame derives most directly, but not exclusively, from activity theory. Each of the major philosophical positions claims to be based "on experience," it is just that different theorists have divergent conceptions of what is learned from that experience. As a psychological rather than philosophical endeavor, the psychology of blame can build a causal thema that takes advantage of the contributions of regularity, necessity, and activity theories, but concentrates on the latter. Our conception of causation thus includes the following three concepts: (1) human agency as the fundamental idea, (2) necessity as part of agency, and (3) temporal priority of cause and effect.

Human agency as the fundamental idea. A person's understanding of causality comes from his or her experience of volitional action. We see ourselves as efficient causes of changes of state, whether those changes take place in our own subsequent actions, in the behavior of other people, or in the states of natural phenomena.

Necessity as part of agency. Without taking a position on the philosophical question of whether necessity is a relation known *a priori* or derived from personal experience with acts of volition, the attributional theory of blame assumes that people will view a cause–effect sequence as a necessary connection, not merely a constant conjunction generalized from the past. We have experience with causality, but we also have an *idea* of what the causal relation involves. This assumption that our notion of causality includes a cognitive factor over and above experience is at once typical of social psychological theory and in direct contrast to the strict behaviorist view of action. The latter, based on a *logical positivism* (the application of principles of logic to the verification of relations among concrete facts) traceable to Hume (1748/1952), and more recently to the Vienna Circle founded by Schlick in the 1920s (Wallace, 1974), would deny the existence of mental structures of any sort.

Temporal priority of cause before effect. Although it is possible that in natural science causes are simultaneous with effects (changes in the pressure and temperature of a gas are an example), in human behavior any potential cause would require a duration of time long enough to support the argument that the "last instant of the cause is the first instant of the effect." The present view of blame thus sides with Ducasse (1969), and Collingwood (1940), against Russell's argument (1925) that there must necessarily be some finite period of time intervening between the termination of the cause and the beginning of the effect (which break would, if it existed, make the identification of *the* cause impossible).

Causality Involves Single Instances

The task of an attributional analysis of blame is to account for people's *explanations* of single instances of causes and effects. Here it is important to distinguish between the scientific goals of the discipline (the development of theories that will generalize across instances of the explanations offered by perceivers) and the goals of the individual perceiver (explanation of particular cause–effect sequences in natural states or in human activities). Thus, while the discipline claims to be searching for general (if not altogether "universal") laws of behavior, it presumes that the individual perceiver is principally concerned with singular events. This presumption is consistent both with activity theory and with Collingwood's first two senses of "cause."

The Cause Is a Subset of the Antecedents

The attributional analysis of blame assumes that an effect will be seen as the consequence not of one single antecedent, but as the consequence of a subset of the possible conditions. The notion that the total set of antecedents of an effect includes both positive and negative conditions is usually traced to Mill (1888), who regarded the causally sufficient subset to include all of the positive conditions. Later writers such as Ducasse (1969) and Collingwood

(1940), however, suggested ways to distinguish among the positive antecedents in order to identify *the* cause.

The possibility of making such distinctions has recently been defended in the philosophy of science by Nagel (1965), in the philosophy of mind by Mackie (1965), and in the philosophy of law by Hart and Honoré (1959). Each of these defenses employs the same sort of "commonsense" view of causality held by an attributional analysis of blame. Although there are some differences across the three presentations in their use of the terms "necessary" and "sufficient," for present purposes I need only note that together the presentations provide ample philosophical justification for the kinds of distinctions I believe perceivers of real events will make. More is said about the uses of "necessary" and sufficient" in Chapter 3.

This chapter began with a single instance of an event to be explained, and that example has served as the vehicle for discussion of the philosophical themata that form the psychological context for a psychological theory of blame. The example is not perfect. It does not do justice to the complexity of many of the philosophical arguments, nor does it represent a moral affront. What it does do is show how each theory might attempt to deal with a common event for which blame is to be assigned.

For the sake of closure, I should conclude with a description of what the "formal" perceivers actually did. Every aircraft accident is investigated by the National Transportation Safety Board, a branch of the Federal Aviation Administration. The Board examines the wreckage of the plane, refers to the on-board recorders of data from mechanical systems and of cockpit conversations, and conducts hearings to obtain information from any potential witnesses. Nearly a year after the accident, the Board issued its report on the crash, finding that *the* cause was pilot error, both in the initial decision to take off and in the subsequent decision not to attempt to abort the take-off roll. Other potential antecedents, such as the severity of the storm, the de-icing procedures, and the long wait to departure, were relegated to the status of conditions, necessary for the accident to have occurred, but not by themselves sufficient. The outcome of the investigation, like the outcome of our excursion into philosophical analysis of causality, emphasizes human agency, the central feature of causality within an attributional theory of blame.

Chapter 3
The Attribution of Causality

A theory of the attribution of blame must describe how people answer three fundamental questions: "What is the cause of this event or action," "Is anyone responsible for its occurrence," and "Who is to blame for the event?" But what exactly is meant by causality? How do perceivers actually use the concept? What is meant by responsibility? What process is involved in the assignment of blame? The philosophical discussion of causality in Chapter 2 permits a more precise answer to the first of these questions. The cause of an event or action must *precede* the event, with the last instant of the causal sequence being the first instant of the effect. The cause will be that single antecedent or group of antecedents that is *sufficient* for the occurrence of the effect. In keeping with the principle of necessity, "the" cause will be considered generative of the effect, rather than being a mere correlate of the effect. If there is to be subsequent blame, the cause must reflect *human agency*. Thus, the initial question becomes "Which antecedents involving human agency were sufficient for the occurrence of the action or event?"

It should be emphasized that this philosophically based question establishes the limits for the causal analysis involved in blame assignment, but its existence does not imply that all perceivers will follow its prescription. People make errors. They sometimes assign blame to individuals only remotely connected with the event. They occasionally deny the blameworthiness of people whose clearly intentional actions have produced a misfortune. Therefore, although the prescriptive definition of a cause (and later, prescriptive accounts of responsibility and blameworthiness) will guide our subsequent theory, that theoretical conception must be tested against the uses to which the term is put by perceivers. The purpose of the present chapter is to describe a social–psychological account of the attribution of causality.

Before turning to explanations of the ways in which people attribute causality, one final word needs to be said about the restriction that in order for blame to be established, the cause must involve human agency. Does this restriction mean, for example, that the destruction following an earthquake has no cause (because no human agent precipitated the earthquake)? Certainly not. Physical events produced by natural forces are no less caused than are behavioral events. Only when human actions are involved, however, does an event become relevant for a psychological investigation of blame.

If the destruction accompanying an earthquake is confined to a wilderness area, the question "What caused the damage?" is purely geological. If, on the other hand, the damage also includes the destruction of buildings, then the question about causality has psychological significance. Should the people have known better than to build a city on a fault? Could more stringent building codes have limited the damage? Has offshore oil drilling enhanced the power of the quake by removing material that would otherwise have stabilized the earth's crust? Such questions make it clear that while the quake itself might have been a purely physical event, the subsequent destruction was a *mixed* case, involving both physical antecedents and some degree of human agency (if only errors of omission). The following discussion specifies how individual perceivers identify the human causes of events.

Personal and Impersonal Causality

Social psychological accounts of the ways in which people come to understand the causes of events began with the seminal work of Heider (1944, 1958), whose book on interpersonal relations is universally regarded as having established attribution theory as a separate enterprise within social perception. This "naive analysis of action" bears a striking resemblance to the "common-sense" arguments that Reid (1863a, 1863b) raised against Hume's (1748/1952) assertion that causality was nothing more than a constant conjunction of like events. Recall that Reid engaged in introspection about the exercise of will, concluding that only a human being could be the (Aristotelian) efficient cause of an event. In an important respect, Heider's (1958) careful analysis of the manner in which terms like "cause" and "responsibility" are used in the language represented the distillation of a more collective common sense, because that language has been shaped by individual experience through the years. Nor surprisingly, Heider's conclusion was much the same as Reid's: True personal causality was equated with intentional action. Excluded from the realm of personal causality were those events brought about by impersonal antecedents (such as forces of nature and physical laws) and those effects in the production of which the person was merely "part of the sequence of events" (Heider, 1958, p. 100).

For Heider, intentional action was distinguished from impersonal causality on two grounds, equifinality and local causality. These related grounds are best defined by an example: If while you are skiing you narrowly escape being buried in an unanticipated avalanche, you are unlikely to conclude that the snow was "out to get you" personally. Although the onrushing snow will always complete its journey at the foot of the slope, showing a version of equifinality common to physical systems, it will not alter its course in response to your changing position on the mountain. Suppose, however, that you decide that you have had enough skiing, leave the lodge, and depress the brake pedal in your car as you back out of the parking lot. You discover that your car suddenly has no brakes. Now your entire explanation for recent events will change. Not only will you conclude that someone *is* out to get you, you may now believe that the someone also initiated the avalanche. "Equifinality" thus refers to a state of affairs desired by a person or persons, and that state of affairs will be achieved despite your best efforts to prevent it. To accomplish their goals the persons will exercise local causality, a feedback-like intervention designed to respond to your attempt at evasion. Unlike physical systems, persons can monitor the progress of events and redirect the process as needed to reach their objective.

Is a limitation of true personal causality to intentional action appropriate for an attributional analysis of blame? Probably not, for two principal reasons. Consider again the example involving the crash of Flight 90. The event to be explained is the crash, a one-time occurrence. Embedded in the idea of equifinality is the assumption that the observer has access to a *sequence* of events, all of which point toward the same end. True, it is possible to describe the crash of the plane as the consequence of a more elementary causal sequence. Only the paranoid, however, would argue that the equifinal objective was prevention of the plane from reaching its destination, such that when the airport was not closed ("event" 1), the plane's mechanical systems did not freeze up ("event" 2) as they were supposed to, the blizzard ("event" 3) did not prevent the take-off, and the contact with the bridge ("event" 4) did not cause the plane to explode, the icy river finally had to finish the job by sinking the fuselage ("event" 5). There is attributional research showing a remarkable consistency in the way individuals "chunk" causal sequences (Newtson, 1976), and one doubts that very many people would subscribe to this rather bizarre chunking. If the plane crash must, then, be considered a single event, the criterion of equifinality, achieved through repeated exercise of local causality, cannot be brought to bear on the judgment of whether personal causality was involved.

The second difficulty with limiting personal causality to intentional action defined by equifinality has to do not with the process but with the presumed objective. No one would propose that the air controllers, the de-icing crew, and the pilots of Flight 90 shared a common intention to crash the plane. It is not completely accurate to describe the result as the unintended consequence of another intentional action (a description that, for Heider at least, would take the crash out of the realm of personal causality). Rather, the crash was the exact *opposite* of what was intended, the last thing any of the participating individuals might have wanted to accomplish. Despite this clear absence of an intention to crash the plane, it is still true that without the pilots' decision to begin the take-off, there would have been no crash. Therefore, by the sufficiency criterion discussed earlier, that decision must be given causal efficacy. This attribution of causality to the pilots is made, admittedly, on logical grounds, but there is every reason to believe that the same attribution would be made by the "naive" perceivers whose inferences the theory will attempt to explain.

Where do these difficulties with Heider's (1958) definition lead us? To the conclusion that intentional action, characterized by equifinality and local causality is the paradigmatic, but not the only, instance of personal causality. An observer given the opportunity to view several events in sequence and note the reappearance of a person who redirects the flow of events until some final state has been achieved can conclude confidently that the person caused the outcome. Perceivers, however, legitimately can decide that a person has caused an event where there is only one element in the sequence, even when the end achieved might not have been desired. What changes across the two cases is not the presence of personal causality. Rather, what changes is the perceiver's confidence that the person in question caused the occurrence and the degree to which that person might be held morally blameworthy. More is said about the confidence in causal judgments later in this chapter. For now it is sufficient to note that the line dividing personal from impersonal causality may be less distinct than either Reid or Heider defined it to be.

The Naive Analysis of Action

To be fair to Heider's account, it should be pointed out that the development of a theory of people's assignment to blame for *events* is not the same as the description of the way in which people might explain human *actions*. Thus, while it is not realistic to claim that only intended events should be attributed to persons, it is reasonable to argue that true personal causality for action might be limited to intentional behavior. Events may have causes other than human actions, and those observable human behaviors may, themselves, have prior causes. As discussed in Chapter 8, however, the logical attribution of *blame* for events does require the judgment that an intentional human behavior was the cause of the event to be explained.

Establishing the basis for the idea that causes of behavior are either internal to the person or external to the person, Heider argued that all human action was the product of a balance between "personal force" and "environmental force." In most of his analysis of interpersonal relations, Heider (1958) considered environmental force to be an *obstacle* to successful completion of desired activities, with the principal component of that force being task difficulty. Personal force, in the form of ability or power, combined with task difficulty in an additive fashion such that if power exceeded difficulty the state of "can" was thought present. Only if a person "can" accomplish an action will his or her intention to do so result in the occurrence of the action. At one point Heider did note that what he called an "action outcome" (what I would call an "event") may be produced in the absence of any exercise of personal force if the effective environmental force "were greater than zero (that is if those environmental factors favorable to x were greater than those unfavorable to x)" (1958, p. 82). For the most part, however, Heider's discussion concentrated on actions, not events, and assumed that environmental force would be acting to prevent those actions.

If a person can perform an action, whether he or she does so will then depend on the motivation ("trying") present, with this motivation consisting of two components, intention and exertion. In this sense of the word, "intention" dealt not with some ultimate objective of the actor, but rather with the specific goal of the immediate action. How intention might interact with exertion was not specified, but together the two were thought to combine in a multiplicative fashion with power, on the assumption that if either power or motivation were zero, no action would result. Both motivation and ability are necessary, neither is sufficient alone.

What makes Heider's work so important as the foundation for attribution theory is not that his analysis of the common sense embodied in language was so clear and cogent as it was, but that the analysis was only the first step. Heider then went on to suggest how a perceiver might *infer* the presence or absence of a particular component from the fact of a completed behavior. That a person has performed an action indicates at least that he or she "can" do so, under the circumstances prevailing at the time. If the person is obviously exerting himself or herself in the direction of the outcome, we would also infer that he or she had intended to produce the results involved. More certain inferences about the individual's ability, intention, and exertion, and about the level of difficulty of the task can be achieved by observing the stimulus person's behavior should the circumstances change, or by comparing that person's actions to the behavior of other people in similar circumstances.

By distinguishing personal force from environmental force, suggesting that attributions might differ in certainty, comparing the attributions made for success with those made for failure, and showing the information that could be gained through comparisons across circumstances or people, Heider laid the foundation for the attributional questions to be asked by a host of later investigators. Heider's "naive" perceiver was soon to become much more sophisticated.

Multiple Events: An Individual Differences View

One of the first problems encountered by a perceiver attempting to attribute causality for an event is to define precisely what "the event" *is*. In discussing the limitation of personal causality to intentional action, I noted that there might have been disagreement about the description of the crash of Flight 90, but for clarity in exposition I simply asserted that the crash itself was the event to be explained. Similar assertions are pervasive in attribution research:

Subjects are given the description of an event and are asked to explain it.

Unfortunately, outside the social psychological laboratory, perceivers are not told by an omniscient third party, "Here is an event, x; now, explain it." Quite the contrary. Our everyday social interaction more closely resembles a process that continues through time rather than a sequence of discrete events. For example, at some point in the development of a dating relationship, two people may discover that they are "in love," but they might be hard pressed to identify the instant at which the change occurred. An employee's yearly "personnel evaluation" becomes institutionalized when the appropriate papers are filled out, but surely there is some judgment of performance taking place throughout the year. A parent's "overreaction" to a child's minor transgression can be understood if it is viewed as the culmination of a thousand minor irritations. In each of these cases the identified "event" might be the single instance or the entire process. Although Newtson's (1976) research shows that perceivers will identify very much the same "breakpoints" in an interaction, there is no research that can presently be used to justify the establishment of criteria by which the boundary between ongoing process and single instance can be predicted reliably. All the social psychologist can do at this writing is raise a caution: Be sure that individuals asked to attribute causality for an event are using the same points in time to specify the beginning and the end of the event to be explained.

If two or more perceivers can agree on *when* an event is taking place, they may not agree on *what* is happening. Suppose that I am spending a windy fall afternoon burning a pile of leaves that I have collected from my yard. What is "the event?" It is certainly true that I am (a) "burning leaves," but I may also be (b) "preparing my yard for winter." My neighbors downwind would notice that I am (c) "filling the house up with smoke," and they might believe I am also (d) "recklessly endangering the dry woods" behind both of our houses. If there is a county ordinance against open fires before 4:00 P.M., then I am also (e) "breaking the law." The action is (f) "contributing particulate matter to the air" and quite possibly (g) "increasing the discomfort of sufferers from emphysema." Finally, if it is a weekday afternoon, I am also (h) "being unavailable to students." Even simple actions can have multiple, often simultaneous, effects, and any combination of these can be used to define "the event." Moreover, many of the different descriptions would lead to different causal attributions, and to different responses from the observers. Someone who considered me merely to be burning leaves would not be likely to take any action. By contrast, a perceiver who considered me to be breaking the law, endangering the woods, or polluting the air might very well call the authorities. But even in this case, *which* authorities were notified—police, firefighters, or the clean air agency—would depend on the particular description of the event.

On what basis is the perceiver supposed to choose one description over another? Unfortunately, in both the philosophical and psychological literatures, there are divergent answers to this question, nearly all of which are based on the same analysis of language in which Heider engaged. The philosophical problem is known as *act individuation*, and using the example above, the first question is "was there one action performed, or were there eight actions taken?" One view is defended by Anscombe (1957), who makes a detailed argument for four contentions: that there is only one act, not eight; that the act performed is the one of which the actor has conscious awareness; that the actor has a reason to undertake this act; and that the actor, himself, is the only "authoritative source" of information about that guiding reason. This reason will be discovered in answer to the question "Why did you do that?"

But not all of the possible descriptions are reasonable answers to this question. If you ask me "Why are you burning those leaves," and I reply "To burn the leaves," you will not be satisfied with the answer. In Anscombe's terms, you really want to know the "intention *with which*" (1957, p. 46, emphasis in original) I am burning the leaves. This final intention "swallows up" previous intentional elements of the action. I intentionally took the rake out of the garage, intentionally raked the leaves into a pile, intentionally took out a pack of matches, intentionally lit a piece of paper placed among the leaves, intentionally fanned the flame until the entire pile caught and burned, and finally, intentionally began to add more leaves (carefully, so as not to put out the fire). My likely claim that I am "cleaning up the yard for winter" would be a quite satisfactory explanation for all of these elements of the action.

There are, however, both philosophical and pyschological problems with the notion that there is only one action, that is, the action I identify in response to the question "Why?" To begin with the philosophical difficulties, Goldman (1970) has argued that any "single act, multiple description" view would require that all of the descriptions refer to an action or event that is *identical* under any description. If "burning leaves" is identical to "breaking the law," then the two actions ought to have all properties in common. But clearly there are ways to break the law that do not involve burning leaves, and just as clearly there can be circumstances under which burning leaves will not be breaking the law. Building on a distinction between "basic acts" and "nonbasic acts" (Danto, 1963) and on what is known as the "by-relation," Goldman would argue that descriptions b–g of the leaf-burning episode are descriptions of nonbasic actions that are accomplished by performing the basic action (a). Indeed, (g) "increasing the discomfort of emphysema sufferers" stands in by-relation not only to (a), but also to (f). Without pursuing this line of reasoning any further, it can be seen that the multiple descriptions are *not* equivalent and cannot, therefore, be explained adequately by reference to a single overriding intention.

It may be true, as Anscombe (1957) has argued, that an observer cannot adduce evidence to *refute* the intention I present in response to the question "Why are you doing that?" Collingwood's (1940) principle of relativity of causes, however, suggests that observers may see in my activities intentions that have as much intuitive force for them as mine does for me. Not only may the police believe that my intent was to break the law and willfully endanger property, they may also be able to convince a judge or jury that their interpretation is the correct one. To argue that a person is the *only* authoritative source of the intention behind his or her action would have the practical consequence of limiting the application of criminal penalties to those few people who came forward to admit their own transgressions.

Turning next to the psychological objections, there are numerous instances outside the courtroom in which actors can be shown to be less-than-perfect reporters of the intentions behind their actions. At the least incriminating end of the scale there is the research reviewed by Nisbett and Wilson (1977) to support their claim that people do not have the kind of access to their ongoing cognitive processes that psychologists (or for our purposes, philosophers) would expect them to have. This claim is controversial (e.g., Smith & Miller, 1978), but none of Nisbett and Wilson's critics would make the kind of "authoritative source" assertion on which Anscombe's (1957) argument depends.

If it is forgivable not to know the answers to questions you are asked, it is somewhat less forgivable to guess. The entire literature that has come to be known as the "psychology of prediction" (Ajzen & Fishbein, 1983; Borgida & Brekke, 1981; Nisbett & Borgida, 1975) illustrates just how mistaken some of those guesses can be. True, very few of these studies have asked subjects to estimate the frequency of their own actions, but some of the same cognitive heuristics that adversely affect judgments about others might also affect judgments about the self. It is, however, when the self-assessments have to do with performance or self-esteem that the individual's own claims about his or her intentions are most suspect. There is a well-documented asymmetry in attributions for one's own performance, with actors routinely taking more credit for their achievements than they accept blame for their shortcomings. Whether this asymmetry is a rather "passive" cognitive artifact, as some have argued (Brewer, 1977; Miller & Ross, 1975), or involves "active" attempts at impression management (Weary & Arkin, 1981) is considered in more detail in Chapter 7, along with some of the cognitive heuristics that might adversely affect judgment. For now it is sufficient to note that either reason could change the answer to the query from "Because I intended to accomplish *x*" to "You're mistaken. I wasn't really trying to do anything like that."

What implications do these objections have for the description of an action or event? The objections lead to what may best be described as an *individual differences* view of action. This view rests on two fundamental assumptions. First, an action by one description is different from "the same" action by a different description. The fine-grained analysis of the descriptions of action shows that because different descriptions are not identical in properties, they should be regarded as reports of related, but distinct, actions. Second, the actor cannot be accepted as the "sole authoritative source" of information about the intent behind the action as he or she would have described it. The actor is certainly a good source, perhaps even the best source, but his or her statement of *the* intent is no less an inference than is the inference that would be made by an outside observer.

The conclusion to be drawn from these two assumptions is this: What we might have called a single, unique event is seen, on reflection, to be a distribution of events as they would be described by the actor and by various observers. The most frequently occurring element of that distribution is what most people would call "the action," and the intent behind that action is the one that would have been inferred by most people. Other observers, responding to their own individual differences in vantage point and objectives, might provide descriptions of the putative event or action, and the intent behind that action, that would differ from this modal element.

The argument that an action or event is more properly thought of as an *event distribution* complicates the task of explanation, but it does square more closely with psychological reality. One does not need to accept the extreme empiricism of Berkeley (1710/1952) or Hume (1748/1952), or to agree with the doctrinaire logical positivism in psychology to which that empiricism led, in order to recognize that the social psychologist's role is to account for the various attributions that are made for actions, not to identify that one unique description that "must logically be correct" in the situation. Certainly it is true that social psychological explanations of the inference process rely on models that specify how such inferences might be made under ideal conditions. Indeed, the theory of the attribution of blame presented in Chapter 8 is just such a rational model. These models, however, are regarded as guides for inquiry, and the possibility of exceptions is explicitly recognized.

Whereas philosophers must wonder whether the contents of mind can be used to say *with certainty* whether an external world exists, psychologists can end their inquiry by describing those mental contents. In the same fashion, whereas philosophy must wonder whether a person's identification of the cause of an action or event would correspond to "the truth" as it might be known by an omniscient deity, social psychology needs only to inquire whether the individual's description of the causes affects that person's subsequent behavior. If I believe my neighbor purposely chose a day on which the wind was blowing my way to burn his leaves, no disclaimers he issues are likely to affect my response toward him. The presumed event and its presumed causes must exist in a single mind in order to affect behavior. Outside the experimental laboratory, it is likely that at least some of the disagreements that arise about causes are really disagreements about the descriptions of the actions or events that have taken place.

Our notion of an event with explanations influenced by individual differences in vantage point and objectives is, on the interpersonal level, quite similar to what Vallacher and Wegner (in press) have described on the individual level as a process of *action identification*. Building on much the same philosophical foundation used here for an attributional analysis of blame (e.g., Anscombe, 1957; Danto, 1963; Goldman, 1970), Vallacher and Wegner argue that the question "What are you doing?" can be answered on any number of hierarchically organized levels.

Vallacher and Wegner give the following example: "Looking for a paper clip" can be described in terms of the discrete muscle movements of the fingers, arms, and limbs; in terms of the "somewhat more recognizable" actions (such as opening and closing drawers) into which those muscle movements can be grouped; or finally, in terms of the "action as a whole" (searching for the paper clip) to be accomplished through these intermediate-level actions. Each succeeding level is related to the preceding level through the by-relation: Searching for a paper clip is done *by* opening and closing drawers, and that, in turn, is done *by* moving various muscles (in press).

The *identity level* given in response to the question "What are you doing?" is defined to be the *prepotent* level. Which level will be prepotent? The theory of action identification proposed by Vallacher and Wegner describes a "fluid system" much like the changing pattern in a fountain. If an action can be identified at both a higher and a lower level, the higher level will tend to become prepotent, reflecting our desire to be informed of what we do "in the most integrative and general way that is available" (Vallacher & Wegner, in press). If, however, an initial high-level identification cannot be maintained as an accurate description of ongoing behavior, then there will be a tendency for a lower level of identification to become prepotent.

For example, I start burning my leaves with the intent of cleaning up my yard before winter comes, so at the beginning of the action I would describe my behavior at this high level of identification. But if a sudden gust of wind threatens to spread glowing debris all over the yard, I will need to concentrate on "keeping the flames from spreading"—an action identified at a lower level. Just as my own action identification can change in this way over time (another psychological reason to distrust me as the "sole authoritative source" of information about my intentions), so another person's description of the action can be affected by his or her objectives or vantage point.

Finally, changes in level of action identification by one person can lead to differences in the person's behavior that are comparable to the differences between people that arise because of individual variations in the descriptions of actions or events. Behavior flows in a stream through time, and action identifications flow in a parallel stream. When the identity level that initiated the action (through an "intent" connection) can no longer be maintained (upon "reflection"), the resulting lower level identification may or may not return to the original position.

The possibility for change is illustrated in studies conducted by Wegner, Vallacher, Macomber, Wood, and Arps (1984). In one study, for example, subjects who had been induced to conceive of the act of "going to college" in terms of its details (like "studying") were more likely to shift to a *new* high-level identification than were subjects who had been induced to conceive of going to college in terms of more comprehensive meanings, such as "preparing for a career." The second study, using "drinking coffee" as the initial identification, showed that these cognitive changes could also be translated into subsequent behavior. No matter whether the divergent descriptions of an action are provided by outside observers or by the actor, the competing descriptions are capable of producing variations in behavior.

To summarize, achieving precision in the description of an event or action requires that such an occurrence be regarded as the modal choice from among an event distribution of possibilities. The actor and individual observers of the action will give accounts that may or may not be identical, and at least some of the disagreements regarding causality may in reality be quarrel over *what* has taken place. Although it is more convenient to speak of "the event" or "the action" as if it were a unique occurrence (and for simplicity's sake I shall often refer to it that way), "the event" is likely to be singular only in an experiment in which it has been specified explicitly. Outside the laboratory the individual differences among observers will lead to alternative descriptions of the event, and these alternative may, in turn, produce variations in subsequent behavior.

Multiple Antecedents of Effects or Actions

Earlier in the chapter I defined a cause as that antecedent or group of antecedents that is sufficient for the occurrence of an event or action. In the rare instances in which there is uniformity of opinion not only about the description of an event, but also about the *single* antecedent that is thought to have brought about the event, the perceiver's task is unambiguous. For example, if I am standing on a street corner in the middle of the day, with numerous people watching me, and I reach down to the sidewalk, pick up a loose piece of concrete from next to the curb, take careful aim, and throw the concrete through the display window of a department store, the observers will have very little doubt that my throwing the concrete was the cause of the window's breaking. These observers may wonder what ever possessed me to do such a thing, but their answers to the question "Why did the window break just now?" will stray very little from "Because that jerk threw a piece of concrete through it!" Even in this example a few of the more analytical individuals may add " . . . and the window was glass" to their account, thus denying that there was a single cause of the breakage.

Most social events, however, cannot be characterized in terms this elementary. From the everyday interaction between two friends to the formal negotiations conducted among nations, there are typically *multiple* antecedents of most events or actions. This multiplicity of potential causes raises two general questions; First, how should true causes be distinguished from mere conditions? The answer to this question relies on a notion of *causal subsets* and will involve a more precise differentiation between necessary and sufficient antecedents than was required in Chapter 2. Second, what processes of social attribution will perceivers follow in order to select one cause, or one subset of events comprising a cause, from among the range of antecedents of an event? This general question must be considered in two separate forms, one form for instances in which repeated observations of potential cause–effect sequences are possible, and one form for cases in which only one observation can be made.

Causes and Conditions

When we attempt to explain the occurrence of any given event or action, we initiate the explanation by asking which aspects of the history, circumstances, and persons involved might be relevant in the production of the event. For any event there will be three mutually exclusive and mutually exhaustive classes of antecedents: potential causal elements, potential obstacles to the occurrence, and elements that are irrelevant (Shaver, 1981). These classes of antecedents are shown in Figure 3-1, and are described in the language of set theory. For any given event E, the universal set of antecedents (U) consists of the union of three mutually exclusive sets. These are the set of j possible causes of the event (C), the set of k potential obstacles to the occurrence of the event (O), and the set of m antecedent elements that are irrelevant to the occurrence of the event or action (I).

   In our example of the crash of Flight 90, the set of potential causes (C) would include such elements (c) as the blinding snowstorm, the possibly faulty de-icing procedure, the long wait after de-icing prior to take-off, the pilots' decision to begin the take-off roll, their subsequent decision not to abort the flight, and the failure of the plane to attain sufficient lift. To this list of potential causes might be added the set of obstacles (O) to the event, factors (o) such as the thrust developed by the engines and the pilots' intention to complete a safe take-off and flight. Whether a particular feature of the setting is a potential cause or a potential obstacle will depend in part on the definition of the effect: The snowstorm is a potential cause of "the crash" but a potential obstacle to "a safe departure." Finally, to the sets of potential causes and obstacles must be added all of the other logically possible antecedents. Some of these (i), such as the fact that the preceding day had been January 12, would be irrelevant under any construction of the event. Others, such as the numerous minor automobile accidents that contributed to the number of vehicles backed up on the bridge, are irrelevant to "the crash," but possibly relevant for an event described as "the rescue of the victims of the crash."

   The potential causes and obstacles are, respectively, what Mill (1888) would

$$U = \begin{cases} C = \{c_1, c_2, c_3, \cdots c_j\} \\ O = \{o_1, o_2, o_3, \cdots o_k\} \\ I = \{i_1, i_2, i_3, \cdots i_m\} \end{cases} \longrightarrow E_n$$

Figure 3-1. The universal set of antecedents of effect, E.

have called the positive and negative conditions for the occurrence of the event. I have previously rejected, on grounds provided by activity theory, Mill's claim that these conditions are indistinguishable from one another and are all indispensable in the production of the effect. Activity theory leads us generally to look for human agency in our explanations of events, just as the National Transportation Safety Board identified human agency, pilot error, as the cause in the specific example. Both that specific finding and the general explanation need to be examined more closely.

To paraphrase an argument made by Mackie (1965), when the National Transportation Safety Board experts found that pilot error was "the cause" of the crash, did they really do so believing that pilot error was, in strict terms, *necessary* for the tragedy? No. Any safety investigator would be able to point to dozens of mechanical failures that could produce the crash of an aircraft in the absence of any mistake on the part of the pilots. So pilot error cannot logically be a necessary condition. If not necessary, was pilot error *sufficient*? Again the answer is negative. If the de-icing procedure had been more effective, the same decision by the pilots would not have resulted in the crash. If the wind driving the snow had shifted slightly, it might have provided enough extra lift to overcome the drag produced by ice on the control surfaces. If pilot error was neither truly necessary nor sufficient, how could the experts and other perceivers as well argue that it was "the cause" of the crash?

Following Mackie's (1965) argument, the question might be answered by identifying a complex collection of antecedents that *together* constituted a sufficient condition for the occurrence of the crash. This collection would include a subset of the potential causes:

c_1 = pilots' decision to take off
c_2 = snowstorm
c_3 = faulty de-icing
c_4 = 45-minute wait for take-off

Also included would be a subset of the potential obstacles (the elements of which together were incapable of preventing the crash):

o_1 = thrust of engines
o_2 = pilots' intention to have safe departure

Thus, the *causal subset* $\{c_1, c_2, c_3, c_4; o_1, o_2\}$ was the sufficient condition for the crash. This causal subset was not a necessary condition, because the crash could have occurred as a consequence of very different causal factors (for example, a severe wind shear that could have caused the plane to crash into the bridge on a clear fall day).

By contrast to the entire causal subset, which is sufficient but not necessary, the central element of the subset (i.e., the pilots' decision to begin the take-off roll) is not sufficient but *is* necessary. This decision is an indispensable element, because without it the entire subset loses causal force. Indeed, the only way that this particular causal subset can produce the effect is for it to include c_1.

Therefore, within the subset, c_1 is necessary; but without the other supporting or contributing conditions, that causal element would not by itself have been sufficient. In Mackie's (1965) terms, the "so-called cause is . . . an *insufficient* but *necessary* part of a condition which is itself *unnecessary* but *sufficient* for the result" (p. 309, emphasis in original). At the suggestion of Stove, Mackie (1965) refers to such a causal element by an acronym for the preceding quoted phrase, using the first letter of each italicized word, "an INUS condition."

The notion of an INUS condition is one to which I shall refer in later chapters, so an additional example will help to make the analysis clear. Three times between October of 1983 and September of 1984, terrorists destroyed American diplomatic and military installations in Lebanon by driving trucks laden with explosives into the buildings. The last of these attacks was made two days before heavy steel gates designed specifically to prevent truck-bomb attacks were to be installed on the road to the American embassy building. The driver of the truck successfully avoided two guard posts, drove around concrete barriers placed in the road to slow down any approach, and survived a hail of machine-gun fire long enough to crash into the building, killing himself and two embassy personnel in the resulting explosion.

At the time of the incident, then President Reagan decried the terrorist attack, but suggested that part of the responsibility for the tragedy should be placed on cuts made by his predecessor, President Carter, in the clandestine staff of the Central Intelligence Agency. The argument was that with a larger group of operatives there might have been better information about the impending attack. Other observers noted that the guard posts had been staffed largely by local militia, not by the Marines who provide security to American embassies, because the Marine contingent had recently been reduced. Still others noted that installation of the various barricades had been "in process" for a period of months, perhaps longer than necessary.

In our terms the suicide driver's actions were the INUS condition for the bombing. Additionally, however, the absence of barricades, the ineffective fire from the militia, and the absence of heavy weapons capable of destroying the truck must be regarded as elements of the causal subset that constituted the sufficient condition for the occurrence. These other elements could not by themselves have produced the explosion, but without their participation the driver of the truck would not have been able to reach the embassy building. The driver's behavior therefore was an insufficient but necessary component of a causal subset that on the whole was unnecessary (a bomb dropped from a plane would also have been sufficient) but sufficient for the tragedy to have occurred.

Minimal Sufficient Causal Subsets

Without multiplying examples any further, it should be clear that for almost any event there are likely to be numerous combinations of causes, obstacles, and irrelevant conditions, which combinations could produce the event in question. Each of these effective combinations of factors is what I have called a "minimal sufficient causal subset" (Shaver, 1981). In more formal terms, given a set of potential causal elements (C) and a set of potential obstacles (O), a subset of the union of these two sets will be a minimal sufficient causal subset if it meets two criteria. First, the subset must be sufficient to produce the event. This would obviously eliminate from consideration those subsets in which the obstacles overcame the potential causal elements. Second, each element of the subset (including any INUS condition that might be present) must be what Scriven (1964) and Mackie (1965) would call "nonredundant." An element is nonredundant if it is able to produce the effect in concert with the other elements in the subset, but incapable of producing the effect by itself.

How many different minimally sufficient causal subsets might there be for a given event or action? The answer to this question depends on the number of individual potential causal elements (the size of set C) and on the number of potential obstacles (the size of set O). Return to the example of the crash, and consider for a moment only the four causes designated as elements of C: the pilots' decision, the snowstorm, the de-icing, and the long wait. Suppose for a moment that the pilots' decision were *not* an insufficient but necessary part of this unnecessary but sufficient causal subset. On the contrary, suppose that any *two* of the four might together produce the crash, although no single causal element could do so alone. The total of minimally sufficient causal subsets would be the sum of (a) the number (six) of possible pairs of elements, and (b) the number (four) of possible triples of elements, or a total of 10 minimally sufficient causal subsets. The order in which elements appear within the subset is not important, so the subsets are counted as combinations rather than permutations. The triples are included because the third element still meets the criterion of nonredundancy—it cannot produce the effect by itself. The one quadruple is not included, because it really contains two pairs, and by definition any pair would have been sufficient to produce the effect. There are six combinations of four things taken two at a time, and four combinations of four things taken three at a time, for the total of 10 minimally sufficient causal subsets. Because the causal subsets are counted using combinations of the elements, the number of minimally sufficient causal subsets would increase geometrically with linear increases in the number of causal elements involved.

If the same nonredundant element is found in every minimal sufficient causal subset, then that element (which may or may not be an INUS condition) will be universally necessary for the occurrence of the event. In the embassy bombing the driver's willingness to commit suicide in an attack is a universally necessary causal element. In more general terms, should there be one or more such elements, then the order of the resulting combinations will be reduced accordingly. I shall return to the issues involved in counting minimal sufficient causal subsets and describe some attributional consequences of various counting methods in the next section.

Specification of the idea of a minimally sufficient causal subset and discussion of the notion of an individually necessary element of such a subset completes the line of reasoning needed to counter Mill's (1888) claim that the various antecedents of an event are indistinguishable from one another. Ducasse (1969) successfully argued that it is possible to identify a single potential cause from among the manifold of antecedents, Collingwood (1940) pointed out that human agency would be a principal nonarbitrary way for making such an identification, and Mackie (1965) showed that a single identified "cause" can be an essential component of the conditions that are (collectively) minimally sufficient for producing the event. Countering Mill's claim in this way makes the logical account of causes and conditions agree with the psychological reality that people *do* identify the individual "causes" of events, even when those individual causes are part of a very complex set of conditions that together produced the occurrence. With consideration of these logical distinctions, the discussion now returns to the psychological processes.

Perception of Multiple Causes

Assuming that perceivers can agree on the time at which an event begins and ends and on the most probable description of that event, how do they choose "the cause" from among the multiple antecedents? The answer, according to Kelley (1973), will depend on whether there is the opportunity to observe repeated instances of the potential cause–effect sequence. When repeated observations are possible, Kelley (1967, 1973) builds on Heider's (1958) suggestion that the perceiver will employ a version of Mill's (1888) "Method of Difference." By contrast, when there is only a single instance observed, the perceiver will use *cognitive schemata*—relatively enduring cognitive structures. These schemata are thought to fill in the gaps in missing data, data that would in principle have been available had there been repeated observations. These two different processes are discussed separately.

Repeated Observations

A perceiver who has the opportunity to observe repeated instances of a potential cause–effect sequence is confronted by the same problem of induction that has plagued formal science for centuries: Can a general principle be abstracted from a series of observations over which the perceiver (or scientist) has no direct control? Contemporary philosophers of science such as Popper (1959) reject induction as a proper method for scientific inquiry, preferring a falsificationist strategy for research. Even if deduction of hypotheses from an axiomatized theory is preferable for formal science, the standard of proof demanded of ordinary perceivers need not be so high as to preclude induction. Consequently, perceivers may—and Kelley (1967, 1973) argues that they do—use methods of inference that are quite similar to the eliminative methods of induction first formulated for science by Bacon (1620/ 1952) and later codified into canons by Mill (1888).

In order to isolate the cause of an effect from the other conditions (what I would call the irrelevant antecedents) present at the time of occurrence of the event, Mill (1888) proposed four fundamental "Methods," only two of which are of any concern to attribution theory. The first of these two, called the "Method of Difference," is stated as follows:

> If an instance in which the phenomenon under investigation occurs, and an instance in which it does not occur, have every circumstance in common save one, that one occurring only in the former; the circumstance in which alone the two instances differ, is the effect, or the cause, or an indispensable part of the cause, of the phenomenon. (Mill, 1888, p. 280)

This method involves a comparison between the occurrence of an event or action and its nonoccurrence, with the circumstances surrounding the nonoccurrence differing in only one respect from those surrounding the occurrence. The canon is stated in such a manner that "the phenomenon" could either be the consequent of the particular circumstance, in which the canon would have isolated the cause, or the antecedent of the circumstance, in which case the canon would have isolated the effect. For the purposes of this discussion, only the former instance is of concern here. It is, as Mill notes, "scarcely necessary to give examples of a logical process to which we owe almost all the inductive conclusions we draw in daily life" (p. 280). What is important to keep clear is that this method deals with a comparison between the *presence* of something and its *absence*.

The second of Mill's canons that is of interest to attribution theory is the "Method of Concomitant Variations," stated as follows: "Whatever phenomenon varies in any manner whenever another phenomenon varies in some particular manner, is either a cause or an effect of that phenomenon, or is connected with it through some fact of causation" (p. 287).

Again, the concern of this discussion is only with causation, not with using the method to identify effects. Here it is important, however, to use Mill's example to convey the central features of the method: If we seek to distinguish the effects of the fact that a body has heat from the effects that would be produced by the body without heat, we cannot use a Method of Difference. It is not possible to remove *all* heat from a body, so the effects that flow from the presence of heat cannot be compared with those that flow from the absence of heat. All that can be done is to observe the properties and effects of the body over a range of possible temperatures.

Mill notes several limitations of this method, two of which are important to this discussion. First, the method logically can discover only correlation. The changes in the presumed effect could be due to the presumed cause, or the concomitant variations in the two could be the product of changes in some third, unmeasured, variable. Second, the conclusions to be drawn from the method can be reasonably certain only within the range of the variations tested. There is always the possibility that the form of a functional relationship could differ beyond the values measured. In attribution a failure to recognize the first limitation can be seen, for example, in the influence that one's expectations for an interaction have on the behavior of the other person, leading to a false confirmation of the expectancy. Failure to recognize the second limitation can lead to the belief that action is the product of personal dispositions, when in fact it has occurred only within the context of a narrowly prescribed set of circumstances.

Each of the methods involves repeated observations of a potential cause–effect sequence, and Heider (1958) suggested that the Method of Difference constituted the procedure through which "in some instances, a percept is attributed to factors within the perceiver, and in other instances to properties of the object or of the mediating conditions" (p. 68). Building on this suggestion, Kelley (1967) formulated the *covariation* principle of attribution, asserting that the "effect is attributed to that condition which is present when the effect is present and which is absent when the effect is absent" (p. 194).

When Mill proposed the Method of Difference as a procedure for formal science, he recognized that it was also the inference process used by laymen in their everyday judgments. Reversing the analogy, Kelley (1967) likened the naive perceiver's use of the covariation principle to the scientist's use of the analysis of variance (ANOVA). Specifically, Kelley proposed that decisions about possible causes were made by examining three different dimensions. The first of these dimensions contained the *entities* in the environment, the second represented the circumstances (*time/modality*) surrounding the attribution, and the third reflected the opinions of other *persons*. As Kelley conceived of it, the event or action was to be the dependent variable in the analysis of variance, and the three dimensions of possible causes were to be the independent variables.

Each of the dimensions had its own criterion; these, respectively, were distinctiveness, consistency, and consensus. As an example of the use of the criteria, an internal state of pleasure following a good meal would be attributed to the food if the attributor found the evening's dish to be particularly enjoyable (distinctive from other foods), if the food was as delightful when consumed from a paper plate at home as when it was eaten from a china plate in a restaurant (consistency), and if other gourmets agreed on the high quality of the dish (consensus). In this example there is change from one food to another, there is no change from one time and set of circumstances to another, and there is no change from one perceiver to another. By the covariation principle the cause of the internal feeling state is that which varied—the food itself.

This intuitive example is straightforward, but the analogy to the analysis of variance is another matter entirely. To begin with, I have noted elsewhere (Shaver, 1981) that the criteria associated with the presumed independent variables were improperly described by Kelley (1967) as part of the error variance: "The first criterion (distinctiveness) seems to correspond to the numerator or between-condition term in the usual F ratio and the last three criteria (consistency over time, modality, and persons) correspond to the error or within-condition term" (p. 198). In fact, variations along each of these dimensions would all be expected to contribute to the *numerator* of the usual F ratio, and in this chapter's example, only the triple interaction (differences in distinctiveness in the presence of high consistency and high consensus) would have been significant. The problem with this corrected example is, of course, that no quantity immediately suggests itself as the analogue for the random within-cell variation that comprises the true error term in the analysis of variance.

In a more recent review of the literature, Jaspars, Hewstone, and Fincham (1983) have also found fault with the ANOVA model. These authors carefully decomposed the elements present in the vignettes used by McArthur (1972) and concluded that her design was in reality an incomplete factorial, some cells of which would have been indeterminate if they had been filled. Virtually all of the research in the distinctiveness–consistency–consensus mold (much of which is reviewed by Kelley & Michela, 1980) has been patterned after McArthur's initial study and therefore suffers from similar problems. Whatever valuable conclusions may arise from that literature, I would agree with Jaspars et al. (1983):

> A strict interpretation of the so-called ANOVA model does not seem to be a likely model for the description of attribution processes. A more simple "natural inductive logic" model, based on the empiricist notion of causality, appears to describe the results of attribution studies fairly well if one takes into account that such a model is sensitive to the personal or situational nature of the cause. (p. 24)

Consequently, while I shall retain the metaphor of attributor as "lay scientist," I shall not refer again to the specific ANOVA model.

The critically important contribution that Kelley's (1967) theory does make to our understanding of causal attribution is the identification of three dimensions along which the Method of Difference, or the principle of covariation, might be employed. First, I *compare* my reaction to one entity with my reactions to other entities, making mental notes of those limited cases in which the effect occurs. For example, I may have had great pleasure at food before, but it has seldom been greater than the happiness this superb chocolate mousse cake brings me. Then I compare my reactions to any distinctive entity over different times and through different modalities. I buy an entire cake, take it home, and delight in eating pieces at different times and in different social surroundings. This set of comparisons is the most literal translation of the Method of Difference and allows me to determine whether my internal reaction remains present in the presence of the entity as different environmental conditions come and go. Finally, I compare this distinctive and consistent response of mine with the responses of others, becoming certain of the cake's delectable nature (an entity attribution) when I find that others' reactions parallel my own. That these three dimensions collectively account for the majority of variance in open-ended attributions of causality (Elig & Frieze, 1975) is testimony to the heuristic value of the three-dimensional classification system.

Single Cases

It does appear that perceivers who have the occasion to view several repeated instances of a possible cause–effect sequence will employ a version of the Method of Difference across dimensions roughly equivalent to entities, circumstances, and persons. But what will a perceiver do when there is only a single observation that can be made? Form an impression, but remain guarded about confidence in that judgment? Withhold judgment entirely until more information has been obtained? Unfortunately, probably neither of these conservative perceptual courses will be chosen. From the "snap judgments" we make informally to the jury verdicts we render with the pomp attendant upon court proceedings, we do make attributions—often rather confident and unyielding ones—on the basis of single observed instances.

We are able to make such inferences, according to Kelley (1972, 1973), because we rely on cognitive schemata that substitute for the data that would have been gathered had repeated observations been possible. Rather than following the covariation principle, attributions made for single cases are thought to follow a principle of *discounting* that serves as a correction for the existence of multiple possible causes and a principle of *augmentation* that compensates for differences in the strengths of individual causes. These principles apply, respectively, in cases of *multiple sufficient causes* (more than a single antecedent sufficient for the production of the effect) and *compensatory causes* (a cause, or multiple causes, powerful enough to overcome obstacles to the occurrence of the effect). Each of these schemata will be considered in turn. For simplicity in presentation I shall limit the number of causes involved in each case, but that limitation changes neither Kelley's description of the schemata nor my criticisms of that description.

To begin with the multiple sufficient causes schema, suppose that a particular action could have been produced by either of two causal elements. In our terms, the set of potential causes (C) consists of two elements, c_1 and c_2, neither of which is individually necessary, and each of which is a minimally sufficient causal subset when taken alone. There are, then *three* ways to bring about the effect: provide c_1 alone, provide c_2 alone, or provide the two causes together in a redundant combination $\{c_1, c_2\}$. The latter circumstance constitutes the schema for multiple sufficient causes, as shown in Figure 3-2. According to Kelley (1973), this schema leads to an attribution governed by

		c_2	
		Present	Absent
c_1	Present	E	E
	Absent	E	

Figure 3-2. Schema for multiple sufficient causes [adapted from Kelley (1972)].

the *discounting* principle, "The role of a given cause in producing a given effect is discounted if other plausible causes are also present" (p. 113).

Two features of this schema deserve more detailed comment. First, each individual cause is what I have described elsewhere (Shaver, 1981) as a *discrete* cause: one that exerts its influence through its presence or absence, rather than through variations in its presumed strength. Consequently, the discounting principle is for an attribution based on a single instance that is the logical equivalent of the Method of Difference for attributions based on repeated instances. Decisions are made on the basis of causes that are present when the effect is present, or absent when the effect is absent. Second, the *degree* to which each individual cause is to be discounted (because of the presence of other potential causes) is, in Kelley's (1973) view, a direct function of the number of alternatives.

For a simple case like that in Figure 3-2, this second claim seems almost trivial. Even in this case, however, there are, as we have seen *three* ways of producing the effect, not two ways. Is each of the two causal elements to be discounted by a factor based only on the number of elements, or by a factor that includes the possible combinations of elements? This question becomes substantially more interesting as the number of multiple sufficient causes increases. For example, with six such causes, should each be discounted by a factor of roughly six (the number of individual elements), or by a factor of roughly 60 (taking into account that there are 63 combinations of ways in which six elements can be grouped into minimally sufficient subsets if redundant subsets are also counted)? In general, is the discounting function a linear change with linear increases in the number of possible causes, or is the function nonlinear? This question deserves more attention that it has yet received.

Whatever the discounting "fraction" might turn out to be, the description of individual causes as discrete entities that are either present or absent is entirely consistent with the initial premise that perceivers follow an analogue to the Method of Difference. Unfortunately, the same cannot be said of Kelley's (1972, 1973) treatment of causes in the schema for compensatory causes. The simplest of these schemata is shown in Figure 3-3, and it contains a single possible cause and a single obstacle (what Kelley refers to, respectively, as a

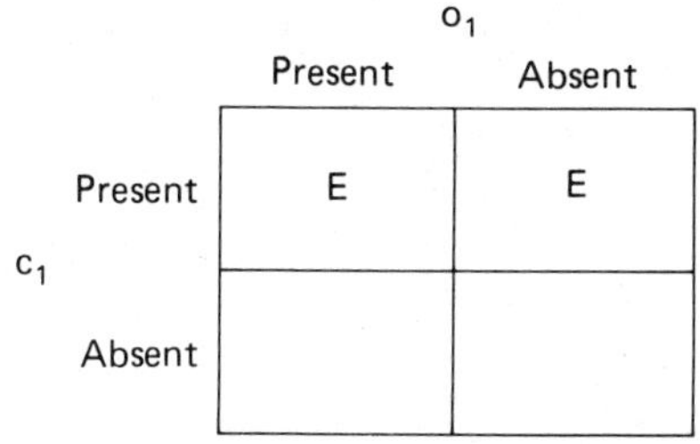

Figure 3-3. Schema for augmentation of a cause in the presence of an obstacle [adapted from Kelley (1972)].

c_2

	Strong	Moderate	Weak
Strong	E	E	E
c_1 **Moderate**	E	E	
Weak	E		

Figure 3-4. Schema for compensatory causes of varying strength [adapted from Kelley (1972)].

"facilitative cause" and an "inhibitory cause"). The entire set of conditions thus consists of the union of a set of causes (C) containing a single element c_1, and a set of obstacles (O) also containing a single element o_1. The cause is individually sufficient, not an individually insufficient but necessary condition, so there are two minimally sufficient subsets for the occurrence of the effect: subset $\{c_1\}$ and subset $\{c_1, o_1\}$.

According to Kelley's theory, the *augmentation* principle holds that the perceiver will believe c_1 to be stronger when the effect occurs in the presence of the obstacle (the second minimally sufficient subset) than when the effect occurs in the absence of the obstacle (the first minimally sufficient subset). This conclusion cannot be based on the Method of Difference, because it involves a comparison between two instances in which the causal element is present. What is really being drawn is a perceptual conclusion based on the Method of Concomitant Variations. There is no question that c_1 is the cause of the effect, there is only question about the magnitude of that cause.

If this were Kelley's (1972) only use of the principle of augmentation, it could easily be reconciled with traditional philosophical analyses of causality. Those analyses, at least from Mill (1888) to the present date, permit causes, once identified, to vary in quantity. What they do not allow, but what Kelley goes on to assert, is that an entity can acquire causal status as a result of variations in strength. This extension of the augmentation principle is shown in Figure 3-4, a schema for compensatory causes that includes two potential causal elements, c_1, and c_2. Each element is claimed to occur in three levels of strength—weak, moderate, and strong. As Figure 3-4 shows, the effect occurs whenever either cause is strong, regardless of the strength value of the other cause. By the same token, the effect is absent when both causes are weak. If the words "present" and "absent" were substituted for "strong" and "weak," respectively, and the moderate strength causes were omitted, then the schema would be identical to the schema for multiple sufficient causes, and there would be no logical difficulties. These problems arise because the effect is also thought to be brought about by the combination of c_1 at moderate strength and c_2 at moderate strength. It is one thing to assert that a cause, once identified, might vary in magnitude (producing corresponding shifts in the magnitude of the effect), but quite another to argue that an entity's causal status will be affected by its strength.

For any theory of causality to be coherent, it must have a logically acceptable definition of its central concept. At a minimum, that definition must provide a rule by which causes can be distinguished from those antecedents that are irrelevant. Unfortunately, as I have previously noted (Shaver, 1981), Kelley's (1972) theory has two different, and mutually incompatible, definitions of cause. The first of these is the one inherent in discounting: Causes are antecedents that *by their presence* produce effects. By this definition it is possible to divide the world clearly into two categories, causes and noncauses (some of the latter might be obstacles, others might be irrelevant). Or is it really possible to do so? What about an entity that is not a cause when it is weak, is a cause when it is strong, and may be a cause (depending on other circumstances) when it is of moderate strength? Such an entity does not fit the category assignment rule.

Suppose the rule were changed to define a cause (as in the case of compensatory causes) as an antecedent that, given sufficient strength, produces an effect. Mere presence is not sufficient (or else the "weak" cause would also produce the effect). This definition, however, would make it impossible to categorize the kind of cause that, in the multiple sufficient schema, produces effects by its mere presence. Regardless of which definition is taken to be the fundamental one, the attribution-theoretical class of causes will include elements that do not meet the defining properties of the category.

Is there a path out of this thicket? Fortunately, both traditional philosophical analyses of causality and more recent work in action theory (e.g., Goldman, 1970) suggest the same solution. Recall for a moment the example of my burning leaves on a windy day. Through a "fine-grained" consideration of that event, it became clear that there were several different actions being performed, not a single action with multiple descriptions. Exactly the same sort of fine-grained analysis can be helpful in the present circumstances. There is good reason to consider the "strong" versions of the causes shown in Figure 3-4 to be different entities from the "weak" versions of the same causes. After all, the two differ not only in characterization, but also in effect (one produces the event, while the other does not). Furthermore, the "moderate" versions of the two causes may be distinguished from the "strong" and "weak" causes on the same grounds.

Adopting this distinction, the two causes (each with three levels) in Figure 3-4 can be rewritten as the six discrete causes in Figure 3-5. The effect always occurs in the presence of c_1 or c_4, so each of these by itself is a minimally sufficient subset for the occurrence of the event. In this representation, however, the subset $\{c_2, c_5\}$ also now constitutes a minimally sufficient causal subset. Neither element can produce the effect by itself, but the two can do so together. What changes in this analysis is not the strength of any particular cause, but the number and nature of the other elements in the subset. Success at a difficult task is achieved not because a cause called "effort" is increased in

	c_4	c_5	c_6
c_1	E	E	E
c_2	E	E	
c_3	E		

Figure 3-5. Schema for discrete compensatory causes.

strength, but because a cause called "intense effort" is present. In this way the person's contribution to the outcome is described in the same manner as the resistance of the task: There are "hard tasks" and there are "easy tasks," and the two are thought to be different. The same should be true for effort.

This revision of Kelley's (1972, 1973) theory accomplishes two important purposes. First, it eliminates the logical problems associated with having mutually incompatible definitions of the central concept of causality. A cause is now any causal element of a minimally sufficient causal subset. That subset may have only a single element, it may have multiple nonredundant elements, one of its elements may be insufficient but necessary for the sufficiency of the subset (an INUS condition), or it may be overdetermined and contain multiple redundant elements. In all of these cases, however, it is the minimally sufficient causal *subset* that is the sufficient cause of the event, not any individual element by itself. The mere presence of any such minimally sufficient subset will produce the effect, and the effect will not occur unless one of the possible minimally sufficient subsets is present. The interplay between elements that Kelley would have described as "strong" or "weak" takes place *within* the subset; a causal element of "intense effort" must be part of any minimally sufficient causal subset that also contains the obstacle "very difficult task."

The second purpose served by conceiving of causes in this way is that the principles of discounting and augmentation may now be described in conceptually equivalent terms. A given minimally sufficient causal subset will be discounted to the degree that other such subsets are also present. When an effect occurs in the presence of an obstacle, the minimally sufficient causal subset presumed to have preceded the effect will be perceived to have contained causal elements that individually or collectively overcame the obstacle. Obviously, if only one causal element is thought present in the subset, it will be considered a strong cause rather than a weak one. In other circumstances, however, that single strong cause might be replaced by multiple causal elements that together overcame the obstacle. Augmentation, then, can be restated as the perceiver's beliefs about the strength of an acknowledged cause or as that person's choice of multiple causal elements. In either case, the criterion at the level of the causal element is presence versus absence, keeping the entire reasoning process consistent with the Method of Difference.

Attribution of Causality

What did the National Transportation Safety Board mean when it stated that "the cause" of the crash of Flight 90 was pilot error? What would it mean to say that the nation's economic policy is the cause of high interest rates? Or to say that mutual incompatibility was the cause of the dissolution of a marriage? Whatever the particular event in question, how might a perceiver have reached the causal conclusion? This question can now be answered: Whether the event to be explained is an accident, a corporate or organizational decision, or an individual person's action, the psychological processes involved in providing an explanation can be represented by the model shown in Figure 3-6. This model borrows from philosophical discussions of causality, and it builds heavily on research and theory in social psychology. It may not be the only account that could be offered for the process, and as shown in later chapters, it will probably require refinements and additions. It does, however, serve as an internally consistent summary of the distinctions that have been drawn in this chapter.

The several elements of the process are listed at the left of Figure 3-6, and the particular content of each step is shown in the body of the diagram. The process of attribution begins at the top of the diagram, with the perceiver's description of the event to be explained. This event is, in reality, an *event distribution*, and the individual differences among perceivers in vantage point and objectives will lead to variations in the description offered. Occasionally, these variations will reflect conscious choices ("Call it what you want to, but for me it is an . . . "), but more frequently the perceiver's description will be so "automatic" that he or she will fail to notice that other interpretations are possible.

When the event is the action of a person, that act will be identified as occurring at a particular level—typically the "action as a whole," but sometimes at a lower identity level. In part depending upon the perceiver's description, the event to be explained will either appear to have an "obvious" single cause (my throwing the piece of concrete through the store window) or possible multiple causes. In those few cases involving single obvious causes, "the cause" is, in our terms, a single *minimally sufficient causal subset* that may have only one causal element or multiple causal elements. Regardless of its constituents, that minimally sufficient causal subset will, for most perceivers, exhaust the universe of explanations. Only if there are multiple causes of the event will there be any further need for cognitive processing.

When there are, potentially, multiple causes for an action or event, the perceiver will need to employ some inductive method to distinguish "the cause" from the other antecedents of the effect. Whether this is the

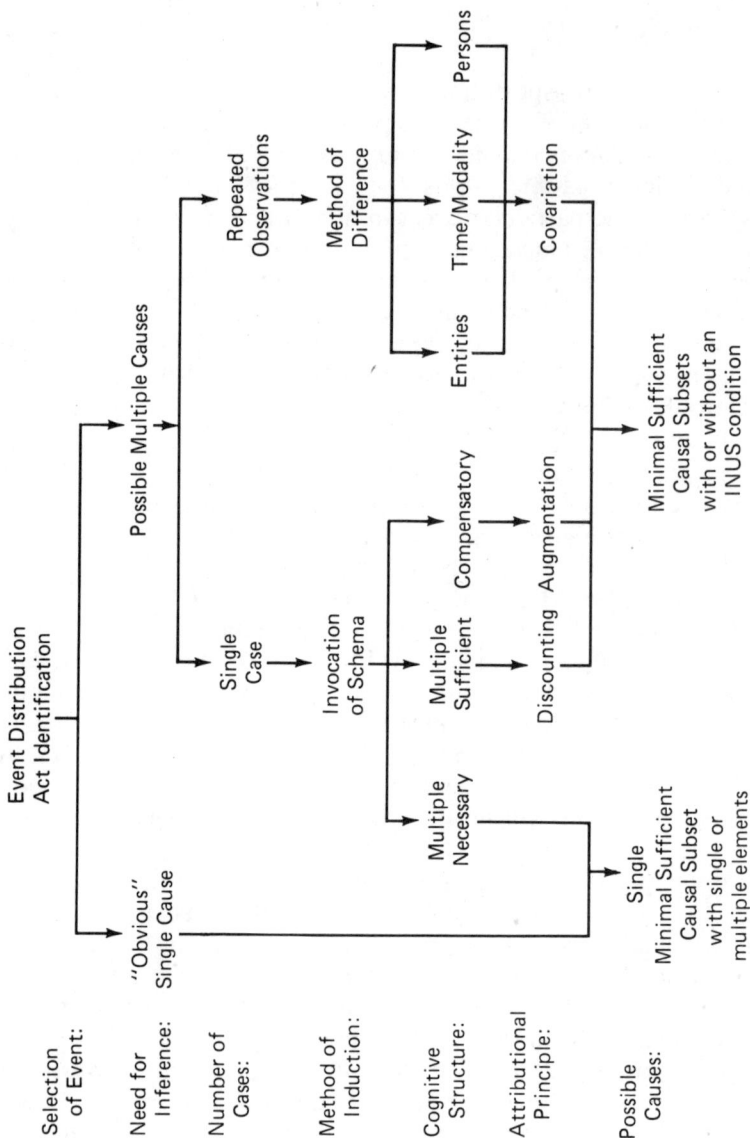

Figure 3-6. A preliminary model of the attribution of causality for an event of action.

psychological equivalent of the Method of Difference, or the invocation of one of the cognitive schemata, will depend on whether or not there are opportunities for repeated observations. With repeated observations the cognitive structure presumed to be involved in the perceiver's judgment is the three-dimensional structure outlined by Kelley (1967). The possible causes will be examined to determine whether they are distinctively associated with the event to be explained or are also associated with other entities. Those possible causes distinctively associated with the occurrence of the event will then be followed through time or across modalities. Finally, the opinions of others will be sought regarding the causal efficacy of the few remaining distinctive and consistent potential causes. Through successive applications of this principle of covariation the perceiver will arrive at a judgment that "the cause" is one of several minimally sufficient causal subsets, or that "the cause" is an insufficient but necessary element within a sufficient causal subset.

A perceiver attempting to explain the single occurrence of an event or action will, by contrast, need to resort to the invocation of one of the cognitive schemata as a substitute for application of the Method of Difference. If the multiple causes all appear to be necessary for the occurrence of the event or action, that minimally sufficient causal subset (with its multiple elements) will be identified as "the cause." If the multiple possible causes each appear to be sufficient, then the principle of discounting will lead to a reduction in the presumed importance of each minimally sufficient causal subset. Finally, if the effect has occurred in the presence of obstacles, or if no individual cause appears sufficient by itself (although one of these could be insufficient but necessary), the schema for compensatory causes will be invoked. In the former case the principle of augmentation will lead either to the choice of a minimally sufficient causal subset containing enough causal elements to outweigh the obstacle, or to an increased weight given to an acknowledged causal element. In the latter case of truly compensatory causes, the perceiver will identify as "the cause" a minimally sufficient causal subset containing enough causal elements to have produced the event. As was true with causes identified through covariation, the causal elements identified through augmentation and discounting might be individually necessary, though individually insufficient.

This model of the process of causal attribution not only summarizes the discussion of causality to this point, but it also brings to our attention a number of questions that have yet to be answered about the process. For example, is there a fixed time-order for the comparisons across entities, time/ modality, and persons? What are the implications for the final causal judgment if the comparison across persons precedes the identification of distinctive causal elements, as might be suggested by the decision-process model of bystander intervention in emergencies (Latané & Darley, 1970), which holds that social comparisons among individuals may help to define whether an event is a real emergency? A second remaining question has to do with the determination of which particular minimally sufficient causal subset will be reported in any judgment situation leading to several possibly influential subsets. Will perceivers refuse to choose among these alternatives, or will their personal individual differences, their initial descriptions of the event, or other factors in the situation lead them to "choose" one of the subsets as being prepotent? A third question deals with the selection among cognitive schemata in the attribution of causality for a single case. The theory makes it clear that the three schemata will, once invoked, lead to differing attributional outcomes. But what characteristics of the event or the perceiver will lead to the use of one schema as opposed to another? Will the original description of the event make a difference? Or will factors such as the perceived intentionality, exertion, or ability (for the case of an action) dictate the choice of a schema?

The answers to these questions, and other features of the attribution of causality, may depend on the content of the attribution and on the *use* to which the perceiver intends to put the result of the causal analysis. For this reason the model will be referred to again only after considering the companion to causality—responsibility.

Chapter 4
Dimensions of Responsibility

What does it mean to say that a person is "responsible" for an event? Does it mean that the person caused the occurrence? that the person should be held legally accountable? that despite any decisions that might or might not be reached by the legal system, the person should be held morally accountable for the event? The question of responsibility, like the question of causality, is a complex one. Consider an example: Suppose that a person raises a loaded rifle, takes careful aim, pulls the trigger, and the bullet that is fired kills another person. Is the one who pulled the trigger "responsible?"

Given only this information most of us would reply, perhaps with annoyance, "of course." But what if we learn that the person who pulled the trigger was a 6-year-old child? Or an adult who was convinced that he or she was helping to save the earth by firing at a dangerous extraterrestrial? Or a perfectly sane adult who was part of a duly constituted firing squad carrying out a legal sentence of death on an offender who had been properly convicted of the brutal murder of an entire family? The fact that most people would answer these questions differently, even though at one level both the act and the result are the same in all cases, illustrates some of the problems involved in the determination of responsibility. Responsibility depends heavily on causality, but the two are not identical. The purpose of this chapter is to examine the concept of responsibility by describing the five related philosophical issues that bear on the determination of personal responsibility: causality, moral standards, determinism, voluntary choice, and extenuation.

As already noted, the first issue that affects the determination of responsibility is *causality*: Are there instances in which individuals can legitimately be held to account for events that they have not personally caused? Ordinarily, the answer to this question is negative, but there are special cases in which there might be an affirmative answer. The second issue concerns the *standards* against which behavior is to be compared: How can we decide which actions should receive censure (or legal sanction) and which should receive approbation? Detailed consideration of this broad ethical question is beyond the scope of our inquiry, but those general ethical principles that are particularly relevant for the punishment that often follows wrongdoing will be noted.

The third issue is the thorny problem of *determinism*: If it can be shown that there is no true freedom of action, can anyone be held accountable for actions that contradict moral guidelines? This is a critical question not only for an attributional analysis of blame, but also for more general psychological theory. On the one hand, if there is not *some* regularity in human behavior, psychologists have no business searching for it. On the other hand, if Freud's (e.g., 1920/1952) internal determinism or Skinner's (1953) external determinism completely accounts for behavior, then no one could be held responsible, either in a moral judgment or in a legal proceeding. The fourth major issue arises only if there is an alternative to this extreme view of determinism. If it is possible in principle for human beings to make free choices, how in practice can those be distinguished from reflex actions and involuntary behaviors: What are the characteristics of *voluntary* action? Truly voluntary behavior will require some knowledge of the consequences of action and at least the opportunity to have done otherwise.

The last major question also assumes that there is an alternative to a complete and mechanistic determinism. What *extenuating factors* might release an individual from the moral or legal responsibility that would otherwise have followed performance of the action? The presence of external coercion may reduce responsibility, and actors may offer either excuses or justifications for their behavior.

Although elements of all five issues can be seen in the preceding example, the elements that are most apparent are the differences in extenuating circumstances across different descriptions of the action. Before considering these five philosophical problems in more detail, it would be a good idea to begin with at least a working definition of responsibility.

Senses of Responsibility

Standard dictionary definitions of "responsibility" equate the term with "accountability," with liability either for praise (if the action for which one is responsible is a socially valued one) or blame (if the action is morally or legally wrong). As Hart (1968) has argued persuasively, however, this simple idea does not really capture all the senses in which people use the term "responsibility." According to Hart, there are four different senses of the word.

In the first, *role-responsibility*, a person is considered bound to perform the duties legitimately attached to his or her "distinctive place or office in a social organization" (Hart, 1968, p. 212). It is in this sense that Hart believes a sentry is responsible for alerting the guard, parents are responsible for the upbringing of their children, or a sea captain is responsible for going down with his ship. Such role responsibility can be as permanent or as temporary as the social role involved, and among the latter Hart would include such transient and informal roles as the role of "host." The extent to which an individual might receive opprobrium as a consequence of a failure to meet his or her role responsibilities could be prescribed by legal dictates, as in the case of a captain who deserted his sinking ship; by moral conventions, as in the case of a person who tells a harmful, but not illegal, lie to a friend; or by neither, as in the case of a host who is routinely impolite to guests. Only those instances in which people with *formal* roles in organizations fail to perform the duties universally expected for role occupants will be of any significant concern for our analysis of blame. Because these will be exceptional uses of the more general term, "responsibility," they will be noted specifically when they occur.

The second of Hart's senses, *causal responsibility*, is one in which the phrase "was responsible for" could be replaced by "produced," with no loss of meaning. In this sense, "not only human beings but also their actions or omissions, and things, conditions, and events, may be said to be responsible for outcomes" (Hart, 1968, p. 214). According to Hart, this sense is almost always expressed in the past tense, and represents a substantial portion (but not all) of the causes that are present in the world. That is, while "was responsible for" can always be replaced by "caused," the converse is not true. In our terms, causal responsibility is nothing more than the identification after the fact of the minimally sufficient causal subset (whether or not that subset is the action of a person). Given a thorough definition of causality, this version of "responsibility" is worse than redundant—it is confusing. So I shall never use the term in this sense.

Now, taking Hart's argument out of its original order, the next sense, *capacity responsibility*, explicates the phrase "she is responsible for her actions." In Hart's view "The capacities in question are those of understanding, reasoning, and control of conduct: the ability to understand what conduct legal rules or morality require, to deliberate and reach decisions concerning these requirements, and to conform to decisions when made" (Hart, 1968, p. 227). The presence of these capacities is argued to be a criterion for moral accountability, and according to Hart ought to be a more generally recognized criterion for legal accountability as well. In the legal system the absence of one or more of these capacities may result in one form or another of a verdict of not guilty by reason of insanity. But the absence of a capacity to conform one's behavior to moral principles, or even to understand what the moral principles are, may characterize young children (or seriously emotionally disturbed adults) who may have committed no particular transgression for which accountability is being demanded. In short, apart from its implications for moral or legal accountability, capacity responsibility can be a description of an individual's psychological state. More will be said about individual capacities in a later section on exculpation, and whenever capacity responsibility is meant, the full term will be used.

Whenever the word "responsibility" is used in an unmodified form, it will refer to Hart's notion of *liability-responsibility*. According to Hart, this sense of responsibility is assigned in the moral realm only if certain conditions are

met. One of those conditions is that the actor possess capacity responsibility—specifically, the knowledge of the potential wrongfulness of the
action for which he or she is to be held accountable and the self-control
required to have avoided the problem. Here, self-control refers both to the
presence of personal skill and the absence of external coercion. A second
condition is that there must be some causal or other connection between the
actor and the person harmed. As we shall see in a later section, the legal
system permits the assignment of "strict responsibility" (legal accountability
without intent) and "vicarious responsibility" (legal accountability without
proximate causation). Neither of these recognized legal principles is, in Hart's
view, acceptable if applied in the moral realm. If the person to be held to
account is not the direct cause of the wrongful act, then at least he or she must
have been able to exercise some control over the actual perpetrator (a control
intentionally or negligently avoided).

It is important to notice that moral liability responsibility is not isomorphic
to causation. Specifically, it is possible both to refrain from attributing moral
responsibility to one who has caused harm, and to assign such responsibility
to one who has *not* directly caused harm. Suppose, for example, that a
political candidate makes statements about his or her opponent that
irreparably damage the latter's reputation. The candidate has clearly caused a
harmful effect, but we would not hold him or her morally responsible if the
statements were true and had been made in good faith. Harm has been caused,
but the "perpetrator" is not morally required to make amends. On the other
hand, suppose the same candidate had in bad faith made obviously false
statements about his or her opponent. We would hold the candidate morally
accountable for the indiscretion, even though no actual harm was caused.

With Hart's distinctions in mind, a working definition of responsibility can
be constructed. The unmodified term, "responsibility," will be defined as a
judgment made about the moral accountability of a person of normal
capacities, which judgment usually but not always involves a causal
connection between the person being judged and some morally disapproved
action or event. Four features of this definition should be emphasized.

First, because the goal of this discussion is to account for the assignment of
blame, a person's potential contributions to positive events can be excluded
from consideration. Positive actions do help establish the limits of what might
have been possible in a situation, and some errors of omission may have
involved a failure to do something positive. But to say, for example, that a
sales representative's efforts were "directly responsible" for the increased
profits of a business is to identify a causal agent who should receive *praise* not
blame. In part because excuses would never be offered for a positive outcome
(cf., Austin, 1961), this use of responsibility is irrelevant to an attributional
analysis of blame.

Second, the causal connection between the potentially responsible person
and the negative outcome must be specified with great care. In simple cases the
potentially responsible person will have performed a voluntary action intended
and expected to bring about the negative outcome. Even in these cases,

however, the intention and volition may be as important to a determination of responsibility as is the actual fact of causality. It must also be remembered that people can be held morally responsible not only for the actions they freely cause but for their intentions in the absence of produced negative effects and for their omissions.

Third, "moral accountability" is not to be equated with blame. Some writers (notably Bradley, 1927) claim that among naive perceivers "For practical purposes we need make no distinction between responsibility, or accountability, and liability to punishment" (p. 4). To the contrary, I shall argue that responsibility is only one *condition* of blame or punishment. We may hold an individual responsible for the occurrence of a negative outcome, yet release that person from blame or punishment because of a satisfactory excuse. Responsibility represents blameworthiness only in the presence of an evil intent and the absence of an acceptable excuse.

Finally, responsibility as used here to describe moral accountability should not be equated with legal responsibility. Because much of the philosophical writing on responsibility has to do with legal sanctions, this last point deserves more detailed attention.

Moral Responsibility Versus Legal Responsibility

Unlike moral responsibility, the meaning of which must be induced from ordinary language, philosophical theories, and psychological processes, legal responsibility has a particular meaning that is prescribed in the common and statutory law (Hart, 1968). With the exceptions to be noted below, a criminal act is considered to consist of two components: an *actus reus* (an overt action that is willfully performed, occurs in specified circumstances, and results in certain harmful consequences) and a criminal state of mind, *mens rea*, with which that act was performed (Williams, 1953). In most instances the *actus reus* and the *mens rea* will both be necessary for the individual to be legally liable. Our earlier example of a person's shooting another involves a crime if that deliberate act is performed outside the bounds of the law and with malicious intent, but it does not involve a crime if, as with an executioner faithfully carrying out his role responsibility, the act is within the law and there is no criminal intent.

The separation of a legally prohibited act into overt and internal components is an important aspect of classical legal theory (Hart, 1968; Kantorowicz, 1958; Williams, 1953). The need to include both observable behavior and unobservable intent arises from the law's objective of balancing a requirement for order with a concern for justice. The first of these has to do, as Holmes (1881) pointed out, with the regulation of external conduct:

> Notwithstanding the fact that the grounds of legal liability are moral to the extent above explained, it must be borne in mind that law only works within the sphere of the senses. If the external phenomena, the manifest acts and omissions, are such as it requires, it is wholly indifferent to the internal

phenomena of conscience. A man may have as bad a heart as he chooses, if his conduct is within the rules. (p. 110)

It should be emphasized that this concentration on behavior is not meant to regulate, as a matter of law, accidental or involuntary bodily movements. For this reason the actor's intentions, capacities, and exercise of will—components of the *mens rea*—must be taken into account. If order requires that conduct be regulated, justice requires that sanctions be applied only to those who truly deserve them.

There are, however, some exceptions to the general rule that both an *actus reus* and *mens rea* are required for full legal responsibility. For example, a particular actor might not be morally blameworthy at the time he or she engaged in a criminal act:

> The rule that law does, in general, determine liability by blameworthiness, is subject to the limitation that minute differences in character are not allowed for. The law considers, in other words, what would be blameworthy in the average man, the man of ordinary intelligence and prudence, and determines liability by that. If we fall below the level in those gifts, it is our misfortune.... (Holmes, 1881, p. 108)

This is another version of the doctrine that "Ignorance of the law is no excuse for breaking it" (Holmes, 1881, p. 47). It is not necessary for the law to show that the individual in question actually had the degree of self-control needed to conform his or her behavior to the dictates of the law; it is only necessary to demonstrate that in the same circumstances a person of "ordinary intelligence and reasonable prudence" (Holmes, 1881, p. 108) would have had that degree of self-control.

In addition to the exception inherent in the "reasonable man" standard for behavior, there are several instances in which criminal liability may be undiminished, even though elements of the *actus reus* or *mens rea* are missing from the case. For example, although the full definition of *actus reus* includes circumstances and consequences, as well as the willful act, some acts are defined as crimes without the need for consequences. Examples are perjury, conspiracy (or a failed attempt), or possession of controlled substances. Another exception to the general rule is that some acts do not change from criminal to noncriminal depending on the presence or absence of guilty mind, but merely change from one kind of crime to another (murder with intent, manslaughter without). Finally, there are some acts that are defined as criminal whether or not there is any guilty mind. Such crimes are usually described by the term "strict liability" (Hart, 1968), and a common recent example is the specification by statute of a particular blood–alcohol content below which there is a presumption that the person might be driving under the influence, but above which there is automatic conviction of the same offense.

Despite these occasional exceptions, the doctrines of *actus reus* and *mens rea* serve the criminal law very well. Why are they not also suitable as a model for judgments of moral accountability? There are three major reasons, two having to do with the process of assigning responsibility, and one having to do with the conceptual terms that are used. The latter centers on the definition of an "act" or an "action." As we have just seen, *actus reus* is not a synonym for what ordinary language would call an act. Rather it is a legal term of art that represents not only the action, but also the circumstances in which that action was performed and the consequences flowing from the action.

The very same act may or may not be an *actus reus* depending on the circumstances. Entering into marriage, normally positively regarded by the society, is a crime (bigamy) if one is already married. What for the law is a single *actus reus* would most probably be described in ordinary language, particularly of the "fine-grained" sort discussed in Chapter 3, as two actions, "getting married"and "becoming a bigamist." Moreover, in ordinary language, a distinction typically is drawn between an action and its consequences. To recall the example from Chapter 3, "burning leaves" is different from "filling my neighbor's house with smoke." In the law, however, that action, its consequences, and the additional circumstance that my neighbor suffers from emphysema, together constitute a single *actus reus* of "reckless endangerment." There are just too many conceptual discrepancies between the ordinary meaning of "action" and the definition of an *actus reus* to permit the two to be used interchangeably.

Even if a way could be found to reconcile the conceptual differences, legal assignment of responsibility as a *process* would still differ from the determination of moral responsibility in two significant ways. First, the legal system must always make a decision, according to prescribed rules. Judges and juries cannot refuse to make the choice between assignment of legal accountability and acquittal just because they have what they (and we) would consider insufficient information on which to base a decision. Nor are they permitted to go outside the prescribed procedures (whether those are of an adversary kind or an inquisitorial kind) to obtain information they might lack. Rather, they are faced with having to do the best they can with the limited information available at the time the decision must be made. By contrast, ordinary perceivers can seek additional information, postpone a formal decision until such material is available, simply refuse to decide, or *alter* a previously rendered decision if it later becomes apparent that an error has been made.

The second process difference arises because the law serves two masters, while the ordinary judgment of responsibility serves only one. A legal tribunal arriving at a determination of legal responsibility, and an ordinary perceiver making a judgment of moral accountability, are both expressing the community's disapproval of wrongdoing. Each in its own way is acting as a moral authority, serving as the instrument (however blunt that instrument may sometimes be) of general moral principles that have been violated. In addition, however, the law is a powerful coercive force, able to impose *punishment* on an offender.

To be sure, moral opprobrium can also be unpleasant, but it can never exceed the offender's limit of tolerance. No amount of moral condemnation can force an offender to make restitution, to redress the balance by doing good deeds for others, or to suffer a deprivation of property, liberty, or life.

The legal system, however, is able to accomplish each of these ends (if the circumstances warrant) over the most strenuous objections of the offender. As Hart and Honoré (1959) put the difference:

> The law is not only bound to follow the moral patterns of attribution of responsibility but, even when it does, it must take into account, in a way which the private moral judgment need not and does not, the general social consequences which are attached to its judgment of responsibility; for they are of a gravity quite different from those attached to moral censure. (p. 62)

Private moral judgments may serve only retribution; legal judgments must also serve justice. Procedures and errors tolerable in private moral judgments would be unacceptable to the law.

Because of these process differences, as well as the differences in conceptual content, the legal model cannot serve as a direct analogue for private judgments of moral accountability (a role strongly suggested for it by Fincham & Jaspars, 1980). Principles of law can be informative or heuristic, as they have been for Darley, Klosson, and Zanna (1978) and Shultz and Schleifer (1983), but they can never substitute for detailed conceptual and empirical analysis of the judgments that perceivers make when determining moral liability responsibility.

The working definition of responsibility thus includes (a) some connection (usually a causal one) between an actor and an occurrence, (b) a generally accepted set of moral principles by which that occurrence is judged harmful, (c) the view that the set of causes of events includes elements produced by human action, (d) the assertion that the actor whose behavior is being judged voluntarily produced (or voluntarily chose not to prevent) the harmful outcome, and (e) an examination of the extenuating circumstances that might release the actor from answerability for producing the outcome. Particularly by contrast to disagreements over the nature of causality, philosophical investigations (e.g., Feinberg, 1981; Ryle, 1949) of the assignment of moral accountability are, in recent years at least, in virtual agreement that these five elements together would comprise an acceptable judgment of "responsibility." Where the accounts differ is in their positions on the form of, or even the possibility of, the individual elements. So it is to these five general questions that the discussion now turns.

Causality: A Precondition for Responsibility?

Philosophical discussions of moral accountability often begin with purely causal questions: What is the cause of an event? How can causes be distinguished from mere conditions? How can "the cause" of an occurrence be identified from among the numerous possibilities? Fortunately, this volume has already dealt with these familiar questions. Thus, in the terms used here "the" cause of harm for which a judgment of moral accountability might be made will be that *minimally sufficient causal subset (or insufficient but necessary element within such a subset) involving human agency, which subset has been identified through processes of causal attribution.* This definition encompasses not only the result of philosophical analysis of the concept of causality, but also the psychological view that the identification of causes is done by individual perceivers who may have an interest in the outcome.

For the paradigmatic case of the judgment of answerability (an instance in which the actor clearly *did* something harmful), the philosophical questions of causality have already been settled. In such a case an attribution of causality can be thought of as a necessary *precondition* for an attribution of moral responsibility. Even in cases where the actor's causal participation is less obvious, that participation might still be presumed necessary for a judgment of moral accountability.

This is the argument advanced by Shultz and Schleifer (1983), who claim that the relationship between responsibility and causality " . . . can perhaps be expressed most efficiently in terms of the notion of *pre-supposition*; a judgment of moral responsibility presupposes one of causation (p. 53, emphasis in original). These authors do note the legal exception, the principle of vicarious responsibility, which holds that a person can be held accountable for the actions of those who are in his or her control (such as a parent's being held responsible for the actions of his or her children, or an employer's being held responsible for the on-the-job behavior of his or her employees). But Schultz and Schleifer argue that because these instances are rare and probably embody causal principles in other forms, they do not provide convincing evidence against the presupposition idea. This may, however, be one place where reliance on legal analogies leads to trouble.

Consider the following questions: "Who is responsible for the dissolution of our friendship?" "Who is responsible for the failure of the company's most recent project?" Or, on an international level, "Who is responsible for successful terrorist bombings of embassies?" Three things should be noted immediately about questions of this kind. First, they are not thought to be nonsense questions. Troublesome, divisive, but not unintelligible. Second, nobody would suggest that the answer should be provided by some legal process. Perhaps there should be a determination made in a court of public opinion, but certainly not in a court of law. And third, they do not involve causality by the potential recipients of censure, at least not a kind of causality that corresponds to any sense in which we have used the term.

The critical point about questions such as these is that they do not arise as the natural consequence of an observation of causality. On the contrary, they arise from a need after the fact to identify someone who can be held to account. In the minds of the persons who ask the questions, *answerability*, not causality, is the issue. If some causal connection can be found, so much the better. But responsibility will be assigned whether or not a causal link can be shown. How rare these examples are in judgments of moral accountability is, of course, an empirical question. They are, however, not so infrequent that they can safely be ignored in theory.

To summarize, there is little doubt that the "standard" attribution of moral responsibility rests on the foundation of a perceived causal connection between the actor and the observer for which he or she is to be held accountable. Nevertheless, judgments of responsibility can be, and are, made outside the boundaries suggested by this prototypical instance. The need to hold *someone* to account for harm may serve as a second general precondition, along with causality, for the determination of moral responsibility. Attributions of responsibility made without clear causal connections may fortuitously be correct, or they may be in error, but they are no less psychologically real.

Standards for Moral Evaluation

Whether the precondition for a judgment of moral accountability is thought to be a causal connection or merely the social need to hold some person responsible for the occurrence of harm, what actually constitutes harm—and what should be done about it—must be determined by reference to some general standard. Philosophical inquiry has for centuries attempted to establish fundamental principles for describing what is good or moral, and although much of that debate continues today, it is not recapitulated here. Only two ethical theories, utilitarianism and retributivism, bear directly on what sanctions might follow a judgment of responsibility, so they are described briefly in the following paragraphs. Even these theories have limited application to the attribution of moral responsibility, in comparison with their forceful implications for the legal system, because such attribution is a psychological process that may or may not follow the dictates of philosophical theory.

Of the two theories, utilitarianism is the most comprehensive, including general standards for moral behavior, principles that might suggest acceptable excuses, and a view of justice that would outline what sanctions might be appropriate for a person who has been judged responsible but whose excuses have not been deemed adequate. The fundamental principle of utilitarianism, originally presented by Bentham (1789/1879) and later extended by Mill (1861/1907), is that of "the greatest good for the greatest number." Although Rescher (1966), for one, has pointed out that this is really a two-factor criterion (the greatest individual good might be achieved by reducing the overall numbers of people involved in the distribution), utilitarian theory would still define "harm" as an action that reduced the happiness of any individual. The more that an action reduced the happiness of a single person, or the more individuals that this unhappiness-producing action affected, the greater the harm caused by the behavior. This is a relatively straightforward (and, its proponents would argue) universal criterion against which any action can be compared to determine whether the actor should be held to account.

The theory's application does not end there. Suppose that a perceiver decided that an actor's behavior ran counter to the utilitarian principle. The actor might even accept the responsibility, admitting "Yes, I did it," but deny his or her blameworthiness on utilitarian grounds: "It is true that this action harmed the one person affected, but at the same time it added to the happiness of these other 10 individuals." Should this attempt at an excuse not be accepted, the perceiver might use very much the same rationale for his or her *own* act of heaping public blame on the original harm-doer. The utilitarian idea is relevant to the initial judgment of the harmfulness of conduct, the excuses that perpetrators offer for their actions, and the perceiver's subsequent explanation to others of why the actor had to be held to account.

By contrast to the relatively unified nature of utilitarianism, retributivism is a collection of differing views (Feinberg, 1980), and its focus is on questions of appropriate punishment for wrongdoing. As such, it does not provide a general standard against which conduct can be compared to determine whether it is harmful. Nor does retributivism give rise to any excuses but the obvious "I was only doing to him what he had previously done to me." What retributivism does suggest is that the degree of moral culpability and subsequent blame or punishment should be dictated by the gravity of the original offense. While the utilitarian view is "forward looking," concerned with the broader effects that assigning responsibility or blame might have, the retributivist view is "backward looking," concerned with the original transgression. Utilitarianism would not suggest a connection between the amount of moral responsibility assigned and the seriousness of the offense, while retributivism would imply proportionate amounts of both responsibility and blame.

The principal difficulty encountered when attempting to apply either of these theories to the attribution of responsibility was eloquently stated in Mill's (1861/1907) recounting of a criticism of utilitarianism: "We are continually informed that Utility is an uncertain standard, which every person interprets differently . . . ." (p. 82). Although Mill takes issue with this criticism, the fact remains that judgments of harm and of the degree of accountability appropriate for specific harmful actions are no less subject to individual differences than are descriptions of events. In short, the attribution of responsibility, the acceptance or rejection of excuses, and the ultimate assignment of blame are psychological processes. Establishing which of several philosophical theories is the best guide for determinations of legal responsibility is a question of substantial import (and considerable controversy). For the individual judgment of moral accountability, however, all that is important is that by some personal standard the act has been judged harmful, so that the actor's responsibility must be ascertained.

As observers of the making of moral judgments, we might legitimately wonder what sort of moral theory could have led a perceiver to the conclusions reached, but an attributional analysis of blame must try to go beyond these idiosyncracies in moral outlook to identify principles of responsibility assignment that are independent of a particular view of morality. This approach contrasts sharply with recent attempts in the study of legal socialization to examine the effects on legal decision making of individual differences in level of moral development (Tapp & Kohlberg, 1971). In that work the focus is on the contribution made by "person variables," while in an attributional analysis of blame, the focus must be on the "situation variables" that are thought to affect judgments of responsibility across individual perceivers. Determining which particular ethical theory—or, for that matter, which level of moral development—provides the foundation for a person's assignment of moral accountability is a concern that must be postponed. What is important for the purposes of this discussion is that any judgment of responsibility presumes that *some* personal ethical standards exist against which the actor's behavior has been compared.

The Dilemma of Determinism

Expecting actors to conform their behavior to a generally accepted moral standard implies that their actions are freely chosen. This implication translates into two fundamental philosophical questions. First, is it possible, in principle, for any human actions to be freely chosen? And second, assuming an affirmative answer to the first question, how in practice can voluntary action be distinguished from involuntary behavior? The first of these questions raises the long-standing controversy between free will and determinism and is discussed in the following paragraphs. The second question calls for criteria by which freely chosen actions can be distinguished from body movements for which the actor should not be held accountable; those criteria are presented in the following section in this chapter.

That the second question can be asked, or more importantly, that an attributional analysis of *blame* is being proposed, assumes that there is at least some human freedom of action. That assumption is one of the thematic foundations for a psychological study of blame, so it deserves attention here. As noted by Berofsky (1966), the formal doctrine of determinism had its origins in the scientific writings of Laplace, who contended:

> that a knowledge of the mechanical state of all particles at some particular time together with a knowledge of "all the forces acting in nature" at that instant would enable an intelligence to discover all future and all past states of the world. (Laplace cited in Berofsky, 1966, p. 3)

The preceding formulation embodies two central principles. First, every event (action or state) has a cause. Second, complete knowledge of the system at one point will lead, through appropriate extrapolation, to an equally thorough understanding of the system at any other point in time. The second principle is the more controversial, because it precludes the possibility for any future human action to alter the state of the world as we would predict it on the basis of full knowledge in the present. In other words, whatever it is that we do, we could have done nothing else.

The effect that this philosophical position has on judgments of moral responsibility is indicated by the dilemma of determinism as presented by Feinberg (1981):

1. If determinism is true, we can never do other than we do; hence, we are never responsible for what we do.
2. If indeterminism [denial of the universal principle of causality] is true, then some events—namely, all human actions—are random, hence not free; hence, we are never responsible for what we do.
3. Either determinism is true or else indeterminism is true.
4. Therefore, we are never responsible for what we do. (p. 328)

Were this conclusion accepted, it would present insurmountable problems not only for any psychological study of blame, but also for any theological system that contained a role for personal choice (e.g., "choosing to love God") and for any legal system that required personal guilt as a precondition for the application of sanctions. In the latter, incarceration merely to incapacitate offenders might still be maintained on logical grounds, if perhaps not on moral grounds.

Despite these difficulties, one of the three major responses to the dilemma that has been defended in the philosophical literature is the outright acceptance of the conclusion. This "hard determinism," or more accurately, *incompatibilism*, encompasses both aspects of the deterministic thesis. Every event has a cause, and the existence of such causes is incompatible with any notion of free will. In classical philosophy this deterministic incompatibilism is represented in the ethical theory of Spinoza (1677/1952). Spinoza's ethical arguments were presented in the style of a mathematical proof and from prior demonstrations that the human mind is part of the infinite intellect of God and that "God alone is a free cause" (p. 326), Spinoza concluded:

> In the mind there is no absolute or free will, but the mind is determined to this or that volition by a cause, which is also determined by another cause, and this again by another, and so on, ad infinitum. (p. 391)

The resulting deterministic doctrine "teaches us to hate no one, to despise no one, to mock no one, to be angry with no one, and to envy no one" (Spinoza, 1677/1952, p. 394).

In other words, transgressions can be committed only because the actor has an imperfect knowledge of God, and because that imperfection (not any willful misbehavior) causes harm, there should be no individual moral accountability. The same sort of incompatibilism, absent the discussions of God, can be seen in the biological determinism of Freud (1920/1952) and the environmental determinism of Skinner (1953). In the recent philosophical literature this incompatibilist position has been most forcefully defended by Hospers (1950), whose philosophical discussion of the tenets of psychoanalysis takes the notion that "the child is father to the man" one step further. In Hospers' view, events that occur during an individual's childhood (for the occurrence of which no one would hold the child responsible) inevitably determine adult behavior. This psychosocial determinism (whether manifest or unconscious) is so complete that neither should the adult be held to account for the present actions thought to arise from events that occurred during childhood.

The second major response to the dilemma is the one that has become known as "soft determinism," a position that accepts the first half of the thesis, namely that events are caused, but rejects the notion that free will is incompatible with the idea of universal causality. Thus, individual liberty is reconciled with the principle of causality. The label is unfortunate, because it suggests either that the evidence for the position is weak, or that the logic of the argument is flawed. In fact, neither of these difficulties is more true here than for any of the alternative resolutions of the dilemma. To avoid the confusion, however, I shall refer to this second resolution of the dilemma by its technical designation, *reconciliationism.*

In classical philosophy this position is characteristic of the British empiricists, notably Hume (1748/1952). When causality is conceived, as it was for Hume, of nothing more than a constant conjunction between a presumed cause and a presumed effect, the human action that follows an exercise of will is no different in principle from the motion of a billiard ball when struck by the cue ball. The constant conjunction is present in both cases, and neither case involves causality in the sense that the term would be used by necessity theory or activity theory. In Hume's view a free action "can only mean *a power of acting or not acting, according to the determinations of the will*" (p. 484, emphasis in original). Because this liberty belongs to everyone "who is not a prisoner and in chains" (p. 484), people should be held accountable for their voluntary actions.

It is certainly true that Hume's version of reconciliationism benefits from his particular definition of "causality," but the general idea of reconciliationism has also been defended by philosphers whose version of causality corresponds more closely to that of activity theory. One such defense was offered by Stace (1952), whose view of causality clearly involves human agency, but whose criterion for whether a person "could have done otherwise" is no less empirical than Hume's:

> It is to be observed that those learned professors of philosophy or psychology who deny the existence of free will do so only in their professional moments and in their studies and lecture rooms. For when it comes to doing anything practical, even of the most trivial kind, they invariably behave as if they and others were free.... This should cause us to suspect that the problem is not a real one.... The dispute is merely verbal, and is due to nothing but a confusion about the meanings of words. (Stace, 1952, pp. 248–249)

If, as Hume also argued, the problem is nothing but a semantic one, how can it be resolved? In an answer that sounds more psychological than philosophical, Stace argued that *"common usage is the criterion for deciding whether a definition is correct or not"* (p. 250, emphasis in original). The proper question is not how philosophers use the term "free will," but how ordinary people use the term in their everyday language. Did a person fast for a week of his own free will, or because he lost his way in the desert? Did a criminal sign a confession of his own free will, or because the police beat the confession out of him? After analyzing these and other examples, Stace concluded that actions ordinarily attributed to free will are those that have as an immediate cause *"psychological states in the agent"* (p. 255, emphasis in original). All events have causes, but some of those causes are internal to the agent. For a psychological investigation of blame, this version of reconciliationism is important, not only because it permits the assessment of personal responsibility but also because of the criterion. We are led to conclude that even though events have causes, individual actors "could have done otherwise," not on the basis of philosophical theory but on the basis of how ordinary perceivers use the language. This criterion will reappear in the discussions of voluntary action and exculpation.

The third major resolution proposed for the dilemma of determinism is that of *libertarianism*, which accepts the principle that human freedom is incompatible with universal causal determinism, but which simply argues that there are instances (namely, some human actions) that by the standards implicit in the deterministic thesis should be regarded as *uncaused*. Here a word of caution is in order. The libertarian position does not argue that human actions occur by random chance in a pattern that no scientist or ordinary person could render intelligible. On the contrary, libertarians recognize the predictability of human behavior, but argue instead against the particular definition of "causality" that determinists have transposed from physical systems to accounts of human behavior. As Feinberg (1981) describes it, libertarians argue that "human actions, unlike other events in nature, are subject to a special kind of explanation: the actor's own *reasons* for acting" (p. 329, emphasis in original).

The classical roots of libertarian doctrine include the writings of Reid (1863a, 1863b), whose "common sense" critique of Humean causality was discussed in Chapter 2 as the basis for activity theory. Recall that Reid distinguished the use of "causality" in physical systems (which he believed to be an improper use of the term) from the true sense of the word, a sense discovered through introspection (or in philosophical language, phenomenological analysis) of "inner experience." Given this philosophical outlook, to say that "friction and gravity caused the pendulum to come to rest at the bottom of its arc" is not to identify a true cause, but rather to state that the movement of a pendulum follows a pattern that can be described by a deterministic law. Indeed, it is only in those rare cases for which no deterministic law appears applicable that a *true* cause can be found, and all of those cases involve human activity. So to employ a meaning of "cause" imported from mechanics—as most deterministic theories do—is to commit a conceptual error.

In the recent philosophical literature a strong libertarian case is made by Campbell (1957), whose discussion of free will extends Reid's prior argument. According to Campbell, arguments about "free will" take place only because the capacity for such voluntary action is recognized as a precondition for moral accountability. The meaning of the term should immediately be restricted only to those cases of moral significance: "the act of *deciding* whether to put forth or withhold the moral effort required to resist temptation and rise to duty" (p. 168, emphasis added). Most of our behavior does not involve this difficult moral decision, and behavior that does not can be predicted successfully by anyone who knows our character and personality well. (Campbell's view on this particular point may be more optimistic than current psychological knowledge would warrant.)

Two questions form the core of Campbell's (1957) argument. First, is it possible for anyone who is in the throes of making a difficult moral decision to *dis*believe that he or she *could be* deciding otherwise? Further, is it possible for that person to *dis*believe that he or she is the sole author of the decision? The answer to each of these questions is a resounding "No!" According to Campbell, the inner psychological state of a person making such a decision is one of conflict between the pressures of character, inclination, and external inducements on the one hand, and the requirements of personal morality on the other. If it is the person's character and inclination, together with external inducements, that lead toward the temptation, then none of these could be the cause (as incompatibilism would argue) of the *resistance* to temptation.

To put the argument in a more contemporary form, if it is really the criminal offender's childhood experiences that have determined his or her adult transgressions, why is the offender able to resist some opportunities while succumbing to others? Determinists would argue that all of the relevant external conditions were not identical, but Campbell would reply that the one essential condition—the inner experience of deciding to resist—can in principle never be known by an outside observer.

> Reflection upon the act of moral decision as apprehended from the inner standpoint would force [a determinist] to recognise a *third* possibility [other than determinism or chance], as remote from chance as from necessity, that, namely, of *creative activity*, in which (as I have ventured to express it) nothing determines the act save the agent's doing of it. (Campbell, 1957, p. 178, emphasis in original)

For the libertarian, even more than for the reconciliationist, it is *psychological reality*, not the internal structure of the philosophical investigation, that provides the ultimate test for the truth value of the claims made. Both alternatives to incompatibilism argue that the original dilemma exists only because of "confusion about the words," both point to the crucial importance of psychological states within the person, and both conclude that it makes philosophical sense (as well as common sense) to hold people responsible for moral transgressions in cases where those people could have done otherwise.

The reconciliationist's version of this standard of conduct is a hypothetical one, while the libertarian's version is a categorical one meant to hold for the actor in question at the time the moral decision was made. Because of its greater assertion of human agency, the libertarian position on responsibility is the most consistent with the causal theory that underlies an attributional analysis of blame. But either alternative provides sufficient justification for proceeding to the question of how "truly voluntary" actions are to be distinguished from other human behaviors for which the performer of the behavior should not be held morally accountable.

Characteristics of Voluntary Action

Reconciliationism and libertarianism establish as a matter of principle that it is possible for human actions to be free of external deterministic causes. They do so by giving special status to the inner psychological life of the individual, an inner experience that is, for libertarianism at least, considered logically inaccessible to the outside observer. Postulation of internal, unobservable, psychological states—unacceptable to Skinnerian behaviorism—is certainly consistent with traditional attribution theory, and presents no insurmountable problems for an attributional analysis of blame. What the assertion of an internal choice between moral and immoral action does require is a set of clear rules that will identify cases in which the free choice that is available in principle has actually been exercised in practice.

Having seen, in the discussion of determinism, the problems that can arise from "mere words," we had better take to heart Austin's (1961) admonition that " . . . words are tools, and, as a minimum, we should use clean tools: we should know what we mean and what we do not . . . " (p. 181). In short, "voluntary" should be defined at the outset. The sense of "voluntary" inherent in this volume's psychological analysis of blame is exactly the one outlined by Ryle (1949) and Melden (1961): it becomes important to know whether an action is voluntary only when that action ought not to have been done. For example, if you have just completed a technically brilliant rendering of a challenging piano concerto, the only person who might ask whether you did so voluntarily would, according to Ryle, be a philosopher who would be stretching the definition. No ordinary person would think to ask the question. Could you have done otherwise? Certainly, but those other possibilities are so obvious (especially to those of us who do not play the piano) that we need not inquire about them. Only if you have taken a hammer to the piano's keys would we want to know whether you had done so voluntarily.

This example not only establishes limits for the domain of actions that might be considered "voluntary," it also suggests that the proper contrapositive will not be "involuntary" alone. Especially for those with a psychological background, the term "involuntary" will usually be thought to represent some fairly spasmodic muscle movements over which the individual could have had no control—a sneeze, the patellar reflex, or an eye blink to an air puff. To this purely physical sense of involuntary, Ryle (1949) would add a sense reflecting circumstances (not movements) over which the person had no control, such as being swept out to sea on the receding tide, or being late for an appointment because of an unforeseen accident. There is, however, another adjective that can be applied to action that is opposite "voluntary," and that is "compelled."

To recall the example from the beginning of the chapter, suppose that a person raises a rifle, takes careful aim, and kills another person. Normally, such action would be considered voluntary, and if the person who performed the act were not discharging legitimate role responsibilities, he or she would be charged with intentional murder. But if a second person had held a gun to the actor's head and had compelled the shooting, the action properly would not be described as "voluntary." Methodical, intentional, but not voluntary. In the discussion to come it should be remembered that voluntary may be opposed sometimes by "involuntary," and sometimes by "compelled," and that its application will be limited to instances of accused wrongdoing.

Not surprisingly, the first philosophical definition of voluntary action was a negative one in terms of compulsion provided by Aristotle (1952) in the *Nichomachean Ethics*: An action is compelled, as opposed to voluntary "... when the cause is in the external circumstances and the agent contributes nothing" (p. 356). But what about the example of an act committed under threat of death? Although the actor certainly contributed something to the action, most philosophical theories would still describe the action as compelled, thus extending Aristotle's definition.

Indeed, some philosophers (e.g., Bradley, 1927; Ryle, 1949) go even further to claim that a coerced behavior is not even what they mean by an action. In Bradley's terms, "Where I am forced, there I do nothing" (p. 6). As useful as it might be to the philosophical thesis Bradley was defending, this exceedingly narrow view of "action" is unacceptable for an attributional analysis of blame for two reasons. First, by Ryle's own criterion of ordinary language, rather than philosophical talk, the very restricted definition does not agree with the common sense use of the term. Second, and more importantly, the restricted definition overlooks the fact that an action may have several descriptions that differ depending on the perspective of the observer. You may not want to consider that a coerced action reflects anything of value about you as a person, but that desire on your part will not prevent others from drawing perhaps erroneous conclusions on the basis of an act that you would disown. Fortunately, the restricted definition of action is not necessary to the argument, which our analysis of blame accepts, that an individual actor can be (correctly) held responsible only in inverse proportion to the amount of external coercion.

If external coercion must be excluded for there to be personal moral accountability, what must be included? Again, the initial answer was identified by Aristotle, who argued that voluntary action required foreknowledge of the consequences. Although a person can be held morally responsible for *being* ignorant of the consequences of an action (the moral equivalent of strict responsibility in the law), an action performed out of that ignorance cannot be described as voluntary. Actions performed "on the spur of the moment" (Aristotle, 1952, p. 357) may be voluntary in the sense that there is no external coercion and the consequences are known, but such acts derive neither from choice nor from deliberation (the translation uses these terms synonymously, but in current usage the latter suggests a longer process, perhaps including seeking others' opinions). A requirement for prior knowledge of the likely consequences is also characteristic of later philosophical accounts of voluntary behavior (Bradley, 1927; Campbell, 1957; Ryle, 1949).

If foreknowledge is necessary, what about choice, or deliberation, or intention? It is easy to think of examples of voluntary action—rubbing one's eyes in the morning, praising the work of a friend, changing lanes in traffic— for which the word "choice" seems inappropriate. After the fact in each case, it would be possible to identify the intention *with which* the action had been performed by asking the person "Why did you do that?" as Anscombe (1957) suggests that we should. Answers might be "I thought it would make them feel better," "I value our friendship," "and "this lane was moving faster," respectively, and both the question and the answer make sense. By contrast, the question "Why did you deliberately praise your friend's work?" might bring the angry retort, "What kind of person do you think I am?" Thus, in cases of actions for which one is not likely to be held accountable for wrongdoing, "voluntary" can be thought of as reflecting the actor's intentions, but not necessarily as involving choice or deliberation. The role of choice is, however, much more readily apparent in the limited sense of "voluntary" that is of interest here. Recall Campbell's (1957) analysis of the creative activity involved in moral decision making. A woman who knows her duty but refrains from doing it and a man who knows that what he is about to do is wrong but does it anyway can each be described as having made a choice. There may not be in either case a decision process extended through time sufficiently to warrant the label "deliberation," but anyone who is aware of the consequences of human action or inaction and is aware of the moral imperatives for the situation cannot *dis*believe that some other choice was possible, unless there is powerful external coercion. For those voluntary actions that might make us answerable to others, choice is not only important, it is virtually a defining characteristic.

What is even more critical than the choice itself is the moral knowledge that the choice presupposes. Not only must an actor know the consequences of action, he or she must also know the view that morality is likely to take of those consequences. It is this very knowledge that provides the bridge between the "inner experience" of the choice and the behavior for which the actor is to be held accountable. In our moral judgments of others we employ an intensely personal version of the law's "reasonable man" standard. We ask ourselves two different questions before holding another person morally responsible for an action. Would *I* have known what the consequences would be? Would *I* have considered those consequences at variance with my moral standards? In short, the philosophical question "Could he or she have done otherwise?" becomes the attributional question "*Would I* have done otherwise?"

The requirements for a judgment of voluntary action are slightly different from those for the possibility of human freedom. To adapt Heider's (1958) phrase to the present circumstances, an attributional analysis of blame is concerned with the "naive philosophy" of voluntary action. That naive philosophy specifies three characteristics of voluntary action: absence of external coercion, presumed knowledge of consequences, and presumed knowledge of the moral implications of those consequences. Given these criteria, immoral action can only be seen as the wrong choice, when the actor should have done otherwise.

Some Warnings About Excuses

The final philosophical issues relevant to the determination of responsibility are those having to do with extenuating circumstances. Few discussions of this topic have been as influential as the one offered by Austin (1961), which is a detailed, psycholinguistically sophisticated analysis of ordinary language. Not surprisingly, the major import of Austin's argument is that we should be very careful about the terms we use. An initial distinction Austin drew was between a justification and an excuse, neither of which is needed unless a particular action is being called to account. Upon such a request for explanation, a response that admits the behavior to have been voluntarily performed—but claims that, contrary to the accuser's moral viewpoint, the act was a *good* thing to have done—is a *justification*. By contrast, an *excuse* is a claim that "it is not quite fair or correct" (Austin, 1961, p. 176) to describe the action in the bald terms the accuser has employed.

Instead of examining the distinctions "that you or I are likely to think up in our arm-chairs of an afternoon" (Austin, 1961, p. 182), Austin catalogued the terms of exculpation that could be found in the dictionary. This technique, typical of the "ordinary language" method, is the philosophical equivalent of the multidimensional scaling procedure that Rosenberg and Sedlak (1972) have used to identify the components of implicit personality theory in everyday language. In short, like so much of the philosophical analysis of responsibility, Austin's work has a decidedly *empirical* character.

Analysis of words relating to extenuation reveals that a high percentage of these are adverbs used to modify the verb that represents the action for which one is being called to account. "I didn't just *do* it, I did it *inadvertently*." Or "incidentally," as I was really doing something else. Not only the presence of such adverbs, but also their placement in the response is important in determining whether the response is an excuse. To borrow from one of Austin's examples, "I clumsily hit him with the stick" is an excuse, but "I hit him with the stick clumsily" is an admission that an intentional action was inexpertly executed. Finally, the sorts of verbs that are modified by various collections of adverbs represent different aspects of "the internal detail of the machinery of doing actions" (Austin, 1961, p. 193). The excuse offered can apply to the planning stage of an action (unknowingly, unwittingly), the choice among response alternatives (thoughtlessly, tactlessly), or the carrying out of the behavior (recklessly, carelessly).

There is, unfortunately, one instance in Austin's otherwise perceptive work in which his own tools were not quite clean enough for the purposes of this discussion. Throughout his discussion of excuses, Austin argued that excuses alter or diminish "responsibility," instead of asserting that they diminish "blameworthiness." To claim that an action was done inadvertently is not to claim that there was external coercion (which would clearly relieve the individual of responsibility), but rather to claim that there was not full appreciation of the consequences (which may mitigate responsibility, diminish the sanctions applied, or do some combination of both). This kind of distinction between the assignment of responsibility and the assignment of sanctions is built into the law and is a distinction that most certainly carries over into everyday life.

When we examine an accused person's excuses, we need to do more than differentiate justifications from excuses. We need to do more than determine whether an excuse has been offered as a defense against a charge of immoral activity, rather than as a defense against a charge of failure to carry through effectively with an intention not perceived as immoral. We also need to be clear about whether the excuse is meant to apply to responsibility, blame-worthiness, or both.

Responses to an Accusation

You stand accused of a moral (not legal) transgression. Shall we hold you responsible? Shall we place moral blame upon you? Given the material considered in this chapter, what, exactly is meant by responsibility? To answer this latter question, examine the answers you might give to the accusation:

1. "I didn't have anything to do with it." This response is more than a denial of personal causality, it is also a denial of any possible connection with the occurence of the event. No matter how strong his or her need to hold someone accountable, an accuser who could accept this answer and yet hold you responsible would be committing a logical mistake. So some connection to the event must be identified for there to be a justifiable assignment of responsibility.

2. "I didn't do it." This is a denial of proximate causality, but not a denial of all other connections to the event. We can accept this claim and still hold you *partially* responsible in one of two ways. First, we might argue that even though you did not cause the event, you are still obligated to make amends. It is in this sense that a later generation of the German people was required to pay reparations to Israel, and that affirmative action guidelines require sacrifices on the part of white males. Second, we could make the stronger causal claim that you were the only insufficient but necessary element involved (or one of several such elements) in the causal subset minimally sufficient for production of the occurrence. This is the moral version of the legal notion of "vicarious responsibility," but the instances in which it might apply have not been specified in advance in our moral code. Regardless of the reason we offer for holding you partially responsible, we should expect you to dispute our judgment, and we might expect other perceivers to do so as well.

3. "I was forced to do it." A response like this acknowledges the causal connection between actor and deed, but seeks diminution of, or absolution from, responsibility on grounds that the action of some *other* agent was the insufficient but necessary element in the minimally sufficient causal subset. If that other agent was a person whose causal contribution was obvious to us, then your responsibility ought to diminish in direct proportion to the extent of

coercion. If, on the other hand, the other's contribution was less clear (or if in an extreme case the other agent was purported to be an evil spirit), then we might give you very little in the way of relief from *responsibility*. Considering, however, the sort of mental state implied by your conviction that shadowy people or evil spirits were forcing you to do things against your will, we might significantly reduce the *blame* we would impose on you.

4. "I didn't *mean* to do it." Again, this answer admits a true causal connection, but it does much more than that. It also admits knowledge that *some* intentional behavior was being performed for which responsibility cannot be denied. What it asserts is that there was an unintended or unforeseen consequence of that intentional action. There is not external coercion, but at the same time, there is no voluntary choice to bring about the consequence that led to the accusation. Depending on the surrounding circumstances, this response may be a request for relief from responsibility, it may be a request for mitigation of blame, or it may reflect some degree of both. Whether any of these requests will be granted will depend on *our* judgment of your possible knowledge of the consequences; you have admitted that the action was morally reprehensible, denying only that you ought to have foreseen the outcome.

5. "It wasn't wrong." This answer admits the causal connection, admits the intentional quality of the action, and accepts the responsibility for the occurrence. What it denies is that the action should be followed by moral opprobrium. Such a response must be accompanied by some *reason* if blame is to be avoided (the sociopath provides no reason, but we do not accept his or her view of morality, any more than he or she accepts ours). That reason could take one of two forms. First, it could be an attempt to specify why our view of the action, or our view of the moral implications of that action, was mistaken. It is important to note that these two assertions that a mistake has been made might have quite different probabilities of being successful. If you could make me understand that my description of the action was wrong and yours was correct, then you would no longer stand accused, so there would be no further need to consider either responsibility or blame. On the other hand, if we agreed on the description of the action, disagreeing only about whether it had been morally correct, you would have to change my mind not only about the action in question, but also about a much wider set of beliefs or values, if you were to convince me to withhold blame. The second general reason you might provide would be in the form of some larger social good (the kind of excuse suggested by utilitarianism) served by this admittedly wrongful single action. Were you to convince me of this view, I would still hold you responsible, but would "understand" you rather than blame you.

Dimensions of Responsibility

Earlier in the chapter, as a result of the examination of causality in Chapters 2 and 3, it was possible to give a one-sentence definition of causality. What these several replies to an accusation make clear is that a correspondingly concise definition of responsibility cannot be offered, even though the term itself might be restricted to Hart's (1968) sense of "moral liability-responsibility." What can be offered instead are the *dimensions* that together can be used to ascertain the responsibility of an individual for a single morally reprehensible act.

The first of these is the *causal* dimension, a measure of the extent to which the actor was the direct and proximate efficient cause of the occurrence for which the accusation is being made. I (Shaver, 1975) have previously described this dimension as having to do with *"local versus remote participation"* (p. 94, emphasis in original), and that remains an adequate statement of the end points of the dimension. This causal dimension represents what I (1975) have called the "production of effects" sense of responsibility, but differs from Hart's (1968) causal responsibility, because the latter also applies to cases of physical or deterministic causality.

A second general dimension on which personal moral accountability can be assessed is *coercion*. This dimension captures the meaning of the assertion that a responsible agent "could have done otherwise." The claim is not meant in its weak (reconciliationist) form, but in its strong (libertarian) form: The actor in question, at the time in question, under the circumstances in question, could have done something different from the action for which responsibility is to be assigned. The likely end points of this dimension would be coerced and voluntary, and research (Shaver, Null, & Huff, 1982) reported in Chapter 7 provides a clear demonstration of this dimension. In my (Shaver, 1975) previous discussion of causality and responsibility, I argued that environmental coercion was a dimension not of responsibility, but of causality. I now believe that position to have been in error.

A third dimension, *knowledge of the consequences*, is likely to be correlated with coercion (in the sense that a person who is completely unaware that his or her actions might have morally reprehensible consequences would not be expected to have considered the possibility of doing otherwise). Labels for the end points of this dimension would include the words "aware" and "unaware," but whether those words would be modified by "was" or by "should have been" might depend on the circumstances of the individual case. Where the observer is certain about the degree of the actor's awareness, the former could be expected to be the modifier; where the observer is ignorant about the actor's true state of knowledge, the latter modifier would be the moral equivalent of the "reasonable man" legal standard. In my earlier work (Shaver, 1975) I also erroneously described this dimension (using the term "foreseeability") as characterizing causality rather than responsibility.

The fourth dimension of responsibility is *intentionality*, and it represents the element of "choice" or "deliberation" in voluntary behavior. The separate existence of this dimension is testimony to the arguments of Austin (1961), Bradley (1927), and Ryle (1949) that "involuntary" is not the conceptual opposite of "voluntary." At the involuntary end of this dimension, the actor will claim that the action was an accident, a temporary muscle spasm, or the product of an external event over which the actor had no control (such as the act of falling into someone's lap when the subway car lurches). If "involuntary" is one end point, then "intended" is the other. Only at the intended end of the dimension does the question "Why did you do that?" make sense (although the actor might not answer the question, and if he or she did, we might not like the answer). As another aspect of voluntary behavior, this dimension should be correlated (negatively) with coercion and (positively) with knowledge of the consequences.

The final dimension on which responsibility can be characterized, *appreciation of the moral implications* of the action, contains the moral accountability analogue of the legal principle that only those who understand that they have done wrong can be held responsible. A young child who behaves in a manner that, were he or she an adult, would be morally wrong, is not typically held to account for the action. Indeed, the adult response "How would you like it if two or three kids pushed *you* down into the mud?" is an attempt to *teach* the very moral principles later to form the standard for adult behavior. End points for this dimension, as described so far, might be "appreciates" or "does not appreciate" that conduct has moral overtones.

Were the dimension used in this way, responsibility would be greatest at the "does appreciate" end, but one can imagine cases in which the dimension would be used in exactly the reverse manner. Were we to encounter an adult who shared a great many of our beliefs and values, only then to discover that such a person was really a sociopath who did not see any of his or her outrageous conduct as morally relevant, the greatest responsibility might be assigned at the "does not appreciate" end in order to teach the person a lesson. Of the five dimensions, this is the only one that inquires about the overall moral character of the actor, rather than relying exclusively on a moral characterization of the action for which that person is to be held accountable.

At this point it would be useful to reiterate two questions asked at the beginning of the book. What is the cause of the event? Is anyone responsible? The form of the first question implies that we can say with clarity what any cause might be, and indeed we can. The form of the second question indicates that we cannot say with equal clarity what responsibility *is*, only how it can be determined. And that, too, turns out to be the case. There is no logical criterion offered by philosophy to distinguish "responsible" from "not responsible," only a varied set of *empirical* criteria. There is no explicit definition of responsibility, only a set of dimensions that should be employed to ascertain whether an individual actor should be held morally accountable for wrongdoing. In the next chapter the discussion returns to the social psychological literature to see just how the evidence suggests that these prescriptive dimensions might be used.

Chapter 5
Attributions of Responsibility

Notwithstanding Hart's (1968) notion of "causality responsibility," there is, as we have seen, a fundamental difference between "caused" and "was responsible for." Many causes can exist independent of intervention by human beings—tornadoes cause extensive damage, bacteria cause disease in animals, lengthening spring days cause new leaves to appear on trees—so the actions of persons constitute only a fraction of the antecedents of effects. Although Reid (1863a, 1863b) was probably correct to argue that our intuitive idea of what is involved in causality arises from the exercise of our own will in doing something, it is still possible to conceive of a cause–effect sequence that does not include even the most remote participation of people. By contrast to this view of human agency as only one of several potential causes, there cannot be responsibility without human participation, either as cause or as perceiver, or both. An assignment of responsibility is a moral judgment, one made about the actions of another (presumably) moral individual. Certainly there are instances of human action for which perceivers will routinely decline to assign moral accountability. But these instances are recognized and debated for the exceptions they are, and even they do not violate the principle that limits "was responsible for" to events involving persons.

The independent existence of causes permits us to ask questions like "What is *the* cause of this occurrence," while the fact that there can only be judgments of responsibility requires that we ask "Given the conditions that prevailed at the time, *how much* can the person be held responsible?" Causes are discrete, but responsibility assignment is continuous. Causes exist in physical reality, but responsibility exists only in social reality. As Fauconnet (1920) put it in the first social psychological treatment of responsibility attribution, "responsibility is born outside of the responsible person. It comes upon him because he finds himself in circumstances that engender it" (p. 91).

These differences between causality and responsibility give rise to the two major objectives of the present chapter: describing the psychological processes involved in responsibility assignment and placing those processes on the dimensions of responsibility suggested by philosophical analysis. First, because of its uniquely social character, the determination of responsibility is best described by attribution processes. The work of Heider (1958) and Jones and his associates (Jones & Davis, 1965; Jones & McGillis, 1976) are particularly relevant and are presented in detail in this chapter. Second, these attributional ideas are recast into the dimensions of responsibility outlined in Chapter 4, to complete the foundation for consideration of recent theoretical controversies that begins in Chapter 6.

Levels of Responsibility

Attributional discussions of responsibility, like those of causality, begin with the seminal work of Heider (1958). Recall from Chapter 3 that Heider's "naive analysis of action" identified two factors that jointly produce effects: personal force and environmental force. The former consists of the person's intention, motivation, and ability, while the latter consists of stable and variable features of the environment, such as task difficulty, luck, and opportunity. If a person's ability exceeds the task difficulty, then a state Heider called "can" exists, and production of the effect then turns on the person's intention and on the strength of his or her motivation.

As a general principle, the person's perceived responsibility for an event will vary in direct proportion to the personal force thought to be involved. There are five "levels" or "successive stages" of personal responsibility, and I shall use the names suggested by Sulzer (1971) for these levels: association, causality, forseeability, intentionality, and justifiability.

1. *Association.* The most primitive level of attribution of responsibility takes place without any reference to analysis of action, because the person is held accountable for an event *not* causally connected to him or her in any way. An example is the United States government's internment, immediately following the attack on Pearl Harbor, of any person of Japanese ancestry who was living on the West Coast. Association can reflect the perceiver's need to hold someone answerable, even someone who has not produced the outcome in question.

2. *Causality.* At this level anything caused by a person is ascribed to him or her. The dispositional state of "can" is present, and although neither intention nor motivation is necessarily ascribed to the actor, that person is seen as (at least) the insufficient but necessary element in the minimally sufficient cause of the outcome. Indeed, the actor need not even be aware of producing the effect, although the causal connection would be obvious to an observer. At this level, the actor's honest response to "Why did you do that?" *could* be "I wasn't aware that I did."

3. *Foreseeability.* At this level of responsibility "can" is also present, neither intention nor motivation is inferred, but it *is* thought that the actor should have been able to foresee the possible outcome. This is the level

represented by the National Transportation Safety Board's finding that pilot error was the cause of the crash of Air Florida Flight 90. The actor is not only the insufficient but necessary element of the causal subset, he or she is also considered "negligent" or "careless" for a failure to have anticipated such a causal role. The actor's intention was to do something *else*, but the side effects of the intended action should have been attended to.

4. *Intentionality.* Responsibility is assigned at this level if the state of "can" obtains, if the actor is thought to have intended the outcome produced, and if there was evidence that the actor was trying to bring about the event. Here the person's behavior may by itself be sufficient for the production of the effect.

5. *Justifiability.* If a person is coerced by illegitimate force or by legitimate authority, even an intentional action will be excused, at least to some degree. From the standpoint of the naive analysis of action, "can" is present, as are intention and exertion, but the direction for the behavior is provided from outside the person whose responsibility is being judged.

There are two aspects of these levels of responsibility that are important for an attributional analysis of blame: Their conceptual status is not as clear as it might be, but their empirical consequences are quite well documented. Let us consider these issues in turn. Heider used two words, "levels" and "stages" to describe the five combinations of personal and environmental force, and compared two of the levels (causality and intentionality, respectively) to Piaget's (1932) stages of objective and subjective responsibility. Are the combinations really stages by the criteria—invariant sequence, incorporation in later stages of all that has gone before, behavioral coherence within a stage, qualitative difference between one stage and the next—that are typically thought necessary?

Looking only at the elements of personal and environmental force that participate at each level, one might be tempted to answer this question in the affirmative. The causality level adds causal force to association; the fore-seeability level adds knowledge (or at least the possibility of knowledge) of the consequences to causality and association; intentionality adds a personal objective to the previous three; and justifiability adds a powerful source of external coercion to the factors present in intentionality. There are, however, some logical problems that appear on closer examination. First, the *kind* of causality changes from one level to another. In the causality level the person's participation is as one of several elements in the minimally sufficient causal subset. In foreseeability, that participation is more appropriately regarded as being an individually insufficient but necessary element (an INUS condition). Finally, in intentionality, the person's action is, by itself, a minimally sufficient condition for the occurrence of the effect. This change across levels would not meet the criterion of incorporating prior causal principles.

Second, as Heider noted, the justifiability level is characterized by the fact that "even p's own motives are not entirely ascribed to him but are seen as having their source in the environment" (p. 114). An intention that arises in part from external coercion may be, in our terms, an external causal element added to a minimally sufficient causal subset already containing the element represented by the individual's own intention. Unfortunately, it is also conceivable that an intention provoked from outside would simply be a causal element *different* from an element representing a wholly internal intention. The internal "for the sake of which" present at the level of intentionality might be *replaced* by an external one at the level of justifiability. That such a possibility exists also argues against a strict "stages" view of the levels.

Finally, true stages are thought to differ from one another in the dependent variables to be examined at each stage. For example, a child at the cognitive developmental stage of formal operations is recognized to have reached that level by his or her newly found ability to solve problems through hypothesis testing, rather than through enumeration of all of the logical possibilities. This skill is one that a younger child is incapable of producing. At each "stage" of Heider's levels, by contrast, the dependent variable—perceived personal responsibility—remains the same. It is, therefore, not surprising to discover that if the research takes careful account of a child's response capabilities, developmental studies using the Heider levels do not show the sort of progression that would be expected from true stages (Fincham & Jaspars, 1980). The claim that the levels are developmental stages must therefore be regarded with suspicion.

A second conceptual claim made regarding the levels is that they reflect a unidimensional scale. This claim, put most forcefully by Brewer (1977), can also be seen in the analysis by Fishbein and Ajzen (1973). In their review of prior research on the attribution of responsibility, Fishbein and Ajzen first proposed that Heider's levels should apply not only to the response given by a subject (or to that subject's cognitive developmental capacities), but also to the context surrounding the stimulus person's actions. On the response side, their argument suggests that "responsibility" should be measured by a multipart question permitting the subjects to say what degree the actor was associated with the occurrence, caused it, could have foreseen it, intended to bring it about, and did so as a consequence of external coercion. The elements of this multipart question are quite similar to the specific items outlined in Chapter 4 as measures of the dimensions of responsibility, but as discussed shortly, there is a critical difference. Turning to the stimulus, Fishbein and Ajzen argued that the attributional level could also be incorporated into the circumstances surrounding the actor's behavior. Thus, depending on the objective of the research, any single experiment ought to make either the response or the stimulus level-specific, while leaving the other free to vary. The advantage of doing so is to avoid confusion in the subject's mind about which meaning of "responsibility" is of interest to the experimenter. As I (Shaver, 1973) have noted previously, however, close specification of the contextual level may render an experiment capable of discovering only that the particular subject population in question uses the scale in the way that everyone else does.

The second proposal that Fishbein and Ajzen (1973) made was to reverse the order of "intentionality" and "justifiability" as they are specified in the context, or stimulus, side. With this reversal a two-way classification scheme can be constructed (contextual level by response level), with responsibility being assigned at a particular response level for any cell on or above the principal diagonal of the matrix. The table thus constructed was claimed to represent "a perfect Guttman scale, suggesting that Heider's levels of causality [sic] form a single dimension of perceived responsibility" (Fishbein & Ajzen, 1973, p. 151).

There are, however, two conceptual problems with this classification scheme. First, there is no theoretical argument advanced for placing the justifiability level between foreseeability and intentionality. Later research by Fincham and Jaspars (1979) has found that when the levels are context-specified in this order, the attributions of blameworthiness do constitute a Guttman (1944) scale, but the attributions of causality do not. These results lend credence to Fishbein and Ajzen's original argument, but they do not solve the conceptual problem, namely, why should a level (justifiability) that includes an *additional* causal element (coercion) be placed on a Guttman scale before a level (intentionality) that includes one less causal element? The second conceptual difficulty with Fishbein and Ajzen's classification scheme is that it predicts an attribution of personal responsibility at the justifiability response level when the context only specifies intentionality. Such a prediction clearly runs counter to Heider's view of what is involved in the two levels of attribution. In short, while the Fincham and Jaspars blameworthiness data did show a Guttman-like increase in the dependent variable, the conceptual case for the classification system remains to be established.

If Fishbein and Ajzen's (1973) characterization of Heider's levels can be described as multifaceted, but still unidimensional, Brewer's (1977) treatment of the levels can be described as almost naively unidimensional. Extending a model developed by Schopler and Layton (1972) for the attribution of power, Brewer claimed that all judgments of responsibility could be represented by the formula $AR = C - PE$, where AR (assigned responsibility) is the amount of responsibility assigned to a stimulus person by a perceiver, C (congruence) is the perceiver's subjective probability that the outcome would have been expected to occur given the stimulus person's actions, and PE (prior expectancy) is the subjective probability that the outcome would have occurred in the natural course of events without any intervention by the stimulus person.

All of the variables that might affect the responsibility assigned (e.g., seriousness of the negative consequences produced, the intentions of the actor, the presence or absence of external coercion) were, in Brewer's model, reduced to the subjective probability associated with the congruence dimension. Indeed, it is probably more accurate to say that these variables were "replaced by" the congruence dimension, because Brewer argued that it is the probabilities, not any of the specific variables they might reflect, that determine the responsibility assigned. Furthermore, Brewer noted that because "the model proposed here equates responsibility judgments with assignment of *cause*, rather than praise or blame, the degree of attributed responsibility does not necessarily have direct implications for the perpetrator's liability to reward or punishment" (p. 63, emphasis in original).

In a careful critique of the model, and of the evidence adduced in its favor, Fincham and Jaspars (1980) showed how it is possible to derive identical predictions without the use of subjective probabilities. They concluded that "the results do not show convincingly that attribution of responsibility is based on subjective probability estimates" (p. 111), although they did allow that the model might have some "heuristic value." Unfortunately, that is perhaps the most positive view that can be taken of Brewer's model. From my perspective the subjective probability model has two fatal conceptual flaws.

First, by arguing that the only difference between unintended, intended, and intended but coerced action is that the former has a lower subjective probability of success, the model overlooks literally centuries of philosophical debate, refinement of ordinary language, and legal tradition. Simplification may have its place in scientific inquiry, but a model that purports to describe human judgment processes ought not ignore judgmental distinctions so frequently made. To accommodate some of the distinctions, Brewer suggests that factors such as intention and external coercion might affect not only congruence probability but also prior expectancy probability.

This solution, however, brings into sharp focus the fact that a key term, "intervention," by the actor, is undefined. If intervention is taken to mean "comes between inadvertently" then intention cannot logically be part of such intervention. The person's intentions would suddenly be placed outside himself or herself, and only the prior expectancy probability could be affected. If, on the other hand, intervention is taken to mean a conscious action intentionally taken by the person, then causal participation at the causality or foreseeability level would be impossible. Only if there are multiple ways in which an individual can participate in the production of an effect (a requirement that brings us back to some version of Heider's levels) can this dilemma be resolved satisfactorily. The resolution can be accomplished, however, only by examining the terms involved, *not* by references to the subjective probability that the outcome will follow the occurrence of the action.

The second critical flaw in Brewer's model is the equation of attributed responsibility with causality. At this point one is reminded of Russell's (1945) characterization of philosophical theories: There are theories that attempt always to be internally consistent, and there are other theories that attempt to describe the world as it is. The latter are internally inconsistent, while the former lead to absurd conclusions. In Brewer's case, if responsibility is really nothing more than a judgment of causality, then ideas like intention and external coercion are superfluous. Either the stimulus person caused the outcome or not (or perhaps had help). A theory that truly believed responsibility to be isomorphic to causality would be internally consistent but would lead to absurd conclusions. On the other hand, if the theory needs, as Brewer's does, to discuss terms like intention and coercion, then responsibility cannot be identical to a judgment of causality. The existing theory, while trying to describe the world, is internally inconsistent. The obvious solution, as taken by most writers on the topic, is to *distinguish* responsibility from causality.

Neither Fishbein and Ajzen's (1973) classification system nor Brewer's (1977) subjective probability notion makes a convincing conceptual case that the factors comprising Heider's levels constitute a unidimensional scale. This point needs emphasis because much of the research employing Heider's levels (in one form or another) produces quite reliable patterns of attributed responsibility.

In the first empirical test of the levels notion, Shaw and Sulzer (1964) presented subjects with a set of 40 vignettes, all concerning the same stimulus person. These 40 vignettes constituted two instances of every combination of (a) level of responsibility, (b) valence of the outcome (positive or negative), and (c) intensity of the outcome (trivial or significant). For example, in several of the serious negative consequence variations the outcome was the death of another person, often occurring under rather gruesome circumstances. The level of responsibility was varied by specifying the appropriate elements of the context. The results of the experiment showed, among other things, that responsibility attributed to the stimulus person increased in a linear fashion from the association level to the intentionality level, and then decreased at the justifiability level to an amount roughly equivalent to that attributed at the forseeability level. This same pattern was obtained in a number of other studies employing the vignettes, but using a variety of subject populations (Shaw, Briscoe, & Garcia-Esteve, 1968; Shaw & Schneider, 1969; Sulzer, 1971).

Indeed, the pattern is so stable that it can be used as an indication of a subject's ability to make the "typical" distinctions among levels. A modified version of the Shaw and Sulzer (1964) materials was put to just such a purpose in a study (Shaver et al., 1984) that successfully attempted to demonstrate a reliable pattern of responsibility attribution among hospitalized schizophrenic patients. Two changes had to be made in the vignettes: one in the stimulus materials themselves and one in the response alternatives available to the subjects. The serious negative outcomes in the original version might have been truly threatening to schizophrenic patients, raising both ethical and methodological questions about the research. The 10 outcomes involved therefore were changed from death of the other person to a milder injury. The original form of the vignettes (the "Perry stories") included a 7-point scale on which the subjects were to determine Perry's responsibility. Pretesting among schizophrenics revealed that these patients were unable to make the distinctions required by a 7-point scale, so the dependent variable was changed to a dichotomous judgment: Was the stimulus person responsible or not? Thus, within each Heider level the schizophrenic subjects made this dichotomous judgment eight times, and the mean number of such judgments (collapsed across outcome positivity and intensity) was analyzed to assess the pattern of attribution.

The results of the study showed that both paranoid and nonparanoid patients attributed responsibility to the stimulus person according to the "standard" pattern: attributions lowest for association, increasing linearly to intentionality, then decreasing with justification. There was, in addition to this main effect for levels of responsibility, an interaction between patient diagnosis and levels, such that paranoid patients were consistently more sensitive than nonparanoids to the differences across levels (lower attributions at association, higher attributions at intentionality). These findings show that even hospitalized schizophrenic patients produce judgments of responsibility that vary as expected with Heider's levels. Furthermore, the differences obtained across diagnoses were quite consistent with the clinical literature showing paranoids generally to be more vigilant and sensitive to external cues than are nonparanoids.

All of this is not meant to suggest that the Perry stories are a perfect vehicle for measuring attributions according to Heider's levels. They are not. As noted previously, the serious negative outcomes may not be suitable for impressionable subjects. There is not the degree of variation in the story content that would be desirable, nor are the individual stories sufficiently detailed. Virtually all of these objections were overcome in another operationalization of Heider's levels by Fincham and Jaspars (1979). Their stories employed only a moderate intensity negative outcome (a bleeding nose or lip) that came as a consequence of the stimulus person's participation in one of the six different activities. The research included Heider's five levels and a sixth "supererogation" level that contained all of the features of the intentionality level, and added an admonition from the (to-be) injured child's mother to the stimulus child to be very careful "as my boy (girl) gets hurt very easily" (Fincham & Jaspars, 1979, p. 1592). Each subject thus read a story from every level, with the negative outcome at each level coming about as a result of participation in a different activity. No important differences were obtained between the intentionality level and the supererogation level, so for present purposes the latter will be ignored.

In presenting their findings Fincham and Jaspars (1979) arranged the five levels in the contextual order suggested by Fishbein and Ajzen (1973), with "justifiability" placed in between "foreseeability" and "intentionality." When their subjects (who ranged in age groups from 6 years old to college age) were asked to attribute *causality* to the stimulus person in the story, there was the standard increase across levels (association lowest, intentionality highest), as in the studies with the Perry (Shaver et al., 1984; Shaw & Sulzer, 1964) stories. The pattern for adults differed from that of children only because of a greater marginal increase from association to causality than the corresponding increase among children. When the same subjects were asked to attribute *blame* to the stimulus person, there was, again, the increasing pattern across levels. Further, there was a significant interaction between age group and level, with younger children differentiating less from one level to another than did older children and adults.

Finally, considering only the results from adults, at all levels except intentionality, less blameworthiness was attributed than causality. Only at the association and intentionality levels was the difference between attributed causality and attributed blameworthiness less than a single scale point (on a 7-point scale). Additionally, as noted previously, the blameworthiness judgments did form a satisfactory Guttman scale, while the causality judgments did not. These findings give further support to the notion that attributions to the potential perpetrator of a negative outcome will increase across Heider's levels (if they are re-ordered). The precise shape of the function, however, will depend to no small degree on whether the dependent variable is causality or blameworthiness (neither of which, from my perspective, can be thought of as identical to "responsibility").

The levels of interaction between personal force and environmental force clearly capture a great deal of what people consider when they are asked questions about the causality or blameworthiness (or even "responsibility") involved in the production of negatively valued events. Attributions made in response to level-specific information virtually always follow the same pattern, regardless of the specific incidents to be judged, and across a wide variety of subject populations, even including individuals hospitalized for what is usually regarded as a profound thought disorder. There are very few principles of attribution that generalize this well.

As positive as most of the empirical findings are, the conceptual status of the levels is all too frequently negatively defined. First, the levels cannot be regarded as true developmental stages. Children as young as age 6 show level-related differences in attribution, the justifiability level can be located in either of the last two positions (thus violating the "invariant sequence" criterion), and the very same dependent variable can be used sensibly at every level. To be sure, there are age-related differences across levels, but these are quantitative, not qualitative, differences.

Second, the levels cannot be considered to be points along some underlying unidimensional continuum. To make this point as clearly as possible, contrast changes in level with changes in some other psychological dimension, say, anxiety, that is believed to be unidimensional. Compared with moderate anxiety, high anxiety is simply more of the same thing. Indeed, the well-known Yerkes-Dodson (1908) "law" that expresses task performance as an inverted U-shaped function of anxiety *depends* on their being only quantitative change from one degree of anxiety to another. By contrast, what distinguishes one of Heider's levels from another is the addition or deletion of discrete elements (e.g., presence or absence of intention). In the terms of this discussion, this change is an alteration in the minimally sufficient causal subset that produces the occurrence. The resulting changes in the *dependent* variable can look like a Guttman scale, but it is highly unlikely that there is the same unidimensional change on the independent variable side. What Heider's levels do appear to be is a set of related dimensions that can affect attributions of causality and blameworthiness, and this positive definition is elaborated in a later section in this chapter.

The Origins of Intention

Whether one considers the legal requirement for criminal responsibility (*mens rea*), or Heider's analysis of the levels of interaction between personal and environmental force, or any of the research derived from Heider's view, it is clear that the greatest amount of either causality or blameworthiness will be attributed to a stimulus person who has intentionally produced a negative outcome. There is, however, one important limitation to this strong relationship between intentionality and attribution: In all cases the presence of an intention is taken as a given. Criminal responsibility follows a judgment that a legally proscribed behavior has been performed by an individual possessing a guilty mind. Because intention is the central feature of personal causality, the greatest personal attribution should follow a judgment of intention. Finally, when subjects are presented with stories at the contextual level of intentionality, consistent attributions of blameworthiness will be made. What if none of this intentionality information is provided? How will perceivers extract the cues to intentional action from the complex events they normally judge? By themselves, Heider's levels provide no answer to this question. Among the major attribution theories, only correspondent inference theory (Jones & Davis, 1965; Jones & McGillis, 1976) suggests what inference *process* might be involved.

In their original statement of correspondent inference theory, Jones and Davis (1965) attempted to specify the reasoning that a perceiver might do to determine, on the basis of observed effects of action, what underlying personal disposition might have been the ulitmate source of those effects. This link between effect and disposition involves observed and inferred components. The effects actually achieved by a course of action are observable, as, in many cases, are the alternative choices open to the actor. There will often be some overlap between the effects associated with the chosen alternative and those associated with various nonchosen alternatives. It stands to reason that these "common" effects cannot have been decisive in the choice. In most instances, however, there will also be effects produced by the chosen alternative that would not have occurred otherwise. According to the theory, it is these "noncommon" effects that will be evaluated to infer the actor's underlying disposition.

There may only be a few noncommon effects (in which case the meaning of the action is clear), or there may be many noncommon effects (in which case the meaning of the choice would be ambiguous). Furthermore, the existing noncommon effects can be classified independently according to their assumed desirability. Such a classification takes into account the "prior probability" that the actor's previous choices, broadly conceived to include things like experience and social role as well as more immediate behavioral choices, will have constrained the desirability of the effects contemplated for a particular course of action. If a perceiver is confronted by few noncommon effects, all of relatively low assumed desirability, then there can be a "correspondent inference": a high degree of certainty that the action and the underlying personal disposition presumed to account for it can be "similarly described."

From the standpoint of this discussion, it is important to notice that such certainty cannot be achieved from an analysis of the observed effects alone. For the inference to be veridical, a particular internal structure must be assumed. Specifically, every action (or, more precisely, every choice between two possible actions) requires the requisite ability, knowledge of the likely consequences, and an intention to produce those consequences. It is this intention that arises from the individual's underlying dispositions. Thus, while a disposition can be thought of as a broad predisposition to behave in, for example, an "ingratiating" manner, that predisposition might lead in specified circumstances to the intentional flattery of a superior. The time sequence inherent in this internal structure is disposition preceding intention, which, in turn, precedes the co-occurring knowledge and ability, which precede the action. I shall return to the problem of a particular inferred time order in a moment. For now it is only essential to note—although the theory does not explicitly say so—that a valid dispositional inference cannot be made in the absence of intention. This is not to say that perceivers never infer dispositions from effects produced accidentally or unintentionally; they do, and do so frequently. But with a central role given to intention, the theory would have to regard these inferences with suspicion.

One of the general principles to arise out of correspondent inference theory is the idea that out-of-role behavior is more informative regarding personal dispositions than is in-role behavior. The latter, by its very definition, is highly desirable for the actor in question, and it may also include a wider array of noncommon effects than would out-of-role actions. When a person does the expected, very little about his or her intentions can be discovered with any certainty. In short, as Jones and McGillis (1976) point out, correspondent inference theory deals with *information gain*.

In order to describe this information gain more precisely, Jones and McGillis (1976) divided the perceiver's expectancy about what an actor might do into two components. The first of these, called the "category-based expectancy," is a probabilistic estimate of likely behavior derived from the actor's readily apparent physical or social characteristics. Age, sex, attractiveness, manner of dress, ethnic origin, known social class, and known occupation are among the variables that might affect this estimate. The theory would suggest that information gain regarding the presence of an intention should increase as the numbers of elements contributing to the category-based expectancy increases: Only if the expected social role is very thoroughly defined will it be possible for the perceiver to distinguish truly out-of-role action from action that is consistent with (some possibly unknown) role.

The second component of the perceiver's expectancy for the stimulus person's behavior is called "target-based expectancy," and is derived from prior experiences that the perceiver has had with the stimulus person in question. If a category-based expectancy resembles a stereotype, a target-based expectancy resembles an implicit personality theory held for a single individual. The comparison of the action performed is made not to the social role of the stimulus person, but to that person's other attitudes, motives, and personality traits. As the perceiver's familiarity with the stimulus person increases, the strength of the target-based expectancy also increases (theoretically predicting larger increments in certainty for actions that violate the expectancy). There is, however, an upper limit to the effects of expectancy disconfirmation. As Jones and McGillis note, any behavior thought to be intentional will require the actor not only to have the requisite ability to perform the action in question, but also to have foreknowledge of the consequences of the action (which consequences the actor intended to bring about). If the expectancy is quite strong, no matter what its base, an action that disconfirms the expectancy is likely to be attributed to a stimulus person's lack of knowledge about the consequences, rather than to a sudden change in all that is known about the person.

In this idea of skepticism about foreknowledge of the consequences, there is a principle of substantial importance for an attributional analysis of blame. An attribution of responsibility, like the description of an event and the identification of its cause, is a judgment made by a perceiver who has his or her own view of the situation. How is it that when learning of an indiscretion on the part of a political figure, the general public brands the person immoral, while the person's friends defend his or her integrity? Is friendship, like love, blind? Or is there some other process at work?

Examine the expectancies closely. The general public has only a vague (even unidimensional) category-based expectancy about the likely behavior of a political figure, while that person's long-time friends have not only a more differentiated category-based expectancy, but also a much more important and long-standing target-based expectancy from years of experience with the person in a wide variety of contexts. Although at times we may doubt it, our category-based expectancy for "holder of a public trust" specifies certain standards of morality for behavior in office. When those are violated, we infer the presence of evil intent, and we hold the individual personally responsible for the reprehensible behavior. On the other hand, if the person is a life-long friend of ours, and in all our past dealings has been forthright and honest, then we attribute a violation of this target-based expectancy either to a lack of foreknowledge of the consequences or to the machinations of our friend's political enemies. As Jones and McGillis stated it, "*differential* knowledge of the target person and his environment" (p. 400, emphasis in original) may be one of the boundary conditions for the attribution of intention based on the disconfirmation of an expectancy. An unanticipated action will be attributed to that class of factors (associated with the person or with the situation) about which the perceiver has the less firm expectancy.

Category- and target-based expectancies not only affect the amount of information gain possible, they also revise the way in which the theory accounts for the assumed desirability of the noncommon effects of an action.

Without specifically describing the process, Jones and McGillis argued that every effect of an action can be given a *valence* derived from the expectancies. The "normative" category-based expectancy against social deviance will lead to a negative valence for any effect of a socially disapproved action, while "stereotypic" category-based expectancies will lead to certain effects' receiving positive valences. Other contributors to the valence attached to effects are those "structural" target-based expectancies derived from observations of the stimulus person's actions in other contexts and "replicative" target-based expectancies derived from prior observations of the person's actions in identical past situations. Once the valences have been determined for the noncommon effects, those valences are summed to produce the predicted choice. Disconfirmation of this prediction, especially if there are few noncommon effects involved, will lead to a correspondent inference.

Thus, in the revised version of correspondent inference theory, the perceiver observes an action that produces identifiable effects within a given situational context. The perceiver's category- and target-based expectancies lead to valences attached to all of the noncommon effects, with the sum of those valences generating the behavioral prediction against which the actor's actual choice is compared. Disconfirmations of all but the most firmly held expectations will then lead to an inference that the action was intentional, and this intention will be seen as the product of an underlying personal disposition. Jones and McGillis are careful to point out that this sequential model is just that—a model. No claim is made that every perceiver will follow all steps in the order specified, or that the process is capable of being verbalized, not to mention conscious.

What the theory does provide is a version of the process that a perceiver *might* employ to infer the presence of an intention from a single instance of observed behavior. Recall, by contrast, that Heider's (1958) criteria for distinguishing intentional action from unintended behavior included one ("equifinality" of the outcome, despite temporary interruption of the flow of action) that virtually requires multiple observations of behavior. In a similar manner, Kelley's (1967, 1973) attribution theory concentrated on covariation among effects and possible causes, resorting to the assumed pattern of data represented by causal schemata when multiple instances were not available.

To be sure, there are important similarities between Kelley's (1967, 1973) approach and that of Jones and McGillis (1976), who argue that their notion of a "replicative" target-based expectancy is equivalent to Kelley's concept of consistency through time. Despite these similarities, the fundamental purpose of Kelley's theory was to "rule out" various possible situational causes of action, while the focus of correspondent inference theory was on the uniquely personal causes of action. This difference has been highlighted by Hamilton (1980), who drew on the legal literature (especially Hart & Honoré, 1959) to note that for correspondent inference theory the comparison inherent in the perceiver's judgment is accomplished by a principle of "could have done otherwise." The action performed is evaluated not against the natural course of events, either in Heider's sense of the multifinal outcomes that typify physical systems or in Brewer's (1977) prior expectancy sense, but against a specific behavioral alternative thought to be available to the actor at the time a *decision* was made. While Kelley's theory is particularly relevant for the "scientific" determination of possible causes, correspondent inference theory is especially well suited to the assignment of responsibility and the sanctions that might accompany a dispositional attribution of "guilty."

As much as it suggests about how intentions might be inferred, correspondent inference theory does have a troublesome conceptual limitation, one created by its restricted definition of intent. By concentrating on those instances of behavior that violate expectancies, the theory claims explicitly that no dispositional information of interest can be obtained and claims implicitly that intentions cannot be discovered from behavior that conforms to expectations. These claims, unfortunately, present both practical and logical problems. On the practical side it is simply unreasonable to argue that the only intentional behaviors people perform are those that violate expectations. How are expectancy-*confirming* actions to be understood? At first glance this practical problem might not be expected to apply to the actions of interest to an attributional analysis of blame. After all, with questions of responsibility arising only when the action being examined is morally or legally reprehensible, doesn't the moral code specify the expected behavior, from which the person's actions can be seen to deviate? Generally the answer would be affirmative, but what about the case, for example, of a "career criminal?" The category- and target-based expectancies for such a person would lead us to be surprised only if he or she did something *positive*. Does this mean that the offender's repeated misbehavior will be seen as unintentional? Certainly not. So the determination of intention in cases of action that agree with expectations remains a practical problem for the theory.

Limiting intention to instances of expectancy violation also presents an important logical problem for the theory. If dispositional properties can be inferred with confidence only from unanticipated actions, how can a firm target-based expectancy be constructed in the first place? Reconsider the case of the career criminal: The first time I encounter such a person, I would have a general category-based expectancy that this would be a "normal" person who shared my moral values. That expectancy would be disconfirmed by the first instance of illegal behavior I happened to observe, and I would conclude that the misconduct had been intentional, perhaps arising from an underlying disposition of dishonesty. On a second, or even a third, encounter, my original category-based expectancy might still hold sufficiently to be disconfirmed by the person's morally objectionable behavior. By this time, however, according to the "feedback" portion of the theory, I would have begun to develop a target-based expectancy about the future.

Imagine that both of these expectancies are plotted in a two-dimensional space in which the ordinate represents increasing strength of (whichever) expectancy, and the abscissa represents increasing familiarity with the person. The category-based initial expectation of moral action decreases with increasing familiarity, while the target-based expectation of immorality increases with increasing familiarity. The logical problem becomes critical at the point at which the two lines would cross. Our pretheoretical idea of what would happen there is that the category-based expectancy of moral behavior would decrease until at some later point it would vanish entirely, while the target-based expectancy would steadily increase with familiarity until it reached some high level. Both of these changes require that we be able to continue learning disposition-relevant information about the person, a feat that is theoretically impossible once the balance of the expectancies tilts toward immoral behavior.

Obviously, the class of intentional actions cannot be confined to "those actions that contravene expectancies." There must be a way to distinguish intentional behavior from inadvertent behavior independent of whether the effects produced violate our expectations. An intentional action is no less planned, no less thoughtfully carried out, just because it happens to produce effects that we would anticipate. Whether it is still informative (in an information gain sense) about an underlying personal disposition is, at this point, an empirical question. But it is certainly possible to imagine attributions, such as those to career criminals, that would increase in confidence even though every instance of behavior agreed with an established expectancy. If this line of reasoning is correct, then some criterion for the inference of intention that does not depend on expectancy disconfirmation must be identified. As discussed in Chapter 6, it is possible to set forth such criteria. For now, suffice to note that the restricted definition of intention is a serious limitation in correspondent inference theory.

Dimensions of Responsibility and Attribution

Philosophical analysis led to the conclusion that responsibility was a process, rather than an entity (like causality), and to the specification of five dimensions that ought to be involved in that process. Recall that these dimensions were prescriptive—factors that an idealized perceiver ought to consider prior to making a judgment of responsibility. The central question for the final section of this chapter is, "How closely does social psychology's description of the real perceiver's responsibility attribution match the template provided by this ideal?" Fortunately, the fit is quite good.

Before proceeding, it would be helpful to recall the prescriptive dimensions from Chapter 4. The first dimension discussed here is the *causal* dimension, having to do with whether the stimulus person is seen as the local versus remote cause of the event for which responsibility is to be assigned. The second dimension is *knowledge*, representing the degree to which the stimulus person was seen as aware (versus unaware) of the consequences of the action taken. Third is *intentionality*, a measure of the degree to which the action will be thought intentional, versus involuntary. Fourth is *coercion*, a measure of the degree to which responsibility for an intentional action can be mitigated by the presumed presence of strong forces within the environment. Fifth is the stimulus person's presumed *appreciation of the moral wrongfulness* of his or her conduct. Philosophical analysis of these terms did not dictate the order in which they will be presented here, but that order most probably corresponds to the one that real perceivers follow in order to assign responsibility.

Causality

Did the stimulus person cause the event? As discussed in Chapter 3, even this question presupposes that most perceivers will have been able to agree on which "event" from the event distribution is to be explained and will also have agreed on the level at which the stimulus person's "act" is to be identified. Neither of these preliminary steps can be taken for granted. In fact, each might be influenced by factors normally associated with responsibility (such as the extent of a target-based expectancy). "Why did she break the law?" is obviously a question very different from "Why did she forget to report all of her financial dealings?"

Assuming, for the moment, that there is agreement among perceivers regarding the description of the event, then the causal dimension has to do with the degree of the stimulus person's participation in the production of the event. Logically, this dimension could vary from a minimum of no participation at all (the stimulus person is truly an "innocent bystander" not associated in any fashion with the production of the event) to a maximum of being the sole cause of the occurrence (the stimulus person's action is the single element in a minimally sufficient causal subset).

Psychologically, however, the stimulus person's causal participation may be a true dimension only in the aggregate, a whole constructed out of a set of discrete parts. Consider the several questions that comprise causal participation. "Can the person be associated with the outcome in any way?" "Were there multiple causes?" "Did these multiple causes include the actions of any other person?" "Were the actions of the stimulus person a true causal element, or were they only a necessary, but insufficient, element of the final causal subset?" Each of these questions calls for an affirmative or negative answer, not for an answer appropriately expressed by variations along a continuous scale. For example, only when the presence of multiple causes has been established does it make sense to ask how many of them were present.

If the analysis is correct, a perceiver who responds to the question "How much was the stimulus person the cause of the occurrence?" by placing a mark along a scale may not, in fact, be answering the question that was asked. To use an architectural analogy, the experimenter was trying to ask, "How far up the inclined plane would you like to travel before stopping?" while the subject was responding by thinking of how many *stair steps* he or she had to climb to reach the stopping place. Not only are the steps individually discontinuous, but also each succeeding step can be thought of as resting on a specified number of preceding steps in a way that differs from the conception of travel up a smooth plane. Let us keep discontinuity and presupposition of prior steps in mind as we examine each element in the psychological characterization of causality.

The first step of any importance is Heider's (1958) level of association between stimulus person and occurrence. Judgments of personal responsibility based on this causal connection alone often have as their justification not a claim that the stimulus person *did* the harm, but on a need to hold someone answerable who can provide moral or financial restitution to the victim. Depending on the nature of the association (again, the decision rule involves the kind of association, not the degree), a person may be held legally accountable according to the principle of vicarious responsibility (Hart, 1968). This sense of responsibility is the one inherent in judgments against employers for transgressions committed by their employees or in judgments against parents for the actions of their children (even if those children are adopted).

What is most perplexing about attributions actually made at this level of responsibility is not that some blameworthiness is assigned, but that the amount of blameworthiness *exceeds* the amount of causality (Fincham & Jaspars, 1979). As confusing as it is for the legal system to assign vicarious responsibility in the absence of causality, at least such an attribution serves the rational goal of deciding who must provide restitution. By contrast, for perceivers to attribute causality at the association level, where there is no evidence of human agency on the part of the stimulus person, does not even serve any obvious rational objective. Even those perceivers, however, would not attribute causality, responsibility, or blameworthiness to a stimulus person not connected in any conceivable way with the occurrence. For this reason, it should be clear that all succeeding characterizations of responsibility presume association.

The next step on the causality staircase is represented by Heider's (1958) second level, causality. The height of the riser for this step will depend on the presence of other plausible causes, the influence of which will be ascertained through some version of Kelley's (1973) discounting principle. If there is no other plausible cause, then the discontinuity between the causality level and the association level will be pronounced. If other plausible causes are present, the discontinuity will still exist, but will not be quite so large. The very fact of this shift may be one of the reasons that Heider's levels, alone, do not appear to form a Guttman (1944) scale.

Recall that in Fincham and Jaspars (1979) data the greatest marginal increase in attribution occurred between association and causality. Such a dramatic increase makes perfect sense: The difference between a person's being remotely and tenuously connected to an event and that person's being a proximate cause is a substantial difference. Indeed, if one were designing a computer program to simulate the attribution of causality, a major branch would be between association and causality, with a high attribution of causality (mitigated only by learning that other people were also involved in producing the occurrence) made after learning that the stimulus person was the proximal cause of the event. This sort of attribution corresponds, as Hamilton (1980) has noted, to the legal assignment of strict responsibility. That sort of legal finding requires no elements of *mens rea*, resting entirely upon the commission of an *actus reus*. Finally, because of the mitigating effect that causal participation of others can have, future tests of Heider's levels should be careful to specify whether or not there were other possible causes present in the situation.

If the causality level of the staircase needs to incorporate some version of the discounting principle to adjust the height of its riser, the next step needs to incorporate the augmentation principle (Kelley, 1973). What changes from causality to this step—Heider's level of foreseeability—is not the degree of the person's causal participation, but our impression of whether or not that person should have known better. If the assignment of responsibility is limited to instances of the production of negatively valued effects, then the foreknowledge that such effects were possible should have been an obstacle to performance of the behavior. According to the augmentation principle, then, the causal force needed to overcome this obstacle will be judged to be greater than the causal force required to perform the action in the absence of the obstacle.

Here, too, it is clear that the attribution of causality cannot always be separated from the attribution of responsibility. Knowledge of the consequences is, after all, one of the dimensions of *responsibility*. Just as foreknowledge is correlated with coercion, it is also implicated in causality, at least at the foreseeability level. On the responsibility side, knowledge of the consequences imposes upon the actor an affirmative obligation to refrain from behavior that could produce harmful effects. Consequently, the legal equivalent of responsibility assigned in the presence of foreknowledge is, again as Hamilton (1980) noted, negligence. The critical point is that the affirmative obligation to avoid producing harm will, through a version of the augmentation principle, affect judgments of causality as well as judgments of responsibility.

A somewhat stronger augmentation will occur at the final step in the sequence of causal judgments, that represented by Heider's level of intentionality. Most of what changes from foreseeability to intentionality is *not* the actual causal force that enters into the production of the effect, but rather the perceiver's certainty that virtually all of that necessary causal force can be attributed to the stimulus person. No longer capable of being viewed merely as part of the natural sequence of events, no longer a necessary but insufficient condition of the occurrence, the stimulus person is now seen as *the* minimally sufficient cause of the outcome. It is in this sense of limiting the alternative explanations that intentionality is, as Heider (1958) described it, the "central feature" of personal causality.

Thus the causal "dimension" of responsibility consists of four major steps, with each step representing an increase in the stimulus person's association with the consequences. Each succeeding step presupposes what has gone before. The second step on this sequence involves discounting, while the third and fourth steps involve augmentation. At the lowest level the stimulus person's actions will not be endowed with causal force, and such attributions of causality as are made (in error) will most probably have arisen as a result of the perceiver's need to justify holding someone accountable for providing restitution. The fundamental question for this initial causal judgment is "Can the stimulus person be associated with the effect?"

At the next level the stimulus person is identified as the proximate causal agent whose immediate actions have brought about the effect. This is the essence of causality, with the last instant of the stimulus person's action being the first instant of the beginning of the effect, with obvious human agency, and with the cause being generative of the effect, not merely correlated with its occurrence. It is, therefore, not surprising to learn that 81% of Fincham and Jaspars (1979) subjects had attributed causality to the stimulus person in their stories by this (second) level. After all, the fundamental question for this level is the typical dependent variable, "Did the stimulus person cause the effect?"

At the third step the person is seen as still more closely associated with the consequences, by virtue of his or her having been aware in advance of the possibility of their occurrence. Because effects for which responsibility is to be attributed are negatively valued, the augmentation principle yields a marginal increase in the causality assigned to the stimulus person. "Did the person know what would happen?" is the question.

Finally, at the intentionality level the marginal increase is brought about not so much by a closer association between the stimulus person and the effect as by the opportunity to exclude from consideration possible causes other than that person's actions. In an important sense the question that defines this level is "Would anything else have made a difference in preventing the occurrence?" A negative answer would produce a judgment of intentional causality.

Although the four levels of causality are discontinuous, there is the possibility *within* each level for variations that would make an imprecise dependent variable appear continuous. Within association, some kinds of connections drawn between stimulus person and event will be more plausible than others, and in the case of the legal system, some associations will produce vicarious responsibility while others will not. Within the causality level, the number of other plausible causes (or, more precisely, the number of other minimally sufficient causal subsets) may temper the judgment of causality that otherwise would have been offered. Next, within foreseeability, the number of obstacles to be overcome will affect the attribution. Finally, at the intentionality level, the presence of the intentional participation of other persons will alter the judgment of causality.

Two words of caution need to be noted in conclusion. First, although several of the steps in the causality staircase have been likened to Heider's levels of *responsibility*, confusion can be avoided if the dependent variable is kept firmly in mind. For example, intentionality is a central feature of personal causality and is a criterion for the most extreme attributions of responsibility. There is no reason to think that intentions are inferred differently in the two cases, so on the independent variable side it is permissible to use the same term to describe the inference. There is, however, a difference on the dependent variable side. When the topic is an attribution of causality, most of the change in judgment arises at the causality level, so adding other features (including intent) makes only a marginal difference in the final attribution. By contrast, in a judgment of moral accountability, the person's intentions should count the most (indeed, in a legal judgment of criminal responsibility intent is often the defining attribute for the crime).

The second caution has to do with the ease of (spuriously) obtaining judgments of causality that appear to represent a true continuous scale. There are two characteristics of the research done to test Heider's levels that will increase the likelihood of this problem. First, there is the tendency to ask the global question, "Did the stimulus person cause the outcome specified?" With such a question there is no opportunity to determine whether variations in the subject's response reflect a perceived increase in the "strength" of one aspect of causality, the perceived addition of another aspect, or a combination of the two. Future studies of Heider's original levels, as well as future tests of the causal dimension of responsibility, will need to include questions measuring all aspects of the stimulus person's causal participation. Second, there is the understandable presentation of the causal judgment data as mean scores collapsed across subjects within a presumed level of responsibility. This aggregation of the data has the effect of smoothing out what might otherwise have been individual step-functions. Future research on the causal dimension of responsibility should report an aggregate number, such as proportion of subjects who have surpassed a specified criterion level of attribution, as well as the more traditional mean scores. Only with these two improvements will it be possible to provide a convincing empirical test of the elements of the causal dimension of responsibility.

Knowledge

"Did she know what she was doing?" Only if there has been a prior attribution of causality to the stimulus person's actions (rather than a claim of causality through association) does it make sense to ask whether that person should have foreseen the consequences of the action. From any single instance of behavior, the only conclusive evidence that a perceiver has that the stimulus person was able to anticipate the consequences of action is an obviously intentional action designed to achieve exactly those ends. Intentionality, however, constitutes a separate, though correlated, dimension of responsibility. A judgment of intention presupposes the stimulus person's awareness of the possible consequences, but reverse is not true. For this reason the knowledge that an actor might have had should be considered in its own right.

Absent a judgment that the actor's behavior was intentional, the knowledge dimension of *responsibility* is a continuous scale that represents the perceiver's view of what a reasonable actor *should* have known. Whether or not the stimulus person really knew of the consequences in advance is not important. This is how the knowledge dimension of responsibility differs from the contribution that foreseeability might make to marginal increases in the attribution of causality. Only if the stimulus person did know of the possible consequences could they have served as obstacles to behavior, thus leading to augmentation of the causality judgment. But action taken despite known consequences is different from action taken in ignorance of consequences that would have been immediately apparent to most observers. Both can magnify a judgment of responsibility, but only the former can augment a judgment of causality.

Perceivers will rely on their own past experience, informal sampling of the opinions of others, and certain category-based expectancies to establish which consequences they believe should have been apparent to the actor. A perceiver who has been in situations very much like the one facing the actor will naturally have a more complete set of expected outcomes than will a perceiver without that experience. The adage that no one is more critical of social drinking than a "reformed drunk" is an illustration of this principle. Without such personal experience, a perceiver may rely on the options of others to establish a set of expected consequences that should have been anticipated by the stimulus person. If everyone I ask about a particular course of action expresses incredulity that anyone would do something so morally suspect, I wonder how the stimulus person could have been paying so little attention that the risk went unnoticed. Finally, perceivers may use category-based expectancies derived from the social role occupied by the stimulus person. In the same way that Hamilton (1978) has argued that an individual's moral liability should be ascribed within the context provided by his or her role, the set of consequences that ought to have been foreseen may be role specific. Indeed, a great deal of professional training—for police officers, rape counselors, or accountants, to name just a few—can be seen as education about the previously unforeseen consequences of action. Against this background provided by the perceiver's own experience, the collective experience of others, and the available category-based expectancies, the more the actor should have foreseen the consequences, the greater the responsibility assigned.

Intentionality

"Did she intend to do it?" This is perhaps the central question in the dimensional analysis of responsibility. It is certainly true that intentionality presupposes knowledge of the consequences, which, in turn, presupposes causality. In our everyday social interaction and in a wide variety of legal judgments, the stimulus person's intention is what separates the reprehensible from the regrettable. How does existing psychological research and theory suggest that it is possible to determine what the intention might be? According to Heider's (1958) theory, intention is to be inferred from the combination of equifinality, local causality, and exertion. Thus, while equifinality and local causality are by themselves sufficient to distinguish personal causality from impersonal causality, evidence that effort was being put forth in the direction specified by the presumed intention is necessary to differentiate intentional action from happenstance.

Unfortunately, this view does not permit us to infer intent in any of the difficult cases. Information about equifinality requires, as we have seen, the repeated observations described in Kelley's (1973) covariation terms. What if our inference must be made from a single instance? We are then left only with local causality and effort. What if the stimulus person happens to be quite expert in what he or she is attempting to accomplish? Experts make actions that would be very challenging for the rest of us look easy. This is most clear in the performance of a socially approved skill, but it applies to negative behaviors as well. For most of us, doing something we know to be morally wrong requires overcoming of socially imposed obstacles. If, however, we were sociopathic (and unencumbered by social restraints), then our performance of wrongful actions would be (and would appear) effortless. Thus, the attribution of intention would rest only on local causality—an unacceptable conclusion.

Is any assistance provided by correspondent inference theory? Again, the answer is disappointing. In the early version of the theory, Jones and Davis (1965) argued that the necessary preconditions for the judgment of intention were a belief that the actor had the requisite ability and knew the consequences of his or her action. Consider first the assessment of ability. Over a long period of repeated observation, it would easily be possible to infer that the actor had the ability, but this inference would require covariation information. Turning to knowledge of the consequences, we have already seen that although such knowledge is necessary for an inference of intention, it is not sufficient. Thus, in the case of a single instance, correspondent inference theory leaves us with a definition stated in terms of deviation from expected behavior. In the later version of the theory, Jones and McGillis (1976) continued this definition, and once again included knowledge and ability as preconditions for intentional action. But even with the distinction between category-based and target-based expectancies, and with the specification of how those expectancies interact with the valences of the effects of action, the more recent version of the theory still leaves us with an incomplete definition of intentional action.

By now it should be clear that providing a definition of intention that is independent of the observable behaviors thought to testify to its existence is a very difficult task indeed. When there is the chance to obtain information over a long period of observations, the judgment of intentionality is simplified (Heider's equifinality, Kelley's consistency, Jones & McGillis's target-based expectancy). Perhaps the difficulty arises from restricting the stimulus situation to a single instance. Yet determinations of intent are made in legal settings without the opportunity for multiple observations. Thorough discussion of this paradox requires more space than is available here, so that task is reserved for a section in Chapter 6. For now, suffice it to note that as the perceiver's belief that an action was intentional increases, attributed responsibility will also increase, with an important exception: coercion.

Coercion

"Was he forced to do it?" As long as there has been human interaction, there has been the possibility of coercion, a fact recognized in both formal and informal attributions of responsibility. Whether it is the philosopher's assertion that coercion changes the fundamental nature of action (Bradley, 1927), Heider's (1958) justifiability level of responsibility, or the legal argument of self-defense, the principle is the same: Responsibility can be mitigated by the presence of coercion. Unlike the causal "dimension," but like the dimensions of knowledge and intentionality, the dimension of coercion is properly regarded as continuous. At the voluntary end, an action will be seen as the result of a free choice by the stimulus person, a choice unencumbered by environmental constraint or threats from powerful others. At the coerced end, the actor will be seen as having had no choice, and may be absolved of virtually all responsibility for the action. As simple as this sounds, there are two aspects of the coercion dimension that deserve further comment.

First, there is the place that the dimension comes into play in the attribution process. We would think it quite strange for a person to try to excuse himself or herself from responsibility by saying "It was an accident, and besides, I was forced to do it" (this remark might not be so strange from a child). For an adult, there must be a *prior* attribution of causality at the intentionality level for the coercion dimension to be at all relevant in the determination of personal responsibility. It should be noted that this assumption represents a combination of social–psychological data and philosophical argument. On the social–psychological side, all of the research testing Heider's levels shows that there will be mitigation of responsibility for intentional actions if there are coercive forces present in the environment. These consistent data are buttressed by our informal understanding that it is nonsense to claim that you were forced to perform some action with which you were merely associated, caused inadvertently, or even caused negligently (without thinking of the consequences). On the philosophical side, only a reconciliationist or libertarian view of human action will support the assertion that there is intentional action or the accompanying assertion that in some cases intentional actions may be excused on grounds of external coercion. For the incompatibilist, by contrast, there is nothing but external control over behavior, so under no circumstances can there be personal responsibility for action.

Second, although threats from powerful others constitute the paradigmatic case of coercion, the dimension needs to be defined more broadly to include other external forces that limit the actor's freedom to choose the moral alternative over the morally reprehensible one. For example, obedience to the requests of an authority can be construed as a response to coercion, even though no threats are involved. An extreme illustration of the power of a situation is provided by Milgram's (1963) study of the extent to which people would provide what they believed were painful electric shocks to another person. Volunteer subjects were told that they were taking part in a study of learning and that their task was to "teach" another person (really an experimental confederate) a series of word pairs. Every time the learner made a mistake, the subject was to increase the intensity of the shock administered.

There were no explicit or implicit threats to the subjects (who were free to leave at any point), and the most the experimenter prodded was to say "the experiment requires that you continue" when subjects showed hesitation in response to the outcries of the victim. The expressive behavior of the subjects clearly indicated that they were wrestling with a wrenching moral choice, but after the fact we can see that the choice was constrained by the situation. This example is not quite as clear as it could be, because surely no subject would have described his intention by saying "I'm trying to hurt the guy as much as I can." In fact, when confronted later by another experimenter, subjects claimed that they were "trying to teach him these word pairs." Nevertheless, subjects *were* intentionally pressing the levers that they knew would deliver shock, so the argument would be over the description of the event, not over the presence or absence of intentional action.

Obedience to authority is only one of many examples of circumstances restricting choice in a way that should limit the personal responsibility of the actor. It is an especially interesting example, however, because it runs counter to an established attributional principle. In his naive analysis of action, Heider (1958) argued that "behavior engulfs the field," by which he meant that perceivers will concentrate on the actor's behavior to the relative exclusion of the situational forces that might be constraining the action. This principle was extended by Jones and Nisbett (1971), and has even been described by Ross (1977) as the "fundamental attribution error."

Just how truly fundamental the error might be remains controversial, but a responsibility version of the argument would hold that actors should be sensitive to all of the coercive forces in their environments, while perceivers should see only the actor's intentional misbehavior. What occurs in the obedience setting, however, is precisely the reverse, at least when all subjects are considered together. Learning that over 60% of the subjects do as they are told, we can see the experimenter's demands for the coercive force that (in that setting) they are. The subjects, however, resort to claiming "he made me do it" only when the unflattering description of their actions is made apparent to them.

Not only does this example broaden the definition of coercion beyond explicit threats, it also makes two important points about how the dimension might operate in the assignment of responsibility. First, it shows that coercion is in the mind of the beholder. As in the case of other aspects of an attributional analysis of blame, it is the *perceiver's* notion of coercion that is critical. If the perceiver believes, either without an excuse from the actor, or after having accepted such an excuse, that there has been coercion, then responsibility will be diminished. Unless it can be entered into the perceiver's record of events, the actor's own view of the presence or absence of coercion will have no effect on the responsibility assigned.

Second, in many cases perceivers will reach their conclusion regarding coercion by examining covariation information. For so many people to have done what they, themselves have thought morally questionable must be testimony to the power of the situation. By contrast, the individual subject has only his one experience in the setting from which to draw attributional conclusions. To the degree that his or her cognitive schemata from prior settings generalize to the present, a subject is likely to recognize what is really happening, but ordinarily that generalization is quite limited. Indeed, one of the advantages of the wide reporting of Milgram's (1963) study is that such reporting provides individuals with the cognitive apparatus necessary to recognize a coercive situation when they face it.

Appreciation of Moral Wrongfulness

"Did she know it was wrong?" Ordinarily, the answer to this question will have been incorporated in the knowledge dimension. Following the lead of correspondent inference theory, the consequences of which the stimulus person is (or is not) aware, are the effects with valences. That those valences are generally regarded as negative contributes through augmentation to the stimulus person's placement on the causal "dimension," and through comparisons involving what would be expected from a reasonable person to enhanced responsibility assignment. There are, however, three exceptions to this general rule that suggest the need for a separate dimension of appreciation of the immoral quality of the act.

The first of these exceptions has to do with what Hart (1968) called "capacity responsibility." A person can be held morally or legally accountable only if that person possesses the requisite experience and understanding to know that the behavior performed contravened normal moral standards. In the legal system, this is the test by which young children, and adults suffering from severe emotional disorder, are excluded from liability for sanctions. What is in doubt for such individuals is not their capacity to recognize that the particular acts in question were immoral, but their capacity to know right from wrong in *any* circumstances. Knowledge of the consequences may or may not be present and the action taken might even have been intentional, but on the grounds of incapacity to appreciate the wrongfulness of the conduct, no responsibility will be assigned.

The second exception to the general association of moral valence with consequences of action occurs when an individual becomes so distraught or desperate that the moral quality of the action temporarily becomes lost in the shuffle. The legal version of this idea is "temporary insanity" or "diminished capacity," both of which assume that the legally proscribed action occurred when the stimulus person was not in possession of his or her normal capacities, usually as a result of an immediate provocation.

It is possible that the moral version of diminished capacity would not need to meet the legal standard of not knowing right from wrong at the time of the action. That standard implies (a) that the individual did not stop to think about the moral character of the action and (b) would not have been able to tell that the act was immoral even if it had been thoughtfully considered. We can, however, imagine instances of the first without the second. Some questionable business practices, some aspects of political maneuvering, and even some instances of teenage pregnancy occur not because the people involved were unable to recognize immorality when they saw it, but because they did not inquire about the action's moral quality at the time they performed it. Indeed, many of these actions can be undertaken only if the actors explicitly put issues of morality out of their minds. Whether perceivers of such actions will be quite so forgiving is an entirely different matter.

The third exception to the usual association of negative valences with effects for which responsibility will later be assigned arises because the perceiver and stimulus person simply disagree on the valence. Both parties would be able to specify the consequences of action, but only the perceiver would believe those consequences to be morally reprehensible. Because of who assigns the responsibility, it is the perceiver's moral standards that the stimulus person will need to have appreciated. This requirement that the stimulus person conform to the perceiver's moral code can present no impediments to a veridical attribution (as in the case of the "obvious" sociopath, whose behavior flouts widely accepted moral standards), or it may lead to an assignment of responsibility idiosyncratic to the particular perceiver involved (as in the case of a parent who believes that a child's listening to a radio constitutes immorality).

What these three kinds of exceptions to the knowledge–valence link suggest is that where appreciation of the moral wrongfulness of an action arises as a separate dimension, the judgment involved will have less to do with the action *per se* than with the overall moral capacity of the stimulus person or the moral code of the perceiver. Could the actor have known this was wrong? Did he or she attend to the moral dimensions of the action when it was being considered? Does the person share my view of what is moral and what is not? The perceived reason for the *failure to do the moral thing*, not the effects achieved through the immoral action, will determine how much responsibility is assigned on the basis of the appreciation-of-moral-wrongfulness dimension.

This dimension will interact with the causal, knowledge, intentionality, and coercion dimensions to produce the perceiver's final attribution of responsibility.

Consideration of social psychological theory and research, like the philosophical review undertaken in Chapter 4, has identified five dimensions that form the foundation for an attributional analysis of responsibility. The causal "dimension" is really a related set of discontinuous judgments about the actor's role in production of the effect, while that person's presumed knowledge of the consequences and appreciation of the moral wrongfulness of the action as well as the possible influence of coercive forces in the environment are all best represented by continuous scales. In each of these cases, it is the perceiver's *impression*, not the "truth" in any objective sense, that will affect the final assignment of responsibility. If the actor's intention is a central feature of personal causality, it is also the principal basis for an attribution of responsibility. Unfortunately, social–psychological research and theory do not provide a completely satisfactory definition of this critical concept. Further examination of the actor's intentions and of motives in general is the subject of the next chapter.

Chapter 6
Rationality and Bias: Intentions, Reasons, and Motives

As shown in discussion of the dimensions of responsibility, a person will be judged increasingly accountable for the production of harm as that person's causal participation and knowledge of the consequences of action increases. This attribution of responsibility will be reduced if the person is thought either not to possess the capacity to know that the action was wrong or to have been forced into taking the action. Our most severe moral criticism, like the most serious criminal penalties, will be reserved for those individuals who are thought to have produced harm *intentionally*. But how can we determine a person's intentions with any certainty? Are those intentions evanescent phenomena that arise as if by whim, and disappear just as quickly? Or do intentions reflect more enduring dispositions within the actors? If such underlying dispositions really exist, by what mechanism do they create behavior? How are our judgments as perceivers likely to be affected by our own intentions and motives? The purpose of this chapter is to suggest answers to these related questions.

Definitions of Intention

Recall from Chapter 3 that Anscombe (1957) claimed that the expression of an intention is one answer to the question "Why are you doing that?" As she noted, this question calls for the actor to identify a purpose for which the action is being performed. How can the purpose be learned by the perceiver? Anscombe's reasoning suggested two very different possibilities. First, she noted that " . . . if you want to say at least some true things about a man's intentions, you will have a strong chance of success if you mention what he actually did or is doing" (1957, p. 8). This description is, of course, congenial to the psychological approach of inferring intent from overt behavior.

Second, she also noted that the only "authoritative source" for the intention was the actor himself or herself. Now, it is certainly true that in many instances actors will be prepared to make public admissions of their intentions, and in these cases Anscombe's (1957) view is quite sensible. Even in those cases of interest to an attributional analysis of blame—cases in which the event to be accounted for is morally reprehensible—some actors may be willing to admit having intended to produce the harm. Especially in those instances the actor will be seen, perhaps through an application of some variant of correspondent inference theory, as an authoritative commentator on the action.

How reasonable is it to expect that people will readily publicize their evil intent? Some proportion of the explanations offered for moral wrongdoing will involve admissions of guilt, and how large this proportion might be is an empirical question that has not yet been addressed. Whatever the proportion might be, it would be a mistake to equate naively the actor's intent with "what he or she says it is." Indeed, if it could be assumed that actors always give "authoritative" answers when asked, there would need to be no "excuses." Theoretical work therefore needs to recognize the need for other man-ifestations of intent.

Social–Psychological Approaches

As Maselli and Altrocchi (1969) pointed out in an early review of the attribution of intent, both the legal system and social psychologists have recognized the need to define intention in a manner that permits its inference by a perceiver, without that perceiver's having to rely on a truthful answer from the actor. Unfortunately, as the discussion of definitions provided by Heider (1958) and correspondent inference theory (Jones & Davis, 1965; Jones & McGillis, 1976) illustrated, that inference may be exceedingly difficult to draw from a single instance of behavior. In Heider's case, local causality can be identified on a single-instance basis, but equifinality and trying require multiple observations. In the correspondent inference theory case, a single instance of action that violates an expectancy can lead to a valid inference of intention, but the same is not true for actions that conform to expectations. No doubt some of those expected actions will be intentional. The theory does not provide a criterion for distinguishing them from actions so routine for the person that the response to Anscombe's (1957) question, "Why?" might be "Oh, was I doing that?"

Is there a different social–psychological approach to the choice between one action and another that points toward such a criterion? Two possibilities suggest themselves. The first of these is Steiner's (1970) notion of perceived freedom, which rests on a distinction between outcome freedom and decision freedom. Outcome freedom refers to the person's capability of incurring the costs that would be required in order to achieve some desirable end. Perceived outcome freedom thus is defined for an available outcome as a function of the formula: (valence of the outcome $\times$ subjective probability of attainment) $-$ cost of attainment. By contrast, perceived decision freedom refers not to the ultimate objective, but to the number of alternatives open to the person at the time of the decision.

Decision freedom thus parallels, in correspondent inference theory terms, a choice between actions that would produce equivalent valences (regardless of the numbers of noncommon effects contributing to those valences). Outcome freedom, in the same terms, represents a choice situation in which at least one alternative has very few noncommon, but highly valued effects. For our purposes here, only decision freedom is relevant for the determination of intent from actions that do not deviate from role expectations.

Just how might an individual's perceived decision freedom affect the attribution made for his or her actions? Consider the "fundamental attribution error." Even when the constraints on a stimulus person's actions are made obvious to the perceivers, they still maintain that the stimulus person must possess at least some minimal degree of the disposition implicated in the behavior. One reason this may be true is that perceivers know enough about psychological research and coercive environments to think that notwithstanding his or her protestations to the contrary, the actor *could have done otherwise.* People who realize that prisoners of war consider it a matter of honor not to reveal to their captors any information other than name, rank, and serial number will certainly believe that the minor coercions inherent in everyday life and social–psychological experiments could be withstood if only the actor wanted to do so. Recall that in all of the research of Heider's levels of responsibility, the attributions made at the justifiability level do not drop down to zero, but just diminish from the level of intentionality. In short, even some "prisoners in chains" have a degree of decision freedom. Thus, to borrow a legal analogy, a stimulus person may not be presumed to be innocent in the production of an action, but may initially be presumed to be guilty *at least* of failing to foresee or prevent the negative effects. The attribution of intention is a smaller cognitive step, given this initial position, than it would be if the actor were truly presumed "innocent."

The second candidate for suggesting a more explicit criterion is the view of a perceiver as a (not altogether competent) mathematician. This alternative arises from the analysis of information gain in terms of Bayes' theorem (cited in Feller, 1968). Bayes' theorem is a principle of mathematical probability theory that expresses the degree to which the subjective odds of an event's likelihood ought to be revised following receipt of new information. In their applications of Bayes' theorem to attribution processes, Ajzen and Fishbein (1975, 1983) point out that the theorem is normative (or in our terms "prescriptive"), indicating how much revision would be expected in the subjective probability estimates made by a completely rational perceiver.

In its simplest form, Bayes' theorem is expressed by the following equation:

$$p(D \mid B) = \frac{p(B \mid D)p(D)}{p(B)}$$

where $p(D|B)$ is the *posterior probability* of the perceiver's estimated likelihood that the stimulus person possesses a particular disposition (D), given the knowledge that the stimulus person has performed a certain behavior (B); $p(B|D)$ is the probability that the behavior will be performed given the existence of the disposition; and $p(D)$ and $p(B)$ are, the *prior probabilities* that the stimulus person possesses the disposition and that the stimulus person will perform the behavior, respectively. If in the language of set theory, D' represents the complement of D, that is, $p(D') = 1 - p(D)$; then the expression

$$\frac{p(B|D)}{p(B|D')}$$

represents the ratio of the likelihood that the behavior in question will be performed given that the person possesses the disposition, to the likelihood that the behavior will be performed given that the person does not possess the disposition. Not surprisingly, this fraction is known as the *likelihood ratio*, and reflects the degree to which performance of the behavior favors the judgment that the person possesses the disposition over the judgment that the person does not possess the disposition. A likelihood ratio > 1.0 would suggest that the disposition is present, while a likelihood ratio < 1.0 would suggest that the disposition is not present.

A concrete example of this way of describing an attribution is provided by the extent to which an out-of-role or socially undesirable behavior is informative with regard to the stimulus person's underlying dispositions. As Ajzen and Fishbein (1983) note, "From a Bayesian point of view, a desirable behavior is one that is likely to be performed whether or not the actor has the disposition in question . . . " (p. 74). That is, the probability of the behavior in persons with the disposition is no greater than the probability of the behavior in persons without the disposition. Alternatively, when the action is a socially undesirable one, the probability of the behavior given the disposition, $p(B|D)$, *is substantially greater than the probability of the behavior, given that the person does not possess the disposition, $p(B|D')$.* In this latter case, the likelihood ratio would be in excess of 1.0, and the behavior would be said to be *diagnostic* of the existence of the disposition.

In their reviews Ajzen and Fishbein (1975, 1983) show that a variety of attributional phenomena, such as the assumed desirability of effects produced, the uniqueness of those effects, and even the actor's perceived decision freedom, can be represented by the diagnostic value of the appropriate likelihood ratios. They also argue, but less convincingly, that a variety of motivational biases in attribution really constitute only differences in the prior probabilities or likelihood ratios. More will be said about the general form of this argument in a later section.

Can the Bayesian approach help us to distinguish between intentional behavior and unintentional action? It could certainly be asserted that the diagnostic value of the likelihood ratio is indicative of the presence of intention. For unintentional actions there should be very little correlation between the presence of the disposition and the performance of the observed action, while for intentional actions a specified set of behaviors should be highly probable in any person possessing the relevant disposition. This relationship could be examined by determining the likelihood ratios for a wide variety of actions.

Without reference to any specific stimulus persons, perceivers could be asked to say, for example, what the probability is that the stimulus person is "untrustworthy," given that he or she has lied to a friend for no apparent reason. Then the same perceivers could make estimates of the stimulus person's likely untrustworthiness, given other contexts varying in apparent external justifications for the behavior. The likelihood ratio averaged across all of these contexts would indicate the "diagnosticity" of lying as an indication of an underlying disposition of untrustworthiness. Average diagnostic ratios could then be constructed for a variety of other actions with negative effects. On the assumption that a likelihood ratio can be *veridically* diagnostic only if the behavior has been intentional, those actions with the highest likelihood ratios could be expected to be intentional, while those with ratios less than 1.0 would be considered unintentional or overly constrained by the circumstances.

Unfortunately, what this example illustrates is a fundamental problem with the Bayesian approach. For most attributional tasks, the approach requires a great deal of effort from both the investigator and the subject in order to get information that could be obtained more efficiently through some other procedure. The method proposed in the example would provide a metric for arranging actions of various sorts according to their perceived intentionality. As an alternative, all the actions could have been listed, and subjects could have been asked simply to say how intentional each was considered to be. Or, in a more sophisticated way, all of the actions could have been compared using paired comparisons or multidimensional scaling, neither of which method would require quite as much from the subject or researcher. The Bayesian approach provides an alternative interpretation of attributional data, but only in the case of "motivated distortion" does this alternative conception lead to differential empirical predictions.

Philosophical Approaches

Whatever their value in suggesting factors a perceiver might consider in making an *inference* of intention, none of the social–psychological theories provides us with a clear definition of what an intentional action really is. To construct a definition it is necessary to examine some philosophical analysis of intention begun in Chapter 3. There I first mentioned the analyses of intention provided by Anscombe (1957) and Goldman (1970), who agree on one critical point but disagree on another. The disagreement was first noted in

Chapter 3 and is amplified in a later section in this chapter; the common ground is discussed here.

Expressing a view widely held in philosophy of mind, Anscombe (1957) and Goldman (1970) both argue that an intentional action is *not* one performed for its own sake. Rather than be an end in itself, an intentional action is a means for achieving some other objective. Building on a distinction made by Danto (1963) between "basic" acts (those that can be done directly) and "nonbasic" acts (those that require something else to be done first, Goldman points out that intentional actions are performed because they can generate some other (nonbasic) acts. For example, imagine that you see me standing on a tennis court holding a racket in my hand, waving my arm in the air. Curious about this movement, you ask why I am moving the racket around. You would accept as a reasonable answer a claim that I was warming up for a match, an assertion that I was getting the feel of a new racket, or even an explanation that I was swatting at some exceptionally pesky insects. But the answer "in order to wave the racket around" would lead you to suspect that I had already been out in the hot sun too long.

The way to make sense out of an intentional action is to inquire about the purpose for which it was performed. Indeed, Goldman (1970) argues that an action is intentional if and only if it meets three conditions: (a) There is a nonbasic act the person wanted to do, (b) the person believed that performing the intentional action would generate this nonbasic act, and (c) this want and belief together caused the intentional action.

What if the perceiver's goal is not to make sense out of an action that has been admitted to be intentionally performed, but (as is the more typical case in the assignment of responsibility) to determine whether an action *was* intentionally performed? In this case the converse of Goldman's first criterion can be quite helpful. If the perceiver cannot identify any purpose that conceivably could be accomplished by an action, then that action will not be considered intentional. The key word here is *conceivably*, and the breadth of that term distinguishes this criterion from the one inherent in correspondent inference theory. The purpose need not be low in assumed desirability, it only needs to be one of the logically possible purposes that the perceiver can imagine under the circumstances. After all, "following the dictates of my social role" is a purpose to be achieved by an intentional action just as "expressing my true self" is a nonbasic act generated by intentional action. It must be emphasized that deciding whether or not an action was intentional is different from deciding which disposition might have been the source of a particular intentional action. The greater the number of plausible effects that follow an action, the more likely that the action will be regarded as intentional, but the less certainty there will be that some specified underlying personal disposition was *the* want that influenced the action.

The perceiver's search for which want might be implicated in the action is simplified to some degree by Goldman's second criterion, the necessity for an actor to have the *belief* that the particular intentional action will accomplish the desired objective. Wants are broadly defined as favorable inclinations toward activities or entities, including feelings that certain behaviors are appropriate and obligations to do one's duty as well as desires. Some wants are what Goldman refers to as "standing" and persist through time, while others are "occurrent," arising and dissipating rather quickly. Whatever its form, a want alone is not sufficient to generate an intentional action. Wants must be combined with beliefs about what basic acts will satisfy the wants.

Together the wants and beliefs constitute an *action plan* that, given a particular set of conditions, can be the cause of an intentional action to be performed at a specified time. Goldman's notion of a belief encompasses two components that attribution theory would distinguish: the ability to perform the actions in question, and the knowledge that performing those actions would lead to the desired consequences. In order to infer an intention, the perceiver need not give equal weight to all of the logically possible outcomes of an action, but can concentrate only on those few outcomes for which it is reasonable to think that the actor had both knowledge and ability.

Constructing a Definition of Intention

There are several features that should be incorporated into a definition that would be satisfactory for an attributional analysis of blame. First, the definition should be independent of inference processes. By themselves, the social–psychological definitions do not satisfy this criterion of independence, describing intentions in terms of elements of the inference process such as equifinality, absence of role constraints, and perceived freedom of choice. Second, while remaining independent, the definition should suggest how inferences about intention are to be made. By themselves, the philosophical definitions do not satisfy this empirical criterion, either by asserting that intentions are not discoverable from the outside or by failing to distinguish between knowledge of the likely consequences of action and ability to bring about those consequences. Third, the definition should be independent of the valence of the outcome of action, to cover cases of deliberate actions undertaken to produce positive effects. The correspondent inference theory definition is particularly weak in this respect, but the other social–psychological definitions are not significant improvements. Finally, the definition cannot require successful completion of the action. A deliberate attempt that results in failure, especially because of intervening circumstances (or the volitional action of another person) is no less intentional than a deliberate action that succeeds in attaining its objective.

Recall from Chapter 3 that actions can be identified at a number of hierarchically organized levels (Vallacher & Wegner, in press), and that according to Goldman (1970) the acts, themselves, can be individuated on corresponding levels (with basic acts leading to nonbasic acts, which, in turn, might lead to still more remote nonbasic acts). Using this notion of levels of action and the four criteria, an intentional action can be defined as an action performed by an agent who (a) believes the action will generate a higher-level act, (b) believes he or she has sufficient ability to bring about this higher-level act, and (c) wants that act or event to occur.

This definition is independent of the valence of the outcome and the success of the performance. People may want things that are either desirable or undesirable, and they may not accurately assess either their full knowledge of the consequences or their capability of bringing those consequences into being. The definition is also independent of the processes that perceivers will employ to infer the intention, although it does suggest what features of action ought to be considered. The intentional action is more than desire, ability, and knowledge of the consequences (indeed, it is a particular combination of all three), but each of those factors identifies a characteristic of the outcome that a perceiver could examine to try to infer intent. If there is any aspect of the definition that is likely to raise criticism, it is the assertion that the person's wants *cause* the intentions. Although this assumption sounds no more controversial on its face than does the traditional attribution theory assumption that a person's underlying dispositions cause actions, it has been the subject of some debate, both within philosophy and within social psychology.

Reasons as Causes

Causal Status of Reasons

There are two fundamental questions that need to be answered in the affirmative if an individual's wants are to be considered (together with his or her knowledge and ability) a cause of intentional action. First, is it logically possible for a mental event to play a causal role in behavior, or, more specifically, can a want serve as the cause of bodily activity? Second, regardless of its status generally, is the notion of a motive-as-cause consistent with the previously given (Chapter 2) definition of a cause?

Much of the philosophical discussion of whether a reason for acting—what Anscombe (1957) would call the "intention with which" the action is performed, what Goldman (1970) would call a "want"—can serve as a cause of action parallels two of the issues already considered in detail. In the first place, if there are no generative causes of events, be those events physical happenings or human behaviors, then it makes no sense to ask about the causal status of reasons for acting. The question, "Can a mental event serve as a cause?" is simply not the sort of question that a regularity theorist would ask. On the other hand, the question is a reasonable one for an activity theorist, such as Reid (1863a, 1863b) or Collingwood (1940) to raise. In the second place, the issue of mental events serving as causes presumes a particular resolution of the dilemma of determinism. For an incompatibilist who would argue that human beings cannot cause events at all, it would make no sense to wonder whether a particular aspect of a person has causal properties. Alternatively, for a reconciliationist or libertarian, the mental events issue is real. Having cast its lot with activity theory and against incompatibilist determinism, an attributional analysis of blame has resolved the most general form of the question in the affirmative.

Deciding the general issue in favor of the possibility of human action does not, however, resolve the matter. Even if human intentions can produce actions (and those actions produce effects) in what Campbell (1957) would describe as "creative activity," can the same thing be said of human *wants*? This is exactly the point on which Anscombe (1957) and Goldman (1970) would disagree. For Anscombe, as well as for others who share her position (e.g., Melden, 1961; Peters, 1958; Ryle, 1949), the intention with which an action was performed is a logically necessary part of the description of the action. To recall the example of leaf burning from Chapter 3, "burning leaves to prepare my yard for winter" *is* the description of the action. Not only is there no intention separate from the observed behavior, it is nonsense to suggest that some underlying motive (like a "want") is the cause of the intention. As Melden (1961) states the argument, "In any simple causal explanation of one event by reference to another, it is not the identity or the character of the effect that is at issue, but the conditions in which it occurs— how it came to be" (pp. 87–88). So if the motive for which an action is performed is, as Melden claims, merely a "fuller characterization of the action" (p. 88), then that motive cannot be a cause of the intention (or the action).

As noted in Chapter 3, Goldman's (1970) objection to this view begins with a disagreement that there is a single action with multiple descriptions, some of which characterize the action in terms of the motives for which it was performed. In Goldman's opinion, and that of other reasons–explanation philosophers (e.g., Davidson, 1963) there are several different actions performed, not all of which share identical properties, and some of which are generated by the performance of others. Further, although the actor's response to the question "Why are you doing that?" is typically a statement of the desire to achieve some future state, the very initiation of the action *presupposes* the existence of the desire (and the belief that performance of the act could satisfy the desire) *prior to* the actual behavior. It is in this way, Goldman argues, that a want can function as the cause of an intentional action. In short, not only can human agents cause events, but the standing and occurrent wants of those agents can cause intentional actions. Philosophically, then, reasons can serve as causes.

Adopting the reasons–explanation view of action establishes the philosophical foundation for the possibility that an individual's motives can serve as the impetus to intentional action, but it does not demonstrate that such motives fit the definition of cause used in the present theory of blame. Remember that a cause must precede the presumed effect, involve human agency, be generative of the effect, and must be a discrete entity (a minimally sufficient subset, or the insufficient but necessary condition within such a subset). Does a human motive or want fit this set of criteria well enough to be considered a cause acceptable to the theory? Accepting the reasons–explanation view of action places the motive temporally prior to the intentional action, and endows that motive with the capacity to generate the action. In addition, there is no reason to believe that an individual's want or motive reflects human agency any less than does intentional action. Indeed, Reid's (1863a, 1863b) description of the exercise of human will (Chapter 3) applies to motives as forcefully as to externally observable intentional behaviors. Only the characterization of a cause as a discrete entity requires further discussion.

On first examination, terms like "strength of character," "possesses strong desires," and "strong-willed" would seem to argue that a person's motives ought to be thought of as varying in strength along some continuous dimension. Consider for a moment what each of these terms actually means. A person who possesses strong desires expresses them frequently and conducts a large proportion of his or her activities with a view toward satisfying those desires. In other words, the strong desires are reflected in numerous—but individually discontinuous—actions. Similarly, a person who is strong-willed will succumb to few external pressures. Again the criterion is not really the degree of continuous variation in response, but the proportion of separate occasions on which the individual's will is asserted despite external obstacles. Finally, one who is of strong character is able to resist temptations that might engage the rest of us, but again the resistance is a matter of the height of the person's threshhold for participation, *not* a matter of some continuous scale along which a behavior, once performed, varies.

This is not meant to rule out the possibility of variations in exertion, only to argue that, consistent with the reasons–explanation "fine-grained" analysis of action, an action done with gusto is *a different action* from one performed perfunctorily. Whether it is an intentional behavior or the motive that presumably gives rise to that behavior, a "strong" causal element is merely one that can produce the effect in the presence of an obstacle. For motives as well as for actions, what changes is the composition of the minimally sufficient causal subset, not the strength of any individual element of that subset.

For a motive-as-cause to be consistent with the causal theory behind the attributional theory of blame, it is only necessary to show that motives are discrete aspects of human agency that precede and generate intentional actions. The fit between the causal theory and the motive-as-cause is even better than that: A motive is a perfect insufficient but necessary (INUS), condition for intentional action. Whether the motive is conceived of as a "want," or as an "underlying personal disposition," it is regarded as (1) a necessary component of intentional action, a component that is (2) insufficient by itself, requiring belief (or knowledge and ability) to complete the causal subset. Thus Goldman's (1970) "action plan" is a minimally sufficient causal subset for intentional behavior. Moreover, because neither action theory nor attribution theory argues that there is a one-to-one correspondence between wants (or dispositions) and intended actions, it is logically possible for a single intentional behavior to have arisen as a consequence of more than a single want. The minimal sufficient causal subset containing the action plan (or the disposition and knowledge) is unnecessary, but sufficient, for the production of an intentional action.

Inference of Reasons

It is clearly possible for a person's motives—his or her reasons for acting—to produce intentional behavior. Thus do an individual's reasons become causes. Those reasons, however, are not the *only* causes of action. Where the action is intentional, the motive must be accompanied, at a minimum, by the belief that performance of the action in question at a specified time will enable the agent to satisfy the want. Often this minimum additional causal element is supplemented by external inducements or other internal desires. Therefore, even when the action is intentional, it might have been brought about by several causes, only one of which is the person's reason for acting. When an action is unintentional, the causes of behavior may be even more complex, including the accidental participation of other people, the past history of the actor (which might lead him or her to ignore potential difficulties in the situation that other actors would have foreseen), or just "being in the wrong place at the wrong time." In Chapters 3 and 5 I discussed some of the factors that might lead a perceiver to attribute a particular occurrence to one cause (including intentional action) as opposed to another, but I have as yet said nothing about how perceivers might distinguish reasons from other causes.

As usual in discussions of attribution, the initial insights on this problem were offered by Heider (1958). In his description of the "underlying concepts," Heider describes both the process of "causing" and the process of "wanting." About the latter he noted:

> Want is also connected with causation in the sense that when one wants something, one wants to bring about a certain state of affairs. Motivational factors in ourselves and in others are often spontaneously recognized. For example, by observing the behavior of another person or listening to what he says and how he says it, we discover that he wants to do something but cannot do it, or does not dare to do it. Or we discover that the change he produced in the environment is exactly what he wanted to bring about; he intended it. (Heider, 1958, pp. 16–17)

This is the same conception of "want" inherent in Goldman's (1970) argument that a resaon for acting can be a cause of action, and Heider reiterates the relationship between motive and intention in several other places throughout his book. In his discussion of the naive analysis of action, Heider argues that intention is the central feature of personal causality, but even here recognizes that an enduring motivational state may exist apart from any specific intentional action: "In the interest of conceptual clarification, therefore, we shall use the term intention to refer to *what* a person is trying to do, that is to the goal or action outcome, and not to *why* he is trying to do it. The latter applies more particularly to the reasons behind the intention"

(p. 110, emphasis in original). Later, in describing desire and pleasure, Heider's discussion presages Goldman's notion of an action plan, "The particular action by which the person tries to reach the goal is a consequence of the wish *and* the way the person sees this goal embedded in the causal structure of the environment (means–end beliefs)" (Heider, 1958, p. 128). Finally, the potential causal force of a want is also indicated by the fact that there can be disharmony between the person's wish and ethical requirements (p. 135), or between the wish and the more generalized social obligations expressed as "oughts" (p. 232 ff.).

It should be clear from these statements of Heider's ideas about wants and motives that (1) a person's general wants and motives (reasons for acting) are distinguished from the causes of particular behaviors, and (2) that in some cases, especially having to do with intentional action, that those reasons can, themselves, serve as causes. Unfortunately, these two principles have not always been as apparent to later writers as one might have imagined them to be. For example, Buss (1978) inexplicably comes to the conclusion that " . . . Heider, unfortunately, did not distinguish between causes and reasons. . . . It has been the perpetuation of Heider's exclusively causal interpretation of action that has contributed to some of the serious conceptual confusion in the field" (p. 1313). Buss begins his paper with Aristotle's four causes—efficient, material, final, and formal—suggesting that the modern versions of efficient and final causes, respectively, would be a "cause" and a "reason." The historical review then shifts to the position of Peters (1958) and Winch (1958), who believe with Anscombe (1957) and Melden (1961) that to state a person's reason for acting is merely to provide a fuller description of the observed behavior. The conclusion of this review is that "reason-type explanations help to make an action intelligible by attaching *meaning* to the action in terms of the rules for social behavior and, as such, are not causal explanations" (Buss, 1978, p. 1314). What Buss does not seem to realize is that Heider's "failure" to distinguish between causes and reasons is a true failure only if the philosophical position requiring such a distinction is accepted. The reasons–explanation philosophers would argue, however, that if reasons can also serve as causes, then Heider's position makes all of the distinctions that are required.

Several replies to Buss's paper have noted errors in his argument (Harvey & Tucker, 1979; Kruglanski, 1979; Shaver, 1981), but one of these (Kruglanski, 1979) continues to ignore the possibility that a person's reason for acting might be a cause of his or her intentional behavior. So, in an attempt to "reconceptualize" the cause–reason distinction, Kruglanski suggests that both causes and reasons be regarded as kinds of *explanations*, where an explanation is "a statement constructed around the connective *because*" (p. 1449). Then, according to Kruglanski, a cause is a generic sort of explanation that has been employed in two senses, an "inclusive" sense that covers any explanation, whether or not it is expressed in teleological terms; and an "exclusive" sense that covers only explanations with no teleological component. The summary of this argument is "that cause simply means explanation, no more, no less" (Kruglanski, 1979, p. 1449). There is no need to consider this view in any detail. Suffice it to say that although Kruglanski's position might be compatible with a modern version of regularity theory, it is indefensible as an extension of any version of activity theory. Because it ignores the generative character of human actions, it is of no use to the attributional analysis of blame.

Fortunately, the most recent discussion of causes and reasons in the social–psychologial literature (Locke & Pennington, 1982) is a collaboration between a philosopher and a psychologist that returns us to Heider's starting position. These authors note three major differences between reasons and causes. The first is that an agent necessarily knows what his or her reasons are (reasons account for intentional behavior, while causes might account for accidents or unintentional behaviors). Second, because an agent knows his or her reasons for acting, that agent does not need to appeal to "empirical regularities" to establish causal connections (this is a weaker version of Anscombe's (1957) notion that the actor is the only "authoritative source" of information about his or her intentions). Third, while causes explain behavior by showing it to be the inevitable outcome of a complex of factors, reasons explain it by showing it to be the only thing a rational agent would do (given an identical set of wants and beliefs). None of these differences, however, constitutes a convincing argument that an individual's reasons for acting cannot also serve as a cause of the ensuing intentional behavior. Indeed, Locke and Pennington claim that "The current philosophical orthodoxy ... is that far from being incompatible, reasons are themselves but one kind of cause" (p. 213).

To bring a bit of order into the reason–cause debate within social psychology, Locke and Pennington (1982) offer a three-tiered division of the possible causes of human action. These possible causes are first divided into those internal to the person and those external to the person. There is no elaboration of the external subdivision, but the internal subdivision is further separated into reasons and other internal causes. Finally, although there is no further specification of the other internal causes, there is a partition of the reasons into what are called "psychological" reasons in one group and "situational" reasons in another. This latter distinction is an attempt to accommodate people's tendencies to describe some of their reasons in terms of the pressures of the external situation (what might otherwise be called "external" reasons), while recognizing that in the strict sense all reasons are internal beliefs held by the agent.

A major impetus to Buss's (1978) analysis, and to those of some of his later critics, was the need to understand why an actor's account of his or her behavior is so frequently at odds with the account that would have been provided by an outside observer. This difference looks less self-centered on the part of the actor if it is presumed that for the actor the question "Why did you do that?" really requests a reason, while for the observer it calls for the statement of a cause. Virtually all who have commented on the problem (Buss,

1978; Harvey & Tucker, 1979; Jones, 1978; Kruglanski, 1979; Locke & Pennington, 1982) agree on the empirical likelihood that the question, "Why?" will mean different things to the actor and to the observer, but disagree on the conceptual necessity for the answers to be different. The position suggested by Locke and Pennington (1982) solves the empirical question just as well as any other approach, and it is much more consistent with neoclassical and modern philosophy than is the solution proposed by Buss (1978) or by Kruglanski (1979). The position that reasons can be causes brings us back to Heider's (1958) original notion that while intentional action is the central feature of personal *causality*, those intentions can, in turn, be caused by the individual's underlying wants, desires, and felt obligations.

There is, however, one remaining problem regarding the process by which the perceiver might infer that these underlying dispositions have affected behavior. What is an observer faced with interpreting a single instance of action to do in order to determine whether that action was intentional? Is there an acceptable substitute for the covariation across time, modality, and circumstances that would provide conclusive evidence of the presence of intention? The answer is a hopeful affirmative that relies on the causal status of wants. In describing the philosophical analysis of motivation, Alston (1967) notes that the list of relevant conditions for the performance of a single intentional action must include not only the want thought to be central to the production of the action, but also other wants (including obligations and aversions as well as desires). In short, "It is *systems* of wants, rather than any one want in isolation, which give rise to action" (Alston, 1967, p. 404).

The key suggested by this analysis is that for most everyday social behaviors, the minimally sufficient causal subset will include multiple elements representing various wants, some of which will be potential causes of the intentional action, and some of which will be obstacles to the performance of that action. By examining those *other* elements the perceiver can accomplish a sort of covariation that would not otherwise be possible. The perceiver faced with a single instance of action can deduce from what correspondent inference theory would call "effects foregone" which wants were insufficient to impel action. Further, to the extent that noncommon effects achieved might reflect multiple wants, the "want system" thus revealed can be examined for internal consistency. Finally, this distinctiveness information from effects foregone and consistency information from multiple wants revealed can be used in a covariation-like fashion to arrive at a final attribution about the likely causes of the intentional action. Obviously, as the distinctiveness of the effects foregone and number of possible wants satisfied increase, so will the perceiver's certainty that the action was intentionally performed. This line of reasoning assumes that most actors will have effects reflective of more than a single disposition, perceivers possess an implicit theory of the mutual association of wants much like an implicit personality theory, and, of course, wants *are thought* to cause intentional actions (an empirical question quite apart from the logical issues involved). At present this use of multiple wants to indicate the presence of intentional action is a theoretical speculation awaiting a proper test.

Motivation of Perceivers

If there is an issue in contemporary attribution theory more controversial than the question of whether reasons can serve as causes, it is the argument over whether or not the *motives* of actor and perceiver can affect the attributions they draw from instances of action. The argument arises in connection with three major domains of inquiry: actor–observer differences, asymmetries in attribution of causality for success or failure, and judgments of the responsibility of perpetrators of harm. The first two are mentioned here briefly, and only the third area is discussed in any detail.

First, there is the comparison between the attributions of actors and those of observers mentioned above. On the one hand, the "rational" argument would take a form very similar to the position advanced by Buss (1978), Kruglanski (1979), and Locke and Pennington (1982), namely that when asked "Why?" the actor believes the question involves a reason, while the observer believes the question involves a cause. Naturally, the two give different answers, and there is no need to involve a possible motivation. On the "motivational" side, the observer is presumed to be "objective," having no stake in whether the attribution ultimately made is dispositional or situational, while the actor is presumed (especially in instances of interest to an attributional analysis of blame) to be "motivated" to minimize his or her causal participation. Even the most rational account of the actor–observer difference relies, as we have seen, on the possibility for an individual's *wants* (a motivation-laden term, to be sure) to cause his or her intentional actions. Even if the two participants (actor and observer) are rationally answering different questions, a strong element of motivation is nevertheless present.

The second domain in which there is controversy regarding the presence or absence of motivation involves the identification of the causes for success and failure. Although the discrepancy has been understood anecdotally for centuries, the specific attributional statement of the problem is once again to be found in Heider's (1958) work, as indicated, for example, by "We need only to recall how often the poor workman blames his tools to realize that the attribution of can, as well as its cognition, is not always as objective as might be desirable" (p. 98). Again, the "rational" position (reflected in the writing of Brewer, 1977; Miller & Ross, 1975; Ross, 1977) holds that people generally expect success (as a logical outgrowth of the fact that most of the time people experience success in their daily activities), so when they do succeed at some laboratory exercise, they claim that outcome to have been due to their own efforts. Similarly, when they experience failure, it is so inconsistent with their own past performance that they naturally assume the outcome to have been the product of external forces beyond their own control.

By contrast, the "motivational" position (represented in the writings of Bradley, 1978; Greenberg, Pyszczynski, & Solomon, 1982; Weary & Arkin, 1981) argues that at least part of the tendency to claim more credit for success than the amount of blame accepted for failure arises from the actor's own personal motives, either to preserve or enhance self-esteem or to make a positive impression on the attending audience. This domain of attributional inquiry, like that of actor–observer differences deals with the question of the *agent's* motivation or lack of motivation. As a consequence, as long as it is presumed that wants can cause actions, the outcome of the success–failure debate cannot eliminate motives from the potential causes of the actor's behavior.

The Rational Perceiver?

The third domain of attributional research in which there is controversy over the influence of motivation has to do not with the motives of the actor, but with the possible motives of the perceiver. This controversy is the most important of the three, because the actors' opinions cannot always be taken as conclusive on questions of their responsibility for harmful outcomes. Should an actor admit having intentionally done harm, that actor will most probably be believed, even though the confession might not have been warranted. On the other hand, should an actor deny intentionally having caused harm, the perceiver's task of determining causality, assigning responsibility, and ultimately ascribing blame will proceed in a manner relatively independent of interpretive contributions offered by the actor.

Are these personal judgments rational reflections of the information contained in the situation to be evaluated, or are the attributions perceivers make subject to bias from what could only be described as the perceiver's *own* motives? That is the critical question for the last section of this chapter.

The notion that the perceiver is an "intuitive scientist," embarked on a search for attributional truth but occasionally suffering from limitations in the method of inference, is embodied in the work of Ajzen and Fishbein (1975, 1983), Brewer (1977), Fischhoff (1976), Nisbett and Ross (1980), Miller and Ross (1975), and Ross (1977). The "weak" version of the rationalist thesis is that the vast majority of a perceiver's attributional behavior can be characterized by a legitimate attempt to understand the actions of others. It is exceedingly difficult to quarrel with this version of the rational observer position. No doubt most of the time our objective as perceivers is to obtain the most accurate information that we can. Even pointing out that we need this accurate information to accomplish our own *goals* in social interaction (a clearly motivational notion) does not change the presumed necessity for accuracy.

The strong version of the rationalist position, however, is quite another matter. This position, stated with varying degrees of force by Ajzen and Fishbein (1983), Brewer (1977), and Ross (1977) is that motivated distortion is conceptually unlikely. Advocates of information processing have been careful to claim only that motivation "is not necessary" to account for research results that appear to demonstrate distortion or to argue that the motivational position is "untenable," not to assert that motivated distortion is impossible. Nevertheless, even the claim that it is unlikely has tremendously important metatheoretical implications. If this argument were correct, attribution processes would be placed in a category by themselves and would have to be regarded as different in kind from numerous other social–psychological phenomena.

Consider some examples. The fundamental principle of cognitive consistency theories is that a person will distort his or her internal attitudes to have them agree with overt behavior. One of the predominant resolutions for perceived inequity is distortion either of one's own or the other person's inputs or outcomes. On a more general level, entire schools of psychotherapy depend for their conceptual foundation on the presumption that people are not wholly objective when it comes to interpreting their own actions (or in some cases the actions of others). It is, to say the least, implausible that the cognitive processes of attribution are so very different from the cognitive processes frequently found in other areas.

The general claim against the influence of motivation must therefore be regarded with some skepticism. What about the specific version of the alternatives to motivated distortion? To the extent that the perceiver's impression deviates from the facts, that deviation is argued to result from the influence of "judgmental heuristics" (Kahneman & Tversky, 1973), not from personal needs that the observer is attempting to satisfy. The three heuristics that might lead to failure of an otherwise rational process are *representativeness, availability,* and *adjustment.* As Ajzen and Fishbein (1983) note, in attribution the representativeness heuristic leads perceivers to assign a dispositional property to the actor not on the basis of the presumed likelihood that the actor possesses the disposition, but on the degree to which the behavior shown is thought to be prototypical of the disposition. Striking another person is more representative of dispositional aggressiveness than is trying to get the person in trouble with the boss. It should be noted, however, that when the action has been intentional, the choice of physical aggression over backbiting *is* informative about the dispositional quality.

The availability heuristic, according to Ajzen and Fishbein (1983), has two implications for the attribution process. First, those dispositions highest in the perceiver's explanatory repertoire will tend to be invoked even in cases where they are inappropriate. Second, the ease with which the perceiver can bring to mind evidence supporting a particular attribution will spuriously inflate the perceiver's use of that disposition. On the one hand there is a sort of "implicit disposition theory" that militates against accuracy, while on the other hand there is a tendency to find what can be found most easily. The third heuristic, adjustment, refers to the perceiver's tendency to search for information that will be consistent with some initial impression, whether or not that information is really germane to the attribution at hand.

How can these cognitive heuristics account for what otherwise might be considered motivated distortion in the attribution of responsibility? It turns out that the short answer to this question is "they cannot." The key is the limitation of the question to the attribution of *responsibility* to another for a negative event with which that other person has been associated. Well over 25 studies have been published in the last 10 years that presume to deal with the issue of motivated distortion. In most of these cases, the attributions are made by actors for their own task successes or failures. Unfortunately, reviews of this literature have typically generalized information-processing alternative explanations for "self-serving" attributions of *causality* to the attribution of responsibility as well (e.g., Ajzen & Fishbein, 1975, 1983; Brewer, 1977; Miller & Ross, 1975; Ross, 1977). If there is anything I have demonstrated to this point, it is that the attribution of causality is substantively different from the attribution of responsibility. The conclusions reached in one domain— especially when those conclusions deal with attributions made for own performance—cannot be transposed "as is" to the other domain.

The Protection of Self

Even if perceivers are rational processors of information most of the time, they will not be so always—unless attribution processes are significantly different from other psychological phenomena. Assuming that attributions are not somehow unique in their lack of motivational influence, the important question becomes "under what circumstances will the perceiver's *own* motives affect his or her judgments about the motives of the actor? Not surprisingly, Heider's (1958) answer to this question dealt as follows with the "affective significance" of the attribution made:

> Thus, there are two factors that determine the selection of the acceptable attribution: (1) the reason has to fit the wishes of the person, and (2) the datum has to be plausibly derived from the reason. The first refers to the affective significance of an event. That reason is sought that is personally acceptable. (p. 172)

It is true that Heider's (1958) synopsis of the effects of motivation on attributions refers to attributions to self, but on the same page Heider argues that "the examples also show the major influence of self-attitudes on the interpretations of the actions of other people" (p. 172). Whether it is our own actions or the behavior of another person, the attribution is susceptible to motivational influence if the perceiver has a personal stake in the outcome. In correspondent inference theory this personal stake is represented in the notion of *hedonic relevance*, a measure of the degree to which the action to be explained carries positive or negative consequences for the perceiver, and by *personalism*, the attributor's belief that the action was uniquely conditioned by his or her presence.

For the purposes of this discussion, the difficulty with the general idea of the affective significance of an attribution is that the idea is *too* general. In Heider's (1958) work this kind of motivational bias is expected to influence attributions of causality and attributions of responsibility, both of which might be made either for one's own actions or for the actions of others. In the Jones and Davis (1965) version of correspondent inference theory (hedonic relevance is not mentioned in the Jones & McGillis, 1976, version) the distortion is limited to the attributions made for another's behavior, but both causal judgments and responsibility judgments are thought to be affected.

The specific question at present, however, concerns only the ascription of responsibility to others, a judgment believed to be affected by two more limited motives, the need to see a person's outcomes as deserved, and the need to avoid the possibility of being blamed oneself. The first of these reflects what Lerner and his associates (e.g., Lerner & Matthews, 1967; Lerner & Miller, 1978) have called the *need to believe in a just world*. The second reflects what I (1970, 1973) have called *defensive attribution*.

Two critical points should be made about these motives before they are discussed in detail. To begin with, neither represents a distortion in the attribution made for an admittedly intentional action. On the contrary, in both instances responsibility is attributed in the *absence* of intention. The need to believe in a just world leads to the assignment of either characterological fault or behavioral fault when the stimulus person's causal participation in the event rarely exceeds the forseeability level. Indeed, the stimulus person is most typically an "innocent victim." Defensive attribution leads to the assignment of responsibility to a person who might have been causally involved in the production of the negative outcome, but under circumstances in which there is the "intervention" of random forces outside the personal control of that person. In neither case are individuals likely to be blamed for something they *did*. The second critical point is that there is a common thread in the two. The one distortion affects judgments of victims whose situation the perceiver hopes to avoid, while the other affects judgments of potential perpetrators in whose situation the perceiver expects to be, but both depend on the perceiver's desire to minimize his or her own personal threat.

The presumed need to believe in a just world depends implicitly on the perceiver's having generally positive self-esteem. The specific threat cited in the literature is a fear of negative outcomes that occur "by chance." If, however, a perceiver had a very low opinion of his or her own self-worth, thus deserving one bad outcome after another, "chance" would not be threatening. After all, chance might occasionally produce "undeserved" positive outcomes. Assuming that the perceiver does have a positive self-image, then it is threatening to believe that bad things might happen (to a good person like me). How can such misfortunes be avoided?

According to Lerner and Miller (1978), the threat can be reduced in one of two ways. First, it can be asserted that the stimulus person made some *behavioral* error that led to the negative outcome. A familiar example of this assertion would be a claim, by other women, that a rape victim must have done something to invite the attack. Second, if prevented from attributing the outcome to some sort of mistake, the perceiver can still maintain a belief that justice was served by attributing to the stimulus person some *character-ological* flaw for which the misfortune is a kind of retribution.

Strictly speaking, the attribution of behavioral fault assumes a different position on critical dimensions of responsibility. To begin with the most important difference, behavioral fault presumes causality, characterological fault denies it. Characterological blame is at the association "step" of this causal staircase, as the individual is affected by, but did not produce, a negative outcome. Because it does not presume causality, characterological fault cannot involve the knowledge dimension of responsibility, nor does it encompass intentionality, coercion, or appreciation of the moral implications of action. By contrast, the behavioral dimension can be claimed to involve causality, typically at the foreseeability "step" on the staircase. This level of causality makes the individual liable for not having known better (the knowledge dimension of responsibility). Even though the actor is not claimed to have intended the negative outcome, it is at least possible to argue that he or she should have known enough to do otherwise.

Because it does not presuppose causality, the attribution of character-ological fault is much more likely to represent a motivated distortion than is the attribution of behavioral fault. The judgment of behavioral fault is usually assumed to be prepotent, so in some of the early research that obtained derogation of victims, it was made quite clear to the subjects that in no sense of the term were the sufferers "responsible" for their subsequent pain. By virtue of their different positions on the critical dimension of causality, it is reasonable to think that the two kinds of fault ought to be inversely related, an assumption that can be seen in the literature (e.g., Lerner & Miller, 1978). Unfortunately, the first study explicitly assessing the correlation between the two (Davis & Shaver, 1982) found them to be positively correlated. Obviously, the nature of the relationship between behavioral and charactero-logical fault needs further attention. Nevertheless, it is clear that the threat inherent in negative consequences can alter the attributions of fault made to "innocent" victims (Lerner & Miller, 1978).

According to the need to believe in a just world, the threat posed by an event with negative consequences can lead to an exaggeration of the responsibility assigned to an innocent victim. But the perceiver's attempts at self-protection do not end there. Following Walster's (1966) idea that perceivers will assign responsibility in a manner designed to protect themselves from threat, I (Shaver, 1970, 1973) outlined a process of *defensive attribution*. Perceivers can be wholly rational judges of another's responsibility for producing a negative outcome only if they can be confident that they will never be in similar circumstances. If, however, the perceivers believe that they might someday find themselves in the same position ("situational possibility"), then their attributions of responsibility to the perpetrator will depend on their perceived similarity to that individual. If the perceiver is certain that he or she is personally different from the perpetrator (suggesting that different behavioral choices would be made), then the stimulus person's responsibility will be exaggerated and the personal differences will be magnified. Alternatively, if under conditions of high situational possibility the perceiver *also* considers himself or herself to be personally similar (and therefore likely to make the same mistakes), then the stimulus person's responsibility will be *minimized*.

Thus, according to the defensive attribution notion, there will be a self-protective denial of a stimulus person's responsibility only in the presence of both high situational possibility and high personal similarity. There is research consistent with the defensive attribution predictions (Burger, 1981; Chaikin & Darley, 1973; Shaver, 1970; Shaver, Turnbull, & Sterling, 1973), but there is also some contrary evidence (Tyler & Devinitz, 1981). More importantly, the combination of situational possibility and personal similarity is just the conjunction of conditions that a wholly rational view of the perceiver (e.g., Brewer, 1977) would claim to lead to a diminution of responsibility. A perceiver who can imagine being in the actor's circumstances is more "familiar" with the setting, and consequently more likely to understand the constraints on action. In the same fashion, a perceiver who is personally similar to the actor will be better able to take that actor's viewpoint (thus, again, more effectively noting how much of the action might have been due to external factors).

On first examination it would appear, as Tetlock and Levi (1982) have argued, that it will prove impossible to distinguish empirically between the motivated distortion position (at least as represented by defensive attribution) and the information-processing position. A recent pair of experiments by Thornton (1984), however, permits a much more optimistic conclusion. In the first of two studies, Thornton asked subjects to evaluate the responsibility of a stimulus person who was in circumstances that could conceivably affect the subjects as well (situational possibility). Personal similarity to this actor was varied, as was the presence or absence of cues that could provide an alternative explanation for any arousal the subjects might experience (from the presumably threatening combination of possibility and similarity). The results of this study were generally consistent with principles of defensive attribution, but the finding of greatest importance for our present purposes concerned the misattribution of arousal. When subjects had been provided with an alternate label for arousal, they attributed *less* responsibility, either of a characterological sort or a behavioral sort, to the stimulus person than when no misattribution of arousal was possible. In the second study Thornton (1984) repeated the personal similarity manipulations in a high–situational-possibility context, but this time substituted an arousal-*enhancing* manipulation for the emotional misattribution conditions of the first experiment. Again, the results were consistent with defensive attribution principles, with similar stimulus persons assigned less responsibility than different ones, and with a relative preference for behavioral fault over characterological fault when the stimulus person was similar. Moreover, there was a main effect for the induction of emotional arousal, such that more responsibility of each kind was attributed in the high arousal conditions.

As positive as Thornton's results are, they alone cannot settle the issue, for two reasons. First, in both of his studies subjects were asked to evaluate the responsibility of a stimulus person who was the *victim* of a rape, rather than to judge a perpetrator of negative consequences. Whether this motivational bias will also extend to perpetrators remains to be determined. Second, it is entirely possible that the findings obtained from any study that has employed rape as the stimulus material will be difficult to generalize to other sorts of negative consequences. This genralization, then, also awaits further research.

What is clear from Thorton's work is that defensive attribution involves a motivated distortion on the perceiver's part. It is certainly true that in most cases perceivers are rational processors of the information provided by the behavior of others. Even when that behavior produces negative consequences, many of the "errors" can be accounted for by reliance on cognitive heuristics, without the need to invoke additional motivational processes. But just as surely as the actor's own behavior serves his or her purposes, the act of attributing responsibility serves the perceiver's purposes. An actor's reasons can cause his or her intentional actions, and in interpreting those intentional actions more than the perceiver's viewpoint must be considered. A comprehensive attributional analysis of blame must include the perceiver's motives in attributing, just as it must take into account the stimulus person's reasons for acting.

Chapter 7
Attributions of Causality and Responsibility: Discovered or Imposed?

A friend does something to shatter our trust. An airliner crashes, killing dozens of passengers. A period of international tensions erupts into a shooting war. What is the cause of each of these events? Who is responsible? Who is to blame? In the preceding chapters I have tried to show how the first two of these questions might be answered, and in the next chapter I shall consider the last question. At this point it is important to emphasize that there have been two parallel kinds of answers to the questions about causality and responsibility.

The first kind of answer has been prescriptive in character, establishing conceptual parameters for causality and responsibility. As shown previously, a cause must be an entity, a collection of conditions that includes human agency. Although they are typically represented in the minds of perceivers, causes do exist independently. By contrast, a responsibility attribution must be just that—a construction in a perceiver's mind. The assignment of responsibility can be described by several dimensions, but there is no external "responsible" that corresponds to a "cause." Finally, it has been established that an individual's reasons can serve as causes of his or her intentional behavior and that a perceiver's own reasons and motives may affect the responsibility judgments that are made.

The second kind of answer to the questions about causality and responsibility has been descriptive, based not on conceptual analysis but on research. Previous discussion has shown how cognitive schemata are called into play to account for the causes of events observed only once, how perceptions of intention and coercion affect the ascription of responsibility, and how a perceiver's own needs do distort the process of judgment.

One of the principal conclusions that could be drawn from a comparison between the conceptual analysis and the empirical work is that the former embodies distinctions that have only rarely been demonstrated in the latter. This is not a novel conclusion, as it has been suggested before for different aspects of the attribution process by Fishbein and Ajzen (1973), Shaver

(1973), Fincham and Jaspars (1980), and Shultz and Schleifer (1983), to name just a few. Nor is the conclusion entirely surprising. After all, the conceptual distinctions are much more easily drawn than tested, so one would expect the empirical work to lag behind.

Although future empirical developments in the attribution of causality, responsibility, and blameworthiness will depend on there being clear conceptual distinctions and sufficient conceptual detail, it is also important to ensure that future research does not impose its conceptual sophistication on the ordinary perceivers whose attributions are the subject of scientific inquiry. In short, while we cannot achieve full understanding of the processes without plenty of "clean tools," we must also refrain from using tools that are inappropriate for the task at hand, merely to justify their continued presence in our workplace.

Accordingly, the present chapter reports preliminary research that has two purposes. First, it indicates, by two quite different examples, how carefully we need to attend to the "match" between our conceptual explanations of the perceiver's behavior and that perceiver's explanations for events of interest. Second, it suggests some of the empirical implications of an attributional analysis of blame. The two studies described (Shaver, Null, & Huff, 1982; Slocumb, Forsyth, & Shaver, 1983) are beginnings, not final answers to conceptual questions, so their conclusions should be regarded as tentative. Retaining the causality–responsibility order, the discussion begins with a conceptual addition that may need to be made to the attribution of causality and concludes with a conceptual warning that should accompany study of the attribution of responsibility.

What Sorts of Causes?

One of the distinctions drawn both by philosphers and social psychologists regarding causation involves the locus of causality. At least when the events being described are those of relevance to a psychology of blame—events that involve the possibility of human agency—there are two predominant categories of causes. Either events are presumed to have been brought about by the actions of persons (*internal* causes), or they are assumed to have been the product of forces *external* to the person. This bifurcation of causes can be seen in Heider's (1958) notions of personal force and environmental force, in the contrast between intentional action and conformity to expectations in correspondent inference theory (Jones & McGillis, 1976), and even in such recent work as that of Locke and Pennington (1982). It is true that operationally "internal" and "external" are no longer regarded as opposite ends of a unidimensional continuum (Miller, Smith, & Uleman, 1981; Solomon, 1978), but rarely has it been suggested that the two categories together do not exhaust the logical possibilities.

There is, however, reason to think that the ordinary perceivers for whose construction of reality attribution theory purports to account might employ at least one additional explanatory category. For example, in a study of accident victims, Bulman and Wortman (1977) found that the most frequent explanation offered for suffering was "God has a reason." Accounting for one's own misfortune is a process that differs in significant ways from the attribution of responsibility and blameworthiness to others, but there is reason to believe that even in the latter circumstances attributions to what I (Shaver, 1979) have called "superphysical" forces might occur with some frequency. Are these attributions to (malevolent) superphysical forces merely another form of Spinoza's (1677/1952) view that God is the ultimate cause of all things positive, are they just a restatement of the determinist position on free will, or are they conceptually *different* from the usual internal and external causes? Because the purpose of the present chapter is to alert researchers to empirical problems in the application of theory, this question will be examined experimentally rather than philosophically.

Even if attributions to superphysical causality are distinct from those to internal and external causes, only the most doctrinaire would assume that they would be a prevalent choice regardless of the circumstances. A more likely outcome is that such attributions might be "prompted" either by features of the setting or by personal characteristics of the perceivers. For example, superphysical explanations are more likely to be offered by individuals who are highly religious for events that contain "prompts" to their use. To test some of these ideas, Slocumb, et al. (1983) asked highly religious and less religious subjects to describe the causes of events with positive consequences. Subjects evaluated two events, the rescue of a child who had stepped in front of a parked car and the remission of an inoperable cancer. For each subject the two events either did or did not also include a religious "priming" stimulus. As an example, one of the brief stimulus stories reported that the stimulus person's inoperable cancer went into remission either after the person had spent time each day "praying" or "reading about cancer cures."

In order to distinguish among possible causes of these events, perceivers were asked how much they believed the outcome was due to external causes (factors in the situation), to internal causes (something about the person), or to superphysical causes (divine intervention). As a control against the possibility that "superphysical" might be nothing more than another external cause, subjects were also asked to complete the 23-item version of the Rotter Internal–External Locus of Control scale (Rotter, 1966). Subjects were also given the Bardis (1961) religion scale, and those who scored either in the top four deciles or in the bottom four deciles were included in the analysis. Finally, as a control against the chance that simply asking questions about superphysical causality might bias the outcome, a different group of subjects was presented with the same stories and questionnaires, except that the questions about superphysical causality were omitted.

Preliminary analyses of the data indicated that there were no effects for order of presentation of the brief stories, and no main effects involving subject gender (there were three interactions involving gender, but these did not form any consistent pattern). As a consequence, the data were pooled for males and females and collapsed across presentation orders. The major hypothesis had been that the more highly religious subjects (those scoring in the top four deciles on the Bardis scale) would use the category for superphysical causality to a greater degree than would the less religious subjects (those scoring in the bottom four deciles).

The first test of this general prediction was provided by an open-ended question asking the subject to provide a cause of the outcome described in the story. Some subjects provided more than a single answer, so there were 218 separate responses produced to the two incidents by the 80 subjects. Responses were coded into five categories: internal cause, external cause, superphysical cause, chance, and "biological cause" (a category of explanation used infrequently, and only when the outcome was remission of a cancer). Two independent raters made identical category assignments for 94% of the responses, and in the other cases were able to agree on an assignment after discussion.

Contingency tables were constructed within events (one for the rescue story, one for the remission story) in which presence or absence of superphysical causes was examined for highly religious and less religious subjects. These unconstrained attributions of causality reflected the story content, with 36% of the remission responses involving superphysical explanations, but only 7% of the rescue responses invoking superphysical causality. In addition, use of the superphysical category for explanation was, as anticipated, related to religiosity. For the rescue and remission stories, respectively, 85% and 83% of the responses that invoked superphysical explanations were provided by highly religious subjects. Obviously, with the order of the stories counterbalanced, the open-ended question in half of the cases followed the closed-ended scales, one of which raised the possibility of superphysical causality. The absolute levels of this explanation therefore may not be reliable. The differences between the attributions made for one story and those made for the other, however, and the differences traceable to subject religiosity, are not affected by the counterbalancing. Whatever else these findings might indicate, they show clearly that the superphysical explanations provided originated predominantly from the more highly religious subjects.

The major dependent variable in the study was, of course, the specific question about the influence of divine intervention on the story outcome. Mean scores on this and other attribution questions were analyzed by a three-factor analysis of variance, with high or low religiosity, presence or absence of religious priming stimulus, and content of the story as factors (the last one within subjects). As predicted, high scorers on the Bardis religion scale attributed more influence to superphysical causes than did low scorers. In addition, the high scorers believed that this influence of divine intervention would generalize to other aspects of the stimulus person's life to a greater extent than did the low scorers. There was also a significant effect attributable to story content, with superphysical attributions invoked to a greater extent for the remission than for the rescue. There were other findings as well, but they do not bear directly upon the issue here. Finally, the superphysical attributions were slightly (but not significantly) higher in the presence of the religious priming stimulus than they were in its absence.

This experiment is subject to several legitimate criticisms. First, there was only one instance of an action (the rescue) and one instance of an occurrence (the cancer remission), so the effects obtained involving story content might not generalize to a different set of vignettes. Second, the Bardis religion scale was administered in the same session as the stories (following them), so there is a small possibility that subjects who had answered the attribution questions in a particular way would respond to the Bardis scale in a manner that would be consistent with their prior attributions. Third, even though there were no differences between the situational attributions made by subjects who were later asked about superphysical causality and the situational attributions made by the control group that did not receive the superphysical questions, it is at least logically possible that merely asking the superphysical question produces answers that would not otherwise have been obtained.

Certainly, future research should attempt to correct these methodological problems, but even assuming the worst about each difficulty, the results still suggest that there are real attributional differences involved. For example, the fact remains that in the open-ended questions the ratio of remission to rescue superphysical explanations was 5:1, and within these explanations the ratio of those provided by highly religious as opposed to less religious subjects was 6:1. On the attributional question itself, the differences based on religiosity were no smaller than the difference in rated personal causality between the rescue and remission.

These results provide encouraging evidence that explanations in terms of superphysical causality respond as expected to the personal characteristics of the perceivers and to the stimulus characteristics of the incidents for which an explanation is sought. The important question that remains is whether superphysical causes are conceptually distinct from other attributions. Or were the "superphysical" causes in this research just another name for the more traditional internal and external categories? This general concern can be separated into two parts: one dealing with an alternative attribution (chance) and one dealing with an individual difference variable (locus of control).

To begin with, it might be argued that attributions to superphysical causes are nothing more than a different sort of attribution to chance by another name. This alternative explanation cannot be ruled out conclusively, but there are aspects of the results of the study that argue against it. Subjects in all conditions were asked to what degree they believed the outcome that occurred might have been attributable to chance, and responses to this question were analyzed by the same analysis of variance performed on other dependent measures. The results showed two main effects, one for religiosity, and one for nature of the event. Less religious subjects attributed more to chance than did highly religious subjects (consistent with the alternative explanation that superphysical causes are the religious person's "chance"), but chance factors were seen by all subjects to be more influential in the remission than in the rescue. That this effect occurred regardless of the religiousness of the subjects suggests that the use of "chance" was not, in fact, equivalent to the use of "superphysical causality." Indeed, the correlation between the two attribution measures was almost significantly negative for the rescue and was significantly negative for the remission, suggesting that at the very least the two were not equivalent.

Not only is it important to show that, on the response side, attributions to superphysical causes are different from attributions to chance, but it is also critical to demonstrate that those attributions are not merely a reflection of another individual difference variable—a generalized expectancy for external control. If "divine intervention" is just one plausible category of external influence on action and events, then the attributions to superphysical causes ought to have been positively correlated with scores on the Rotter Internal–External Locus of Control scale, on which higher scores represent a more external orientation. The correlation between I–E scores and superphysical attribution for the rescue story was virtually zero, and the same correlation for the remission story was low negative, with neither even approaching statistical significance. Because this alternative explanation would predict a strong positive correlation between I–E score and use of the superphysical attribution, it does not seem tenable. There are, of course, other versions of the locus of control scale that have individual subscales that might have correlated more highly with superphysical attributions (e.g., Collins, 1974, personal efficacy subscale; the God control scales used by Pargament, Steele, & Tyler, 1979), but such correlations are not damaging to the present argument. Indeed, the very need to develop a *separate* scale to measure beliefs in "God control" suggests that such beliefs are conceptually distinct from the usual beliefs in external control. The existence of that difference is just the point.

Recognizing that the Slocumb, et al. (1982) study is only a first step—a step that involves *positive* outcomes, not the negative outcomes typical for attribution of blame—does it nevertheless carry implications for the study of responsibility and blameworthiness? Probably so. At the very least, the study shows that an attributional category of divine intervention is, for highly religious subjects, a meaningful addition to the conceptual tools available to explain events. If with the necessary methodological improvements the results of the study should be replicated for negative occurrences, then the warning to those interested in a theory of blame would be clear: Do not assume that "internal" and "external" will necessarily exhaust the *psycho*logical possibilities for the explanation of actions. The internal–external distinction will continue to be an essential one, especially where coercion might be concerned, but our theories must not fall victim to the availability heuristic, making the error of assuming that what is most familiar to us is all there is.

Dimensions of Responsibility

The likelihood that the distinction between internal and external causes will need to be supplemented by inclusion of a category of superphysical causes that is neither really internal nor external suggests a limitation in theory. In this case the limitation arises because the conceptual foundation is not as finely differentiated as the attributional behavior of the perceivers. Ironically, there is also a case in which contemporary theory can be accused of making distinctions that the ordinary perceivers do *not* make. An example of this problem is provided by the research of Shaver et al. (1982), in which the distinctions drawn by attribution researchers among various responsibility-related words were compared with the distinctions drawn by ordinary perceivers.

This research was designed to answer two questions. First, are the people who establish the theoretical language of attribution still using the distinctions inherent in everyday speech about responsibility? Whether the perspective is philosophical (e.g., Austin, 1961) or psychological (Heider, 1958), the resulting theoretical refinements have been thought to reflect the features of ordinary language. Is this still true, or have attribution researchers begun to speak a language of their own, a language no longer explicitly tied to the "naive" analysis of responsibility? In any scientific discipline, of course, there is a need for "terms of art" that facilitate precise communication among the experts. Attribution theory therefore is entitled to a certain amount of it own jargon. On the other hand, attribution theory purports to account for the way in which ordinary perceivers explain the causes of their own actions and the behavior of others. Consequently, the terms it would place into the mouths of perceivers must closely resemble terms that those perceivers would have used on their own.

Second, what exactly do people mean by "responsibility?" Ever since some of the early critiques of research in responsibility attribution (e.g., Fishbein & Ajzen, 1973), it has been recognized that the global term "responsibility" has had numerous, and often quite different, meanings. As I noted earlier (Shaver, 1973), most researchers have probably meant "moral accountability" by their use of the term, a construction equivalent to Hart's (1968) moral-liability responsibility. Unfortunately, not even this limited claim is entirely true, with Brewer's (1977) equation of responsibility with causality and Shultz and Schleifer's (1983) inclusion in "responsibility" of any personal participation at the level of foreseeability or above as predominant examples of some of the inconsistencies still found in theoretical statements. If there is confusion about the use of the term in theory, there is virtual ignorance about the ways in which the term might be used by perceivers.

To examine the possible meanings of "responsibility" while comparing the technical language to the ordinary language, Shaver et al. (1982) asked "attribution experts" and college undergraduates to estimate the dissimilarity of a variety of responsibility-related terms in a paired rating procedure. The attribution "experts" were the authors of recent attribution publications in the *Journal of Personality and Social Psychology* and the *Journal of Experimental Social Psychology*. The senior researcher (in cases of multiple authorship) was sent a package containing two standard paired comparison forms, with a request that he or she (a) make the dissimilarity judgments on one form, and (b) pass the second form on to a coauthor or a colleague who was expert in attribution. Ten such packages were sent out, but only six completed sets of dissimilarity judgments were received in return.

The undergraduate students were all enrolled in introductory psychology courses at the College of William and Mary. Seventy-four such students participated in the study in one of three experimental conditions. Instructions in the first of these conditions only asked that the subjects perform the dissimilarity judgments (a control condition, $n = 25$, that corresponded to the instructions provided to the experts). In a second condition ($n = 23$) orienting instructions asked subjects to assume while they were making the dissimilarity judgments that they were members of a jury attempting to decide the fate of a defendant (Hamilton's 1980, "intuitive lawyer" notion). The purpose of these instructions was to focus attention on issues of intentionality, culpability, and moral blameworthiness. Finally, a third condition ($n = 26$) presented subjects with orienting instructions asking them to assume that they were scientists attempting to explain the actions of a person. In contrast to the second experimental condition, this treatment was designed to lead "intuitive scientists" to concentrate on questions of causality and on possible constraints on action.

Stimuli for Judgments

In all cases subjecs were asked to estimate the *dissimilarity* of 18 responsibility-related words taken from the literature. The words were the following: at fault, blameworthy, caused, coerced, controllable, culpable, foreseeable, guilty, intended, legally accountable, legally responsible, liable, morally accountable, morally responsible, obligated, punishable, responsible, and voluntary. Subjects were asked to estimate the dissimilarity of all 153 possible pairs of these words, with every subject receiving a different random order of the pairs. Within each pair, the order of presentation of the two members was also randomly determined.

After subjects had made the dissimilarity judgments (on an 11-point scale), they were asked to list up to three characteristics of the stimuli (a standard task for attempting to identify the dimensions that subjects might have used for the dissimilarity ratings). Then subjects rated each of the 18 stimulus words on their "most important" characteristic, using an 11-point scale that ran from "contains very little of" (0) to "is extremely much like" (10) the characteristic. This rating was then repeated using the subject's second-most important characteristic, and it was intended that the two sets of ratings would suggest interpretations of the dimensional solutions to be obtained from the multidimensional scaling (MDS) procedure.

Judgments of Experts

The dissimilarity judgments of the experts (and those of the naive perceivers as well) were analyzed using both individual differences nonmetric multidimensional scaling for groups of subjects and nonmetric MDS for each subject. All analyses were performed separately by two different scaling programs, one named for its alternating least–squares scaling method (ALSCAL, Takane, Young, & deLeeuw, 1977), and one named for people on whose work it was based—J.B. Kruskal, F.W. Young, R.N. Shepard, and W.S. Torgerson (KYST, Kruskal, Young, & Seery, 1978). In neither case were the three-dimensional solutions for experts or naive perceivers an improvement on the explanatory power provided by the two-dimensional solutions, and only the ALSCAL two-dimensional solutions are discussed here.

Analyses of the expert judgments (Figure 7-1) showed a consistent and meaningful two-dimensional solution (average individual fit to that solution produced stress = .27, and r^2 = .78). The first of these was exactly what would have been expected on the basis of the dimensional analysis of responsibility outlined in Chapter 5. The end points for this dimension were "voluntary" and "coerced," clearly representing the degree to which a person described by the dimension could have done otherwise. Note that "obligated" is out at the coerced end of the dimension, suggesting that the experts believe that the requirements of an internally felt duty might be only slightly less controlling than the presence of a clear external coercion.

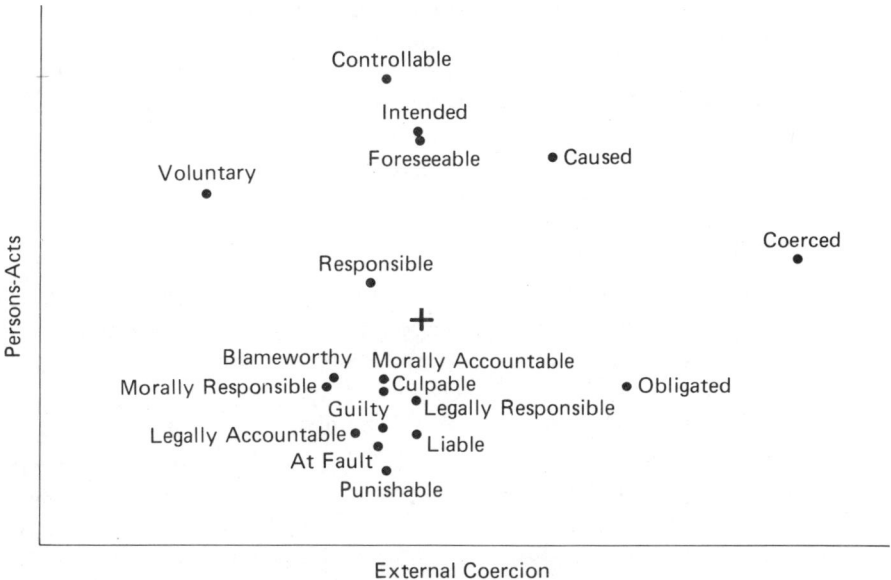

Figure 7-1. Two-dimensional ALSCAL solution for six attributional experts.

Note also that the global "responsible" fell not at the voluntary end of this dimension, but rather slightly left of the origin. This suggests that while "responsible" has overtones of moral accountability, it is susceptible to so many different interpretations that it cannot be located reliably on any single dimension. Finally, notice that the more precise terms "blameworthy" and "morally responsible" virtually overlapped, and fell to the left of "legally responsible." This is a pattern, like the voluntary-coerced dimension itself, that recurred in the plots for naive perceivers.

The second dimension inherent in the expert solution was the almost-vertical line bounded by "controllable" at the top and "punishable" at the bottom. This dimension is not so easy to characterize as the coercion dimension, but in general terms it represents a difference between the characteristics of *acts* (controllable, intended, foreseeable, caused) and the characteristics of *persons* (liable, at fault, guilty, punishable). Notice that intended and foreseeable virtually overlapped, suggesting that the experts might not have regarded the two as being quite as distinct as Heider's (1958) analysis would suggest. The end point of the dimension that describes persons contains an entire cluster of terms related to blameworthiness and liability for sanctions.

What, then, do experts seem to have meant by responsibility? First, they quite clearly employed "could have done otherwise" as a dimension on which to characterize the various descriptive terms. Given the internal–external emphasis in most of the attribution literature, this only shows that the experts have learned the language well. Second, the experts distinguished the characteristics of an action performed by a person from the dispositional culpability of that person, perhaps recognizing, for example, that a person can be "responsible" in either the legal vicarious or strict responsibility sense without having performed an intentional misbehavior, and recognizing that an individual's liability to sanctions might also be relatively independent of his or her causal, or even intentional, participation in an act. This is the beginning of the distinction between responsibility and blameworthiness.

Naive Conceptions of Responsibility

Knowing what attribution experts mean by the word "responsible" is not the same as knowing what the ordinary perceivers, whose attributional behavior is being explained, mean by the term. It had been anticipated that the solution achieved for subjects in the control condition, and the comparison between that solution and the expert solution, would establish what ordinary perceivers meant by responsibility. Comparisons between the control condition solution and the solutions obtained in the jury and scientist conditions were supposed to show how the "normal" meaning of the term might be affected by the specific setting instructions designed respectively to emphasize sanctioning and explanation.

These planned comparisons across experimental conditions, however, depended on there being relatively consistent individual solutions within each condition. Unfortunately, there was much less consistency than had been anticipated. To check on the level of agreement, the solution obtained for each subject was compared with the solution obtained for every other subject within the same experimental condition. There are, of course, $n(n - 1)/2$ such comparisons within conditions (300 for the control condition, 253 for the juror condition, and 325 for the scientist condition). The measure of internal consistency is actually a measure of *inconsistency*, the normalized *residual* remaining after overlapping variability between subjects is taken out.

The smallest such residual was noted for each subject, and the means of these minimum normalized residuals were computed for the three experimental conditions. These means are shown in the first row of Table 7-1, and for each condition the mean score is unacceptably high. One of the explanations for this within-condition inconsistency that immediately suggests itself is that there might be bias contributed by the particular multidimensional scaling program employed (ALSCAL), so the solution for each subject from ALSCAL was compared to the solution for each subject provided by KYST. The mean normalized residuals for this comparison are presented in the second row of Table 7-1, and they are well within acceptable limits, suggesting that there was, in fact, no analysis method bias.

Given the degree of inconsistency within conditions, there are two ways to proceed. Either the single solution for the "best fit" subject in each condition could be identified and examined, or the combined solutions for the several subjects in each condition whose responses have been described reasonably well could be examined. Primarily to retain as much data as possible, the latter alternative was chosen. There are three criteria that can be used to determine quality of fit (Kruskal & Wish, 1978). The first of these involves the characteristics of the nonmetric transformation of the subjects' raw dissimilarity scores that the MDS algorithm uses to obtain the dimensional structure. If too many of the subjects' different dissimilarity ratings are assigned the same transformed value or if too many of the subjects' same ratings are assigned different transformed values, the transformation of the subjects' data will not be a meaningful representation of the original. Using

Table 7-1. Mean Minimum Normalized Residuals From Motion Obtained for Comparisons Among Subjects Within Conditions and Across Methods

	Experimental Conditions		
Comparison	Control ($n = 25$)	Juror ($n = 23$)	Scientist ($n = 26$)
Among subjects within conditions	0.636	0.644	0.634
Across algorithms (ALSCAL–KYST)	0.228	0.179	0.146

transformation characteristics as the criterion, "ideal" groups could be created out of the three conditions, providing eight, seven, and 11 subjects, respectively, for the control, juror, and scientist conditions.

The second and third criteria involve the amount of variance explained in the individual's responses by the group solution and the expert solution, respectively. The former is essentially a part–whole comparison, and asks how much of each individual's solution is accounted for by the group solution for the person's experimental condition. With a criterion of $r^2 > .40$, this criterion produced ideal groups in the control, jury, and scientist conditions of 12, 12, and 12 persons, respectively. On the assumption that the ultimate goal of the study was to compare the solutions for naive perceivers with the solution for experts, the amount of variance accounted for by the expert solution can be considered a form of part–ideal whole correlation. With the same numerical cutoff ($r^2 > .40$), this third criterion produced groups of 13, 12, and 11 subjects in the control, juror, and scientist conditions, respectively. Although the "ideal" individuals selected by each of the three criteria were not always the same persons, there was a substantial amount of overlap.

The choice of examining the solutions for the best-fit single subjects versus examining the solutions of the best-fit group of subjects was a simple choice to make—retain the greatest amount of data. The choice of an "ideal" group for comparison to the expert solution was not quite so simple.

The transformation characteristics criterion does not consider the correspondence that might or might not exist among members of the group so selected. The group variance criterion does consider internal consistency within the treatment condition, but it does not include a baseline that is constant across experimental conditions. To establish a group on this criterion would be to enhance the possibility of obtaining between-condition differences at the expense of seeing how each condition might compare to the expert judges. Alternatively, to establish the ideal groups on the basis of the third criterion, proportion of variance explained by the expert solution, would be to minimize the opportunity to obtain differences between conditions while maximizing the chances of clear comparisons to the solutions provided by experts. So the choice was dictated not by the technical features of the various ideal groups, but by the value judgment of which comparison was most central to the objectives of the research. On that ground it was decided to examine the groups constructed on the basis of the third criterion—variance explained by fit with the expert solution.

Even with the choice made on fit between the "ideal subjects" and the experts, the degree of correspondence was not nearly as high as would have been desirable. The mean amount of variance explained (r^2) in the individual solutions for subjects in each treatment, given an individual differences model, was .52 for the control condition, .55 in the juror condition, and .57 in the scientist condition. Not surprisingly, given the amount of variance accounted for in the individual solutions within conditions, the group solutions for the "ideal subjects" showed a pattern that was predominantly circular, rather than dimensional. Therefore, the first conclusion that must be drawn from the study is that the naive perceivers do not make the kinds of distinctions that are made by attribution theorists.

The Importance of Coercion

Despite this overall inability to find a clear dimensional solution involving all of the responsibility-related words, the solutions for ideal groups of subjects in the three conditions did show some patterns of interest. In every condition of these ideal subjects, there was a strong difference between voluntary and coerced, and the position of the line drawn between those two words was the same in each of the three solutions. The solution for the 13 best-fit subjects in the control condition is shown in Figure 7-2, and as was the case with the experts, the voluntary–coerced dimension was the most important one. Again, "obligated" was far toward the coerced end of this dimension, and the controllable–foreseeable pair was slightly above the line formed by the dimension, although the members of the pair were reversed. The morally responsible–legally responsible pair was in the same position with respect to the coercion dimension as for the experts. Finaly, the unmodified "responsible" was again near the origin of the solution, suggesting that it was no more distinctive to these subjects than it had been to the experts.

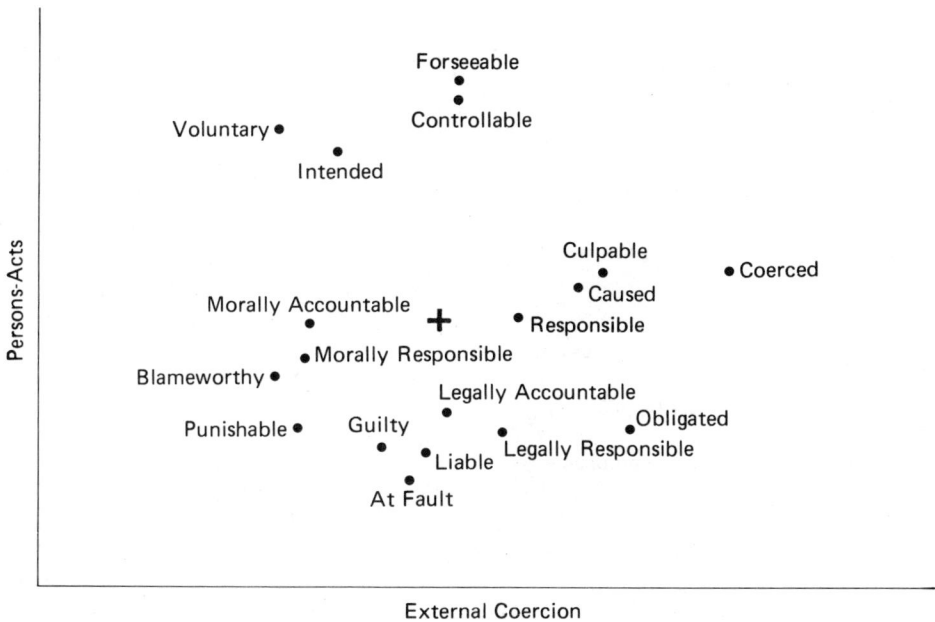

Figure 7-2. Two-dimensional ALSCAL solution for 13 best-fit subjects in control condition, initialized by solution for experts.

The solution for the 12 best-fit subjects in the juror condition is presented in Figure 7-3, and although it differs from the control condition solution in a variety of respects, it shows the same important coercion dimension falling into the same location in the two-dimensional space. Again, "obligated" was near the coerced end of the scale, and the foreseeable–controllable pair was in the same location as it had been for the experts and the control condition subjects. The morally responsible–legally responsible pair was where it had been for the experts, although as would be expected from the condition instructions, the distance between the members of this pair was greater in the juror condition than in any other condition.

Finally, the solution obtained from the 11 best-fit subjects in the scientist condition is shown in Figure 7-4. Again, there were numerous differences between this solution and the others in the placement of various stimulus words. Notwithstanding these differences, the coercion dimension appeared in the same location as before, and it represented the largest distance between members of any pair. Although not displaced quite as far from the origin as it had been before, "obligated" did appear near the coerced end of this dimension. The controllable–foreseeable pair was located as it had been in other conditions, and now it was accompanied by "intended" as it had been in

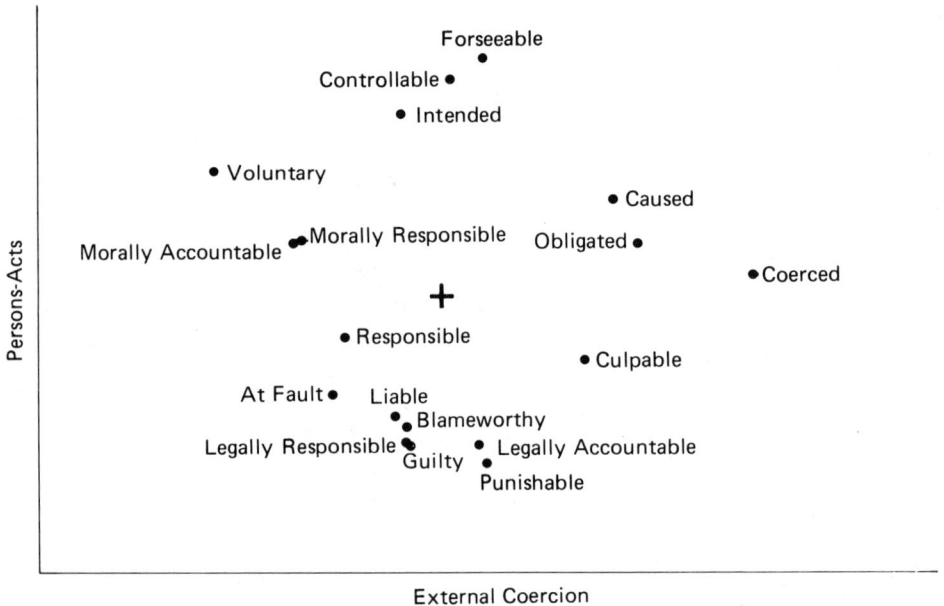

Figure 7-3. Two-dimensional ALSCAL solution for 12 best-fit subjects in juror condition, initialized by solution for experts.

the expert solution (but not in either the control or juror conditions). The morally responsible–legally responsible pair was in the same location relative to the coercion as it had been in the other conditions, although morally responsible was now closer to the voluntary–coerced line.

Versions of Responsibility

Before discussing the general conclusions that can be drawn from this research, it is important to note some limitations in the method. The principal conceptual limitation is the possibility that the degree of agreement between the views of experts and those of the naive perceivers might have been overstated as a consequence of the criterion for constituting the three "ideal" groups of subjects. Recall that the extensive individual differences among subjects in the three experimental conditions made it impossible to construct any group solution that would adequately reflect what would have amounted to the central tendency of the judgments within that condition. The criterion ultimately selected to construct the ideal groups was proportion of variance explained by the expert solution, so some similarity between the solution of experts and those of the naive perceivers was built into the method.

On the other hand, it should be emphasized that the "proportion of variance accounted for" criterion does *not* dictate the particular form that each

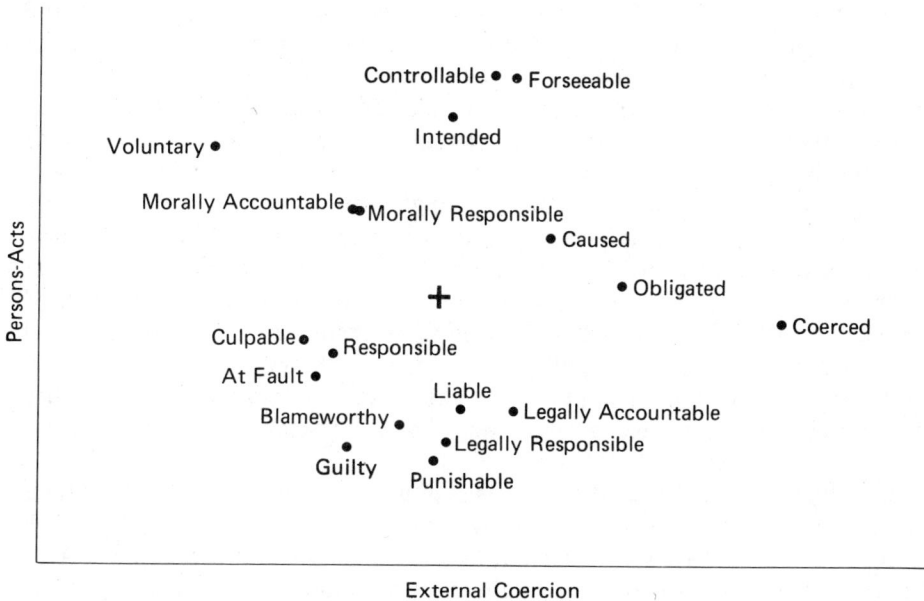

Figure 7-4. Two-dimensional ALSCAL solution for 11 best-fit subjects in scientist condition, initialized by solution for experts.

condition solution would take. For example, if all "ideal" naive perceivers had believed "obligated" to be at the *voluntary* end of the voluntary–coerced dimension, the square of this negative relationship to the expert solution would have produced exactly the same proportion of variance accounted for by the ideal solution. Or, as still another alternative, the fairly low values for r^2 obtained could have come about as a result of agreement between ideal naive perceivers and experts on the placement of terms *other than* voluntary–coerced, obligated, and morally responsible–legally responsible. While the selection criterion generated the degree of similarity, it therefore did not dictate on which particular comparisons that similarity would be manifest. Furthermore, in at least the one experimental condition (juror) most relevant to an attributional analysis of blame, the analysis of all 23 subjects showed precisely the same voluntary–coerced dimension, with obligated at the coerced end, obtained among the experts.

Although the method for selection of the ideal groups makes it more likely that there will be correspondence between the expert solution and those in the experimental conditions, some aspects of the experimental procedure work against the discovery of any correspondence at all. For example, it typically takes subjects as long as 40 minutes to complete the judgments. (There are, certainly, other experimental tasks that require that amount of time, but typically these other tasks can be broken—in the subject's own mind, if not also in the procedure—into smaller segments.) Consequently, fatigue can be a problem. There can be no systematic effects of fatigue, because every subject is presented with a different random order of the stimulus pairs, and the members of each pair are also randomly ordered. As the subjects tire of the task, however, their willingness to attend to the fine distinctions often drawn among some of the terms involved would dissipate. If this change were sufficiently prevalent, it could work against discovery of dimensions that would otherwise have been differentiated.

In much the same way that fatigue might obscure dimensionality, sheer vocabulary limitations might also obscure dimensionality. The attribution experts are not only more "knowledgeable" users of the technical language of atttribution theory, they are also bound to have been more sophisticated speakers of nontechnical English. It would, for instance, be surprising to find an attribution expert who did not know the meaning of "culpable." By contrast, many of the naive perceivers expressed very low confidence values for pairs involving this word, suggesting that they simply did not know what the word meant by itself.

Finally, the words selected for use as stimuli were chosen without the benefit of any of the theoretical distinctions that have been drawn in this book between causality and responsibility, or among senses of "responsible." As a consequence, some words that might now be omitted were included, while others that would now be included were not. Examples of the former are "liable," which would be omitted because it does not distinguish vicarious responsibility from strict responsibility from blameworthiness; and "at fault," which does not distinguish characterological from behavioral blameworthiness. An example of the latter is "involuntary," now recognized as different from the negation of "voluntary." Furthermore, some of the words that were included would need to be changed in form in order to make the comparisons more precise. Examples are "caused," which would become "local" versus "remote cause of"; and "foreseeable," which would become "aware of" versus "not aware of the consequences."

As is the case with virtually any single piece of research, hindsight suggests that this study could have been improved. Despite the limitations, it is possible to draw two valuable conclusions from the study. First, there was support for the coercion dimension of responsibility. That dimension played a significant role in the solution for the experts, it appeared in each of the three groups of ideal subjects, and it also was a prominent feature of the group solution for all subjects in the juror condition. A portion of this consistency might have been due to the method used to identify subjects for inclusion in the ideal groups, because the dimension comprised such an integral part of the expert solution. Nevertheless, it does appear that voluntary actions are reliably distinguished from those produced either through external coercion or through the weight of internally felt obligations.

Unfortunately, the second general conclusion is not quite so optimistic. This section opened by questioning how closely the technical language of attribution theory corresponds to the language that everyday perceivers use to describe notions of responsibility. The answer is "not well enough." Even among subjects for whom the expert solution was a reasonably good predictor, there was no equivalent to the persons–actions dimension in the expert solution. Moreover, the amount of variance in these selected individual judgments that was explained by the expert solution was not impressive. For both of these reasons, it appears as though the scientific language of attribution theory might have assumed a life of its own, taking a critical step away from the "naive" analysis of action. This tendency will need to be countered if the field is to retain its contact with the ordinary explanation of human behavior.

The study of superphysical causality and the multidimensional scaling of responsibility-related words would, if considered as narrowly as possible, seem to point to opposite conclusions. On the one hand, the traditional attribution categories of internal–external do not seem to capture the kind of causality inherent in superphysical explanations of events. In this instance the technical language of theory is an inadequate representation of the distinctions that are made by ordinary perceivers. By contrast, the multidimensional scaling of responsibility-related words, taken alone, would suggest that there is a proliferation of technical distinctions well beyond those needed to account for the ascription of responsibility among the same naive perceivers. When the two studies are considered together, however, a more important general point emerges: Researchers must be careful to avoid *imposing* any conceptual structure on the attributions made by perceivers.

Thus, the research presented in this chapter accomplishes its two purposes. It identifies some of the limitations inherent in present conceptions of the attribution of causality and responsibility, and it suggests tentative directions that future research—now informed by the conceptual foundation of an attributional analysis of blame—might take. The theoretical structure must be specified with sufficient precision to be able to describe whatever processes are involved, but it cannot safely be assumed that this structure will always be exhaustive, or that all of its distinctions will always be needed. With this caveat in mind, the discussion now turns to a theory of the attribution of blameworthiness.

Chapter 8
A Theory of Blame

One of the most intriguing aspects of the assignment of blame is the contrast between the apparent simplicity of the everyday assertion or avoidance of blame and the complexity of the theoretical structure needed to account for the process of assigning blame. On the one hand, it is a rare child whose early repertoire of sentences does not include "It isn't *my* fault!" and the companion "*You* did it." On the other hand, a theoretical analysis of blame assignment involves sophisticated questions about events, their causes, and the dimensions of personal responsibility. Is this contrast merely an example of complexity invented as a substitute for clear thinking? Or are the distinctions drawn to this point really necessary for a complete understanding of the process?

Naturally, those who study the attribution of causality, responsibility, and blameworthiness believe the theoretical distinctions to be required. Fortunately, in this case, there are both anecdotal and experimental data suggesting that the everyday assignment and avoidance of blame are not so simple as they would appear. A substantial fraction of the practice of civil and criminal law is designed to determine "fault" in instances where there are competing claims. Even the parent's response to a child's denial of blameworthiness is often "No, you're mistaken. It *was* your fault, because. . . . " In the experimental literature the robust differences in attribution in response to variation in Heider's (1958) levels of responsibility and the fact that the subjects of Shaver, et al. (1982) did not see all of those responsibility-related words as synonyms indicate that the theoretical distinctions reflect real psychological differences.

Why do these real psychological distinctions exist? Two possible answers to this question suggest themselves. First, in keeping with principles first identified by studies of linguistic relativity (Brown & Lenneberg, 1958; Whorf, 1958), the number of linguistic distinctions required varies in direct proportion to the importance of the issue. Eskimos have specific words for different kinds of snow, because snow is a central fact of life and the distinctions are necessary. All of us can tell the difference between voluntary and coerced misbehavior, both because morality is a central fact of our lives, and because the distinction is necessary.

Second, with only a few exceptions, the assignment of blame reflects a *disagreement* between the actor and the perceiver. To the extent that the two individuals share a common view of morality, the perceiver's assignment of blame is a claim that the actor has done something for which he or she ought to be ashamed. One obvious way in which the moral offense can be noted by both, but with a minimum of residual antagonism, is for a precise characterization of the action to be negotiated. Such precision demands a large number of causality, responsibility, and blameworthiness words. It must be recognized that there can be different descriptions of any one event, events can have multiple causes (which causes are determined through attribution processes), causality is only one of the several dimensions of responsibility, and the perceiver's motives (as well as the stimulus person's reasons for acting) will affect judgments of responsibility and blameworthiness.

As useful as they are in their own right, the conceptual distinctions drawn to this point also serve as the foundation for both the metatheory and the theory of blame attribution that are the subject of the final chapter. First, both the philosophical and psychological discussions have identified *metatheoretical* issues for an attributional analysis of blame. Assignment of blame is a social judgment, one that must incorporate decisions about causality and responsibility, Specifically, the actor's view of the world, the perceiver's vantage point, and the fact that the two are likely to disagree about the attribution of blame must all be considered. In addition, an adequate notion of blameworthiness cannot be established without attention to issues of causality and responsibility. These metatheoretical ideas are examinied more thoroughly in the first major section of this chapter.

Second, the model of causal attribution outlined in Chapter 3 and the dimensions of responsibility discussed in Chapter 5 provide much of the structure for a formal theory of blame. As we have seen, these ideas need to be supplemented to include the motives of actor and perceiver and need to be qualified by the admonition to avoid either adding to or subtracting from the perceiver's actual judgment. They also need to be extended by a more detailed discussion of exculpation. They are, however, an excellent beginning for the theory outlined in the concluding section of the chapter.

Metatheory for the Attribution of Blame

Psychological Context Revisited

Early in Chapter 2, I noted that an attributional analysis of blame would make certain metatheoretical assumptions, including a specific view of what is involved in the causation of events. Like any other endeavor in the behavioral sciences, this theory of blameworthiness has empirical, theoretical, and thematic elements. Following Holton's (1973) lead, the empirical elements can be thought of as falling on the abscissa or *x* axis of a three-dimensional space. These empirical elements are, in terms familiar to psychologists, the outcomes of operations conducted to measure the dependent variables. The theoretical elements occupy the ordinate or *y* axis of the space and are of two general kinds. First, there are the rules of correspondence for translating the conceptual terms into empirical ones. Second, there are the elements that link one facet of the theoretical structure to another, relatively independent of the manner in which any single concept might be operationalized in particular research study. Finally, the third dimension of the proposition space, a *z* axis that can be thought of as extending out from the page toward the reader, contains the *themata* or metatheoretical assumptions.

The psychological context can now be made much clearer with a concrete example. Consider the statement "I blame you less for breaking that vase than for lying to me about it." This admonition contains two separable parts: the blame assigned for the initial occurence (the carelessness involved in breaking the vase) and the blame assigned for the attempt to hide the damage. The two parts can be represented in the proposition space as shown in Figure 8-1. Beginning with the purely empirical content of the compound statement, there is an amount of "blame" assigned for breakage of the vase, and that amount is less on the *x* axis than the amount assigned for lying. What makes the compound statement a scientific one, rather than just an empirical one, is that it has a value greater than zero on the *y* axis as well. Specifically, there are at least two ways in which the statement has theoretical implications.

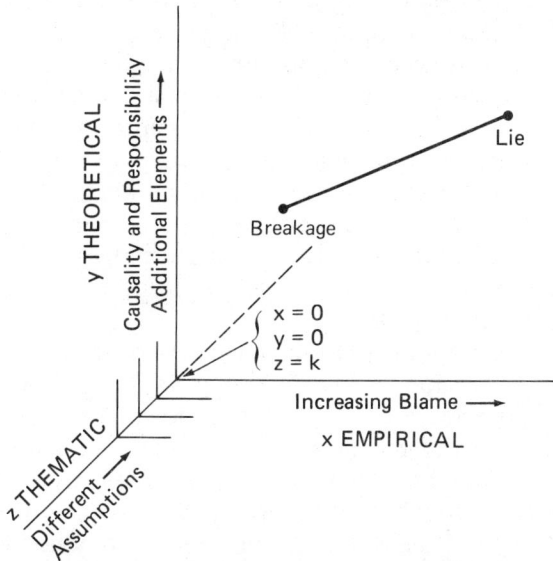

Figure 8-1. The proposition space representing the statement "I blame you less for breaking that vase than for lying to me about it."

First, there are the theoretically specified rules of correspondence by which blame measured on the scale can be translated into blame represented at the conceptual level. These rules of correspondence, which do not appear on the diagram of the proposition space, dictate that "blame" should be measured in each case by an equivalent procedure. This requirement is best illustrated by a negative example. Suppose I have you read a vignette written at Heider's (1958) level of "causality." Then if I ask you "What is the cause of the event?" you will most probably believe that question to mean "did the stimulus person really produce the effect, or was the effect a chance occurrence?" Now suppose that I have read a vignette written at the "intentionality" level and again ask you "what is the cause of the event?" In this case you are likely to believe that question to mean "did the stimulus person really *intend* to produce the effect?" Because of the context provided by the accompanying story, my same words are not interpreted to mean the same thing.

Not only do the rules of correspondence require that the same construct be measured on both occasions, they also require that the construct measured have an appropriate relationship to the theoretical structure. This is also best illustrated with a negative example. There might be some circumstances in which the theoretical structure would lead to questions about "causality," but the example in Figure 8-1 is not one of those cases. Much of the conceptual case that has been made to this point suggests that causality is not equivalent either to responsibility or to blameworthiness. So to ask "what is the cause?" is, in the words of Cook and Campbell (1979), to employ an "inadequate explication" of the concept of blameworthiness.

Finally, the rules of correspondence specify how sensitive the measuring device must be. For example, if the theory makes ordinal predictions, then a dichotomous dependent variable will not be satisfactory. In an attributional analysis of blame it is acceptable to talk about *which* elements comprise the minimal sufficient causal subset, but responsibility and blameworthiness must be assessed with measures that will permit comparisons between the *amount* of responsibility or blameworthiness present on one occasion and the amount present under other circumstances. To paraphrase Holton's (1973) discussions of the empirical axis, the rules of correspondence require that the same "meter" be read in both cases, specify which meter that ought to be, and dictate how finely it should be calibrated. None of that is included in the empirical dimension by itself.

Identification of rules of correspondence is not the only contribution that the theoretical dimension makes. It also contains definitions of accidental occurrences, negligence, intentional action, and volition. These definitions are a critical part of the theoretical predictions that are ultimately made. For example, consider the causal dimension of responsibility. The person's causal role in the breakage would fall at the causality step of this dimension, while the person's production of the lie falls at the intentionality level of the dimension. Thus, although the person is "the cause" in both cases, that causal participation is different in kind, and the difference should be reflected in the blame assigned. There would be corresponding differences between the two cases on other dimensions of responsibility as well, with the lie reflecting greater presumed knowledge of the consequences, greater volition, and perhaps even a more thorough consideration of the moral quality of the act (notwithstanding the fact that the "immoral" choice was made). The theoretical elements that differ across the two situations will, naturally, lead to different degrees of attributed blameworthiness. So the theoretical prediction that would have been made—greater blame for lying than for causing an accident—is consistent with the statement represented in Figure 8-1.

All of this sounds so reasonable that it is easy to lose sight of just how much the theoretical–empirical conjunction depends on the particular metatheoretical assumptions. Suppose, however, that instead of considering human agents to be causes of events, we were to adopt the view of "hard" determinism. In any system dependent on that thematic element, the lie would be no more reprehensible than the accidental breakage, because both would have come about as a function of "causes" external to the person. A critical aspect of the attributional perspective on blame, my belief as a perceiver that, at least in the case of the lie, you "could have done otherwise," would be missing. In a system governed by the thema of incompatibilism, it might be acceptable to assign more blame for one occurrence than for another, but only if there were some larger social purpose (e.g., restitution) to be served. No "backward-looking" determination of individual blameworthiness would be appropriate. The fact that this deterministic thema and others are possible is indicated in Figure 8-1 by the three additional x–y origins drawn on the thematic axis, and by the fact that the origin of the example has $x = 0, y = 0$, but $z =$ some *nonzero* value k.

Particularly by contrast to a deterministic view of morally relevant events, the metatheory for an attributional analysis of blame thus takes a position that combines elements of activity theory with elements of reconciliationism and libertarianism. There are cases in which human beings the causes of events, and in some of those the humans "could have done otherwise." Not all of the metatheoretical assumptions require the extended discussion that has been necessary for the notion of causality. One of those assumptions, however, is as critical to the character of the theory as is the presumed nature of causality, and it is to this assumption that the discussion now turns.

A Disputed Social Judgment

Whether the cause of an event is a natural happening or an intentional human action, that cause exists independent of any perceiver of the causal connection. By contrast, a judgment of moral responsibility—and an assertion of blameworthiness—exists only because of the psychological activity of a perceiver. Responsibility in Hart's (1968) capacity-responsibility sense is (with the exception of the temporary lapse characteristic of "diminished capacity") a relatively enduring property of the actor. In a similar fashion, role responsibility comprises a set of expectations that adhere to the role occupant for at least as long as the role is held (occasionally longer). Only moral-liability responsibility is a situation-specific judgment.

There is, however, no philosophical argument to *prove* that judgments of moral responsibility and blameworthiness exist within the mind of the perceiver. Nor is there, with current (or even anticipated) psychophysiological technology, a method for demonstrating empirically that such judgments exist within the perceiver. So the assertion that responsibility and blameworthiness exist only as the result of a perceiver's cognitive process is, like the assertion that human actions can be causes of events, a metatheoretical assumption of the psychology of blame.

This assumption is as important for what it denies as for what it asserts. It claims that the ascription of responsibility and the assignment of blame are always processes that occur within perceivers (including in principle the actor as a perceiver of his or her own behavior). It denies that the judgments involved can ever be verified to anyone's complete satisfaction. The physical causes of events are visible to all those who search for them. Some causes of human action (e.g., coercion from powerful others) have a similar "public" quality to them. Other causes (e.g., a person's reasons for acting) can only be inferred, never seen. Judgments of responsibility and blameworthiness are, according to the assumption, purely private events within perceivers. They are, in short, *interpretations* of events, interpretations that are open to *dispute* either by the actor being judged or by other perceivers of the actor's behavior. Earlier chapters discussed some of the ways in which disputes between actor and perceiver might arise, and it will be useful to review these here.

To anticipate the model outlined below, an assignment of blame begins with a particular description of the event that occurred, continues with the identification of a minimal sufficient causal subset thought to have produced the occurrence, contains a judgment about whether the outcome had been foreseen or intended, considers the likelihood of external coercion, rests on a decision about responsibility, and finally takes into account any relevant excuse or justification that might be offered. Disagreements between actor and perceiver (or, for that matter, between one perceiver and another) can happen at any one of these intermediate steps.

If actors could be relied on to give utterly honest answers, they would be the only *truly* authoritative sources of information about their reasons for acting, and their intentions in performing a particular act in question. There are, however, reasons to regard an actor's own view of his or her behavior with some caution. Not only might an actor be engaged in conscious impression management, his or her report of the situation might be adversely affected by vantage point or cognitive heuristics. Perhaps because intuitively we recognize the possible limits on an actor's accuracy in describing his or her own morally questionable actions, we all too seldom ask for the actor's intentions or reasons.

Indeed, our *inference* process begins with the description of the event for which blame may be relevant. Events can be named, as noted in Chapter 2, by a distribution of descriptions. Because there is no objective standard by which one description can be declared "correct," the first possibility for disagreement between actor and perceiver is in the definition of what event actually took place. There is a consensual criterion for the correctness of both the event description and the level at which the action is identified. If the actor and the perceiver describe the event in identical terms, then the fact that other descriptions are logically possible is irrelevant to the judgment of blame at hand. If the actor and perceiver offer different descriptions of the event, then the one whose characterization best approximates the consensual standard will be seen as "correct."

Even if the actor and perceiver agree on the description of what actually took place, they can easily disagree on the presumed cause. This kind of dispute can take one of the two general forms. First, the two parties might not identify the same entity as "the cause" of the occurrence—a disagreement on the components of the minimal sufficient causal subset, or on the insufficient but necessary condition thought to have been the "single difference" between the state of the world prior to the event and the state of the world at the time the event occurs. Second, although they might agree on the presence of one causal element (such as the actor's clear intention to bring about a particular state of affairs), the actor and perceiver could still disagree on the relative importance of that intention—a dispute over the presence of other elements in the minimal sufficient causal subset.

Should the actor and perceiver happen to agree on the description of the event and on the cause of the occurrence, they can still differ on the responsibility that should devolve on the actor. Here the disagreement can occur on any of the five dimensions of responsibility. The actor might claim a smaller causal contribution on his part than the perceiver would think appropriate. As discussed in Chapter 5, the actor might also claim lack of knowledge of the consequences of the action, or less freedom to do otherwise, or an intention to accomplish something other than the production of the event for which blame is to be assigned. Finally, the actor might simply claim, on grounds of a different view of morality or because of a justification or excuse, that moral outrage is not appropriate under the circumstances.

Suppose that an assignment of blame is a social judgment open to dispute. What follows from this metatheoretical assumption? Most importantly, the assumption leads to a conception of blameworthiness that must of necessity include prior consideration of causality and responsibility. Both because the assignment of blame is regarded as a *process* that occurs through time, and because there is the potential for disagreement between actor and perceiver at *any* stage in that process, no comprehensive view of blameworthiness can ignore questions of causality and responsibility.

This is true not only on the conceptual level, but also on the empirical level. Research designed only to investigate causality does not need to consider responsibility or blameworthiness; work on responsibility must contain causal questions, but not necessarily questions about blame; investigations of the assignment of blame, however, must incorporate measures of causality and responsibility. A comprehensive theory of blame must encompass all of the human judgments about all the elements of human agency that lead to moral offenses, whether or not an individual perceiver might "short-circuit" some of those intermediate steps in coming to a snap judgment about an actor's blameworthiness.

A Theory of Blame Assignment

Having considered the two central metatheoretical assumptions that comprise the context for a theory of blame, the discussion now turns to the theory. First, distinctions are drawn among "causality," "responsibility," and "blame-worthiness," and then the path that a judgment of blameworthiness might follow is traced in detail. Along the way, some of the complications of the model are identified and discussed.

Justifications, Excuses, and Blame

Questions about blameworthiness arise only when at least one of the causal elements participating in the production of the effect for which blame is to be assigned is a human action. This instance of human agency can, as we have seen, be the sole causal element, one of several causal elements comprising the minimal sufficient causal subset, or an insufficient but necessary condition within that subset. Whether or not this causal element is accompanied, it can be an act of comission that *produces* the effect, or it can be an act of omission that fails to *prevent* the occurrence of the event. In either case the human agent involved can be seen as a cause of the event, as potentially responsible for its occurrence, and as potentially to blame. Once the person has been determined to be "a cause" of the occurrence (excepting, of course, those rare instances of the moral equivalent of legal vicarious responsibility), the person's perceived position on the dimensions of responsibility will lead to a judgment of just how "responsible" the person is for the occurrence.

Once a person has been found responsible for a morally objectionable occurrence, that person stands liable for *blame*. Stating the principle in this way makes it clear that blameworthiness and responsibility are not identical, either in the sort of judgment that is made or in the number of cases for which that judgment is appropriate. Unfortunately, the distinction between the two—like the distinction between causality and responsibility—has not always been drawn as carefully in the literature as it should have been. Too frequently, the conceptual arguments presented in research studies have spoken of "responsibility," while the dependent variables have dealt with "blame," or "punishment." For example, in an otherwise conceptually sophisticated paper, Shultz, Schleifer, and Altman (1981) drew on the utilitarian philosophy of Bentham (1789/1879) and on the legal philosophy of Hart and Honoré (1959) to assert that "Responsibility, within the present model, is conceptualized in terms of a moral evaluation of the protagonist's action. In the case of harm-doing, this is most commonly construed in terms of blameworthiness" (Shultz et al., 1981, p. 239). What these investigators did do, as few others have, is provide subjects with definitions of all the concepts, including a statement that "The question of *moral responsibility* refers to the extent to which the protagonist is *worthy of blame*" (Shultz et al., 1981, p. 242). This view of moral responsibility and blameworthiness as equivalent continued in Shultz and Schleifer's (1983) theoretical paper and is also inherent in the review of responsibility attribution research by Fincham and Jaspars (1980).

Whenever there is a consistent failure to recognize a conceptual distinction, it is important to wonder whether the differentiation suggested is really a distinction without a difference. In the case of the conceptual confusion between causality and responsibility, the answer is clear: It is a serious error to use these terms synonymously. What about the morally responsible–blameworthy pair? Here, too, there are good reasons to separate the two terms, reasons that have to do with what Austin (1961) would have called justifications, and with what he would have called excuses.

First, consider the matter of justifications. As noted in Chapter 4, a justification for a morally reprehensible action is a claim that contrary to the perceiver's opinion, the action taken was a *positive* one. Such justifications could take one of two forms. In the first place the actor might argue that the perceiver's characterization of the narrowly defined individual act was incorrect. This would be a disagreement about the description of the event, a dispute perhaps arising from the possibility that actor and perceiver held different views of what constitutes moral action. The disagreement could only be resolved by comparing the moral characterizations offered by the two parties to the consensual characterization offered by others informed about the occurrence.

The second sort of justification would be the actor's claim that although the single act might have been reprehensible, it served a larger positive social purpose, the value of which would be recognized by the perceiver. Unlike the first kind of justification, this assertion of larger social purposes admits the reprehensible quality of the single act, but places that act in an acceptable context. The critical point for our purposes is that in either case what the justification diminishes is the actor's *blameworthiness*—his or her culpability, liability for censure, or liability for punishment. It does not alter the actor's moral accountability. Indeed, it is precisely because of that moral-liability responsibility that (a) the perceiver made the initial accusation, and (b) the actor responded with a justification.

If an actor called to account for a moral offense chooses not to offer a justification, that actor can still request dimunution in the blame to be assigned by identifying an *excuse* likely to mitigate the blame. The domain of possible excuses encompasses virtually all of the potential sources of disagreement between actor and perceiver that I have discussed above. These excuses were discussed in greater detail in Chapter 4 and so will only be reiterated here. The actor can claim, first, that he or she was not really performing the action the perceiver has called into question: "It may have looked like that to you, but I was really doing something quite different." The fact that such excuses are not always successful in mitigating blame indicates that perceivers, at least, can find instances in which actors are not to be regarded as the authoritative source of information about their actions and reasons. Another choice the actor has is to deny or minimize his or her causal role in bringing about the event. The actor can claim that he or she was only an innocent bystander. Or, more frequently, claim that her or she was an insignificant part of many causal elements (such as the congressional representative who claims that he, personally, cannot be held to account for the passage of an unpopular measure, because he was "only one of 435 people who voted on the issue").

The final strategy for minimization of blameworthiness involves a denial of intention, the familiar "I didn't *mean* to do it." Even with an admission of intentional participation in the production of the action, the actor can minimize his or her potential culpability by asserting the importance of the causal role of others. This assertion may be a claim of external coercion (and here the research on superphysical causality suggests that "external coercion" may, for some actors and some perceivers involve intangible forces), or it may be a claim that another person has intervened in the process between the actor's own behavior and the production of the outcome. As Shultz and Schleifer (1983) note, the voluntary intervention of another human agent is an excuse with a thorough grounding in the law.

Certainly this list does not exhaust the possible excuses, although it should be a relatively complete catalogue of the available *categories* of excuse. For our purposes, all of these excuses have two properties that should be noted. First, if they are accepted, they all have the effect of mitigating not only the actor's blameworthiness, but also that person's moral responsibility. Indeed, considering the excuses alone one might well wonder why a distinction between responsibility and blameworthiness is needed. The second property of the excuses, however, provides an answer to this question: Excuses are offered only after an accusation has been made, an accusation that by its very nature *presumes* a prior judgment of moral responsibility. People do not offer excuses for their morally reprehensible actions at the very same time those actions are being performed. Rather the time sequence is action, judgment, accusation, excuse. Once the excuse has been offered, if it is accepted the perceiver's initial judgment of responsibility will be adjusted downward at the same time that the judgment of minimal blameworthiness is made.

What we learn from an analysis of justifications and excuses is that the assignment of blame is the last step in a process of social judgment. Blame depends on a prior attribution of moral responsibility in the same fashion as that attribution depends on a prior judgment of causality (again, with the exceptions that have been noted). If moral responsibility represents the actor's answerability for his or her behavior, blameworthiness is the actor's state after the answers have been given.

That final state is frequently, though not necessarily, achieved through an interpersonal exchange that can be characterized in the terms that Goffman (1959) used to describe the corrective process that follows one person's temporary loss of face in an interaction. In the case of a morally offensive action, the "challenge" is the perceiver's accusation, based on a preliminary judgment of moral responsibility, that the actor has committed a moral error. The actor's "offering" is his or her assertion of a justification or an excuse, and the perceiver's "acceptance" of that offering is a judgment of blameworthiness that is less severe than it would have been without the "interchange." These theoretical terms borrowed from Goffman's analysis of self-presentation fit the assignment of blame quite well, precisely because the determination of blameworthiness involves a disputed social judgment.

There are, of course, limits to the analogy. In the attribution of blame the accuser does not need to be the person who has been harmed by the alleged moral offense. Nor is there the same presumption that the two individuals have been interacting successfully in the past and have a mutual commitment to further contact. The excuses for the actor's misbehavior may in some instances be offered by a third party, not by the actor, personally. In addition, the actor will not always be informed of the perceiver's final judgment. Despite these differences between the two settings, there is the important common thread: In principle, if not always in practice, both situations deal with negotiations between the two parties. To equate blameworthiness with moral responsibility is to make the mistake of ignoring this interpersonal exchange. Moral responsibility is an intermediate step in a process that terminates in an attribution of blame. With this distinction in mind, it is time to turn to the complete theory of the attribution of blame.

The Assignment of Blame

Having examined "what is the cause?" and "who is responsible?" and having distinguished blameworthiness from moral responsibility, we are now prepared to answer the final question in an attributional analysis of blame: "Who is to blame?" Even though the assignment of legal responsibility is, as noted in Chapter 5, an imperfect representation of the ways in which people decide the moral accountability of others, there is still some general similarity between the two processes. Because of this similarity, the model of blame assignment (Figure 8-2) given here is patterned after the well-known diagram of case flow through the criminal justice system (President's Commission on Law Enforcement and Administration of Justice, 1967). The present model of blame assignment is a summary of all discussion in the preceding chapters,

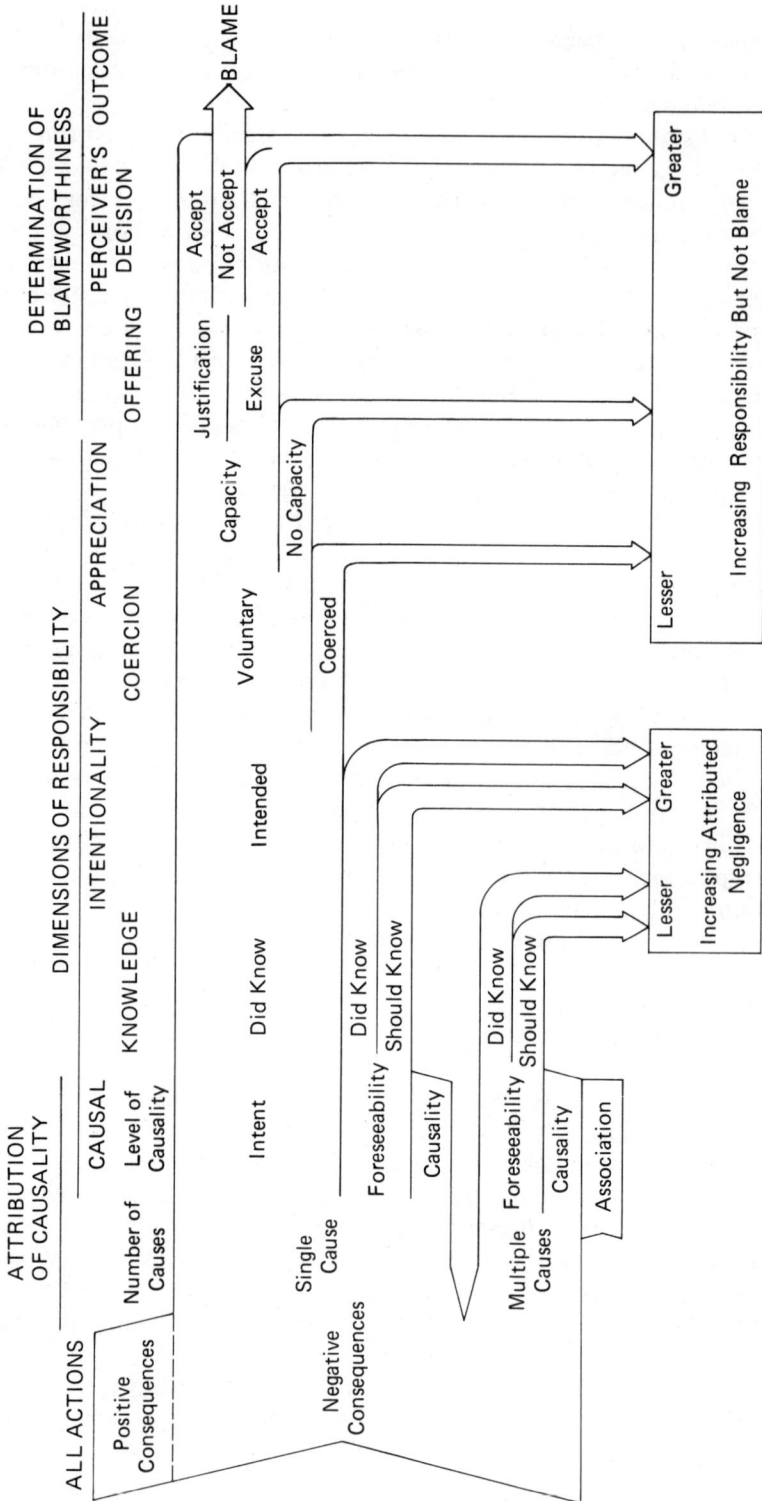

Figure 8-2. Sequential model of the attribution of blame.

and it traces the sequence of judgments a perceiver is thought to make between the observation of an action with negative consequences and the assertion that the actor was "to blame" for the occurrence.

A diagrammatic summary tends to assume a life of its own, so a few preliminary words of caution are in order. First, it is simply impossible for any brief model to do justice to the complexity of the attribution processes involved in the identification of causes and the assignment of responsibility. Indeed, the extensive discussion from Chapter 3 of the attributions inherent in discovering "the cause" is represented in Figure 8-2 by a single column entitled "Number of Causes." Nothing is said here about augmentation and discounting, nor is there detailed presentation of the five dimensions of responsibility. The fact that an actor's reasons can serve as causes of his or her behavior is not explicitly discussed in the model, although it is certainly present in the conception of intention and in the likelihood that an excuse will be accepted. The possibility that perceivers will believe in malevolent superphysical intervention is implicit both in coercion and in an assertion that the actor lacked the capacity either to appreciate the moral wrongfulness of his or her behavior or to resist the temptation. All of these complexities are important, but must necessarily be omitted from a diagram summarizing the major elements of the argument.

One of the specific concessions made for simplicity of presentation is the inclusion in Figure 8-2 only of the judgments that would be made by an "ideal" perceiver. It is not claimed either (a) that all perceivers will follow this model or (b) that any individual perceiver will follow the pattern specified by the model in all of his or her judgments of blame. What is asserted is that deviations from the model are more likely to involve errors than are judgments that follow the pattern implied by the model. Differences that might arise among perceivers in the initial description of the event are omitted, as both the event and its consequences are assumed at the beginning of the diagram. Cognitive heuristics (availability, representativeness, anchoring), the fundamental attribution error, and the tendency to seek confirmation for preexisting hypotheses about social behavior are excluded. Individual difference variables that might influence the attribution process, such as perceiver religiosity, expectancies for locus of control, or cognitive complexity, have also been left out. Finally, the possibility that a perceiver's personal needs and motives— self-presentation, defensive attribution, need to believe in a just world—might affect the outcome is also not represented in the diagram. Like the complexities of the attribution process, these various deviations from "ideal" cannot be included in a brief summary, although they must be considered in the theory and research.

Despite the necessary simplification, what Figure 8-2 does show is that the attribution of blame for a negative occurrence is the result of a *process* that requires a particular prior attribution of responsibility, which judgment, in turn, rests on particular attribution of causality. The process is summarized in Figure 8-2. The attributional sequence starts at the left, with all actions a potentially blameworthy stimulus person might have performed. Those with positive consequences receive no further attention. Only the actions with morally disapproved consequences need to be examined. In theory, the series of judgments proceeds through time from left to right, beginning with the attribution of causality, shifting to the dimensions of responsibility, and ending with the determination of blameworthiness. At various points along the way, particular sorts of actions do not meet the successive tests for potential blame, and those actions split off to lead to the alternative attributions specified. Let us trace the process in more detail.

Attribution of Causality

Beginning with the sum total of all actions at the far left, it is assumed that agreement either between perceiver and actor or at least among perceivers, has already been reached regarding the description of the events, and the levels at which the actions taken are to be identified. The horizontal line dividing actions with positive consequences from actions with negative consequences is shown as a dashed line to indicate that it is an empirical rather than logical division. That is, in practice the perceiver is assumed to use his or her own judgment and moral standards to decide which acts are "positive" and which are "negative." The relatively large size of the area of the diagram devoted to actions with negative consequences obviously represents the principal interest of the theory, not the ratio of negative to positive actions presumed to exist in people's normal behavior.

After the characterization of all actions, comes the attribution of causality for those with negative consequences. This subsidiary process of causal attribution was described thoroughly in Chapter 3, and it involves the separation of events into those for which the stimulus person's action was the single cause (a single element in a minimal sufficient causal subset) and those for which the person's action was only one of the elements of the causal subset. If there are multiple possible causes, the perceiver will, where possible, follow the covariation principle to decide which proportion of the minimal sufficient causal subsets really involve the causal element of the stimulus person's action. If repeated observations are not available, one of the three cognitive schemata (multiple necessary, multiple sufficient, or compensatory) will be invoked to account for the occurrence of the effect. To keep the blameworthiness diagram manageable, the case of a single minimal sufficient causal subset with multiple elements, such as the case of the airline crash described in Chapter 2, is regarded for present purposes as a case of multiple causation rather than single causation.

Once it has been determined whether there are multiple causes or only a single cause, the next step is to identify the particular level of causal force exerted by the stimulus person. As the overlapping headings in Figure 8-2 indicate, this specification of the causal level is both part of the attribution of causality and the first of the five dimensions of responsibility. This level of causal force is the staircase described in detail in Chapter 5.

Looking first at the bottom of this column, the causal level of association appears outside the realm of the actions of the stimulus person, and there is no attribution of responsibility or blameworthiness to be made veridically from that level. In this respect moral accountability differs from legal account-ability, because in legal terms "association" is the equivalent of vicarious responsibility. The difference is that there are no statutes for moral behavior that establish which kinds of association should lead to liability and which should not. In their absence the choice is too likely to be dictated not by the features of the situation, but by the needs of the perceiver, and those needs are omitted from the diagram.

Moving up from association, within the category of events for which the stimulus person's action is one of the multiple possible causes, the two major causal level possibilities are causality and foreseeability. If the stimulus person is one of the several causes of the negative event, and is not believed to have had foreknowledge of the consequences of his or her behavior, there will be no further attribution of moral accountability.

If, on the other hand, the perceiver believes that the actor might have been able to foresee the outcome, then the "knowledge" dimension of responsibility will need to be considered. If the stimulus person only "should have known" of the consequences (but did not know), then there can be an attribution of minor negligence, as indicated by the arrow from the "should know" portion of foreseeability. If the perceiver believes the actor did know of the possible consequences, and carelessly went ahead, then there is a slightly greater attribution of negligence. Note that in neither case did the actor intend to produce the consequences (e.g., they might have been the side effects of his or her doing something else), but the negative consequences still occurred.

Once again the case of the Air Florida crash is useful to the discussion: Some of the complexities in the process are indicated by the fact that the negligence of the Air Florida pilots would most probably fall *between* these two stated alternatives. Any pilot "should have known" the possible consequences of remaining on the taxi-way for so long after de-icing, and the information from the cockpit voice recorder suggested that the pilots *did* notice that the plane was lumbering along, once the take-off roll had begun. Thus the pilots were not only "the cause" of the crash, in the sense that their decisions provided the individually insufficient but necessary condition for the occurrence, but they were also "responsible" for the occurrence, in the sense that their negligence was morally reprehensible.

Moving up in the level of causality column still further, where the actor is the sole cause of the event, causality alone again does not lead either to negligence or to any form of responsibility or blame. As with multiple causes, the degree of negligence attributed if the actor is thought to have been able to foresee the outcome will depend on the presumed state of the actor's knowledge. Regardless of whether this state of knowledge is "should have known," "did know," or even something in between, the amount of negligence attributed will be greater than before, because now the actor's behavior was the sole cause of the occurrence.

Finally, there is the level of causality represented by the actor's intention to produce the outcome that occurred. The intentionality level is most typical of instances in which the actor's behavior is the single cause of the event, although infrequently, intention might also be found among the multiple causes of a negative occurrence. Were the actor's intent to be only one of the multiple causes, unless all of these were necessary, the perceiver would have a difficult time justifying a judgment of blameworthiness. While it is logically possible for the actor's intent to commit harm to be accompanied by other causes, that combination of circumstances occurs so seldom that it is omitted from the diagram.

Dimensions of Responsibility

If the level of causality is judged to be intentionality, this level naturally presumes that the actor did know of the consequences of his or her action, and intended at least to some degree for those consequences to be produced. The difference between the two is that at the level of causality, intent is regarded as dichotomous (present or absent), while as a dimension of responsibility intentionality may vary in degree. This is, admittedly, a distinction that embodies very little real difference. But to notice that the two uses of "intent" are highly correlated is only to recognize one of the primary reasons that an attributional analysis of blame needs to deal with causality and responsibility as well as merely with blameworthiness: The judgments made in one of these settings are *not* independent of the judgments made in another.

On numerous occasions throughout this volume I have pointed out that beliefs about causality will affect responsibility judgments, the dimensions of responsibility, themselves, are frequently interrelated, and the acceptance of an excuse against blameworthiness is also likely to mitigate (retroactively) a judgment of responsibility. On this last point, Lloyd-Bostock (1983) has taken an even stronger position, arguing that the need to blame a person will affect the atribution of causality as well as the attribution of responsibility. I would disagree that blame can *precede* causality, but would not argue that initial judgments of causality could not be subject to the same sort of retroactive modification that takes place with responsibility. The perceiver's task is not only to assign blame (or not) but also to do so with a modicum of internal consistency, if only so that the resulting moral opprobrium can be justified.

Moving to the right in Figure 8-2, a certain portion of the events for which the intentional actions of a person are the single cause will involve coercion. The paradigmatic example of coercion is the irresistible threat from a powerful other person, but coercion can also include the restrictions of freedom of action inherent in the situation (Chapter 5) and the instructions an actor might think he or she was receiving from some superphysical force (Chapter 7). There are, however, two aspects of coercion that need to be emphasized. First, although it is coercion as perceived by the *actor* that might have initiated the action, it is coercion as perceived by the *perceiver* that will serve to mitigate responsibility and blameworthiness. Whether or not there are really any external (or insurmountable internal) forces influencing the actor is one of the many aspects of the situation on which the actor and perceiver might disagree. For the determination of blameworthiness, however, it is the perceiver's conception of possible coercion that is critical.

The second aspect of coercion that deserves comment is the timing of whatever influence occurred, regardless of the source of the influence. If coercion were regarded as acting simultaneously with the actor's intention, then the minimal sufficient causal subset would include at least those *two* different elements. This would dictate changes in attribution of causality, following the discounting principle, that were identical to the changes that would occur in the presence of any other causal element. This is not, however, an accurate description of coercion. In fact, coercion is a perfect example of Collingwood's (1940) second sense of causality—"affording him a motive" for doing something. The coercive force is itself "the cause" of the actor's motive, and that internal reason for acting can, as shown in Chapter 6, serve as the cause of the actor's behavior. The coercive force and the intentional act are in sequence, not simultaneous, making it possible to consider the effects of coercion in conjunction with an intentional act described as the single cause of the resulting event.

To the degree that the perceiver believes the actor's behavior to have been coerced, that behavior should no longer be liable for blame. There is no doubt that the actor was the proximate cause of the event, but because of the duress involved, the actor should be assigned only minimal personal responsibility and no blame. This prediction is derived from the definition of responsibility as "answerability." If a person holds a pistol to your head and says "do this or I'll kill you" and you comply, in *principle* you "could have done otherwise." Not that anyone will be surprised at your choice, and not that anyone will "blame" you for taking the action you did. By contrast, if your action appears entirely free of coercive influence, then that voluntary behavior *is* subject to further consideration and possible blame.

Following the voluntary action to the right in Figure 8-2, the last dimension of responsibility represents the degree to which the perceiver believes the actor shares his or her appreciation that the action was morally wrong. As noted in Chapter 5, there are at least two different senses in which the actor might not appreciate the wrongfulness of the action. The first of these is a limitation in what Hart (1968) would have called "capacity responsibility." In the legal system this limitation is reflected in the various assertions of diminished capacity (the plea of "not guilty by reason of insanity," the plea of "diminished capacity," or the verdict of "guilty but mentally ill"). As I have noted elsewhere (Darley & Shaver, 1983), part of the difficulty with the legal system's use of these concepts is that with the exception of the guilty but mentally ill verdict, the legal outcome has the effect of denying *causality* rather than culpability. People who are acquitted of criminal charges do not claim that "the government failed to convince them to convict me." They claim to be "innocent." A literal interpretation of this word would require not only the absence of blameworthiness and responsibility, but also an absence of causality. This conclusion makes no attributional sense, a fact that has not been lost on a public growing increasingly distressed with the traditional insanity plea. Whether the guilty but mentally ill verdict will resolve the public opinion problems while still providing the protection necessary for those individuals who are truly unable to comprehend the quality of their actions remains to be seen. In attributional terms alone, however, the new verdict at least has the virtue of not being internally inconsistent. Its moral equivalent is indicated in Figure 8-2: A person who lacks the capacity to appreciate the wrongfulness of his or her action should be assigned some responsibility (at least at the causal level, for example), but should receive no blame.

The second sense in which an actor may not appreciate the wrongfulness of the act is merely a disagreement between perceiver and actor over the moral standards that apply in the situation. This disagreement could be over the absolute value of the action (the perceiver considering it negative, the actor considering it positive), or it could be over the degree to which both parties believed the action to be negative. In either case, it is the perceiver's moral standards that apply, so this sense of appreciation of the moral quality of the action is not likely to mitigate blame, and consequently has been omitted from the judgments to be made.

Determination of Blameworthiness

Examination of whether the actor possessed the capacity to know that the action was morally reprehensible ends the discussion of dimensions of responsibility and leads to the determination of blameworthiness. When an intentional, voluntary action taken with full knowledge of the consequences and the capacity to understand those consequences is the sole cause of a negative occurrence, the actor is justifiably liable for blame. By these precisely described preconditions, the pilots of Flight 90 are not blameworthy, although they were negligently responsible. Veridically assigned blame requires still more than this set of preconditions. Once the actor stands accused, he or she may say nothing in defense, simply accepting all of the blame that is to come. Or the actor may provide either a justification or an excuse. If either of these replies is accepted by the perceiver, there will be an assignment of substantial moral responsibility, but still no *blame*. Only if the perceiver rejects the justification, or rejects the excuse, will there be the final assignment of blame.

It should be emphasized that while a justification and an excuse are mutually exclusive response alternatives, neither is categorical. An actor may offer a justification or excuse intended to absolve himself or herself of *all* blame, or the offering may be more limited. Regardless of the degree of justification or excuse claimed by the actor, the perceiver will make his or her own determination of just how extensive the absolution should be. Both the actor's offering and the perceiver's decision, shown for convenience in Figure

8-2 as dichotomous, therefore need tó be thought of as continuous scales, with the resulting blame assigned varying as the inverse of the degree to which either offering is accepted.

Even for a rational "ideal" perceiver, the assignment of blame thus reflects a complex process of social attribution. It presupposes a particular set of actions (those that produce negative consequences), a specific level of personal causality (single causation at the intentional level), a special combination of the dimensions of responsibility (causation, knowledge of the consequences, intentionality, voluntary choice, and the capacity to distinguish right from wrong), and the failure to have an adequate justification or excuse. In the theory's own terms, *each of these conditions is a necessary element of the minimal sufficient causal subset that, itself, is the cause of a veridical attribution of blame.* By specifying the components of a judgment of blame, and by specifying the time order in which those components should be considered, the theory of blame assignment establishes a prescriptive standard against which a perceiver's attributions can be compared. Thus, to the degree that blame is assigned in the absence of any one or more of these elements— for unintentional behaviors, for accidents in the defensive attribution mold, or despite a satisfactory excuse—the perceiver has committed an error.

It is important to remember, however, that the process of blame assignment is one of a disputed social judgment. While a perceiver who attributes blame in the *absence* of one or more of the necessary elements has clearly committed an error in judgment, a perceiver who has combined all of these elements in an idiosyncratic fashion has not so obviously made a mistake. If I blame you for something you did not do, my error will be easy to discover. If I claim your action was intentional, while you (and others) claim it to have been inadvertent, it becomes quite difficult to determine just whose version is correct. My disagreement with you might be testimony to your vested interest in avoiding blame, but my disagreement with other (presumably "objective") perceivers raise doubts about my own characterization of the incident. What the model does do is suggest where we should begin to look in any attempt to resolve discrepancies in the accounts offered by different perceivers.

Conclusions

The assignment of blame to a person who has helped to bring about a misfortune or morally reprehensible event is, as we have just seen, a highly *social* process. There are frequent opportunities for the actor and the perceiver to disagree about causes, responsibility, and even blameworthiness. The perceiver's final judgment, while it follows a version of the process presented in Figure 8-2, is subject to errors created by the perceiver's vantage point, enduring personal characteristics and beliefs, and transient personal needs. What the theory provides is a basic structure, in the terms of which these errors can be examined and understood.

One person's judgments of causality, responsibility, and blameworthiness may or may not agree with the judgments that would have been made by a different perceiver. Nevertheless, because the attribution of blame follows a predictable pattern, there will be underlying similarities among individual judgments of blame. If one's objective is to describe the process in more detail, the regularities are likely to be of primary interest. If one's objective is to determine the "truth value" of a particular perceiver's attribution of blame, then the differences will be of principal concern. The major advantage of having a thoroughly specified model of the assignment of blame is that the model can serve as the starting point for either sort of investigation.

What have we learned by examining the causes of action, the assignment of responsibility, and the determination of blame? We have discovered something about the process of blame assignment, but I think we have also learned something about social psychological theory and something of value in our everyday social interaction. Let's begin by considering just two implications that a psychology of blame has for more general psychological theory. First, within social psychology the study of the attribution of causality has generally followed Kelley's (1967, 1973) lead, concentrating on the attributional criteria of distinctiveness, consistency, and consensus, and ignoring such critical problems as whether these distinctive, consistent, and widely recognized effects were *intentionally* produced or not. This omission is appropriate when the perceptual task at hand is identification of the causes of an internal feeling state ("Is it something about that external entity, or is it some personal predilection of mine?"). When the perceiver's objective, however, is the determination of the causes of another's actions, the failure to consider intentionality severely restricts the usefulness of any conclusions that might be drawn.

By contrast to the study of causality, the social psychological study of responsibility attribution has typically been conducted either in the tradition of correspondent inference theory (Jones & Davis, 1965), or in the area of motivated distortion of responsibility for accidents (Shaver, 1970; Walster, 1966). This work has often considered the possible intentions of the stimulus person, but it has typically ignored the important distinctions between situations involving single causality and those involving *multiple* causes. Despite several efforts to bring the two literatures together (Hamilton, 1980; Jones & McGillis, 1976), there are still too few conceptual bridges. One important contribution of an attributional analysis of blame is to provide an additional bridge by showing the interdependence of judgments of causality and responsibility.

A second theoretical implication of the model of blame goes beyond the study of attribution within social psychology. Thorough specification of the nature of causality is, as we have seen, essential for establishing a clear description of the process of assigning blame. Many of the same philosophical distinctions, however, are important for other psychological theories as well. Should theories of human behavior pattern themselves after the principles of causality, including the notion of a "universal law of nature," that provides the foundation for physical science? There is a tradition in psychology, dating back at least to the Vienna Circle and presently represented in deterministic behaviorism, that would answer this question in the affirmative. There is also the Freudian tradition that, while disagreeing with many of the tenets of behaviorism, nevertheless embodies a similar deterministic view of human behavior. Whether the determinism is environmental or biological, it still precludes the exercise of volition and the subsequent need to assume personal responsibility for action.

In rather direct contrast, the philosophical foundation for a psychology of blame views human activity as the product of *creative* choices made by individual agents who must assume the responsibility for their behavior. For any theory with this view of human nature, the model provided by physical science must be regarded as wholly inappropriate. To be sure, the study of human behavior can only proceed if there are regularities there to be discovered, but the possibility of human choice is one of the regularities that must be included. There is no dearth of prior discussion of causality in psychological theory. What the present analysis suggests is that investigators should reverse the traditional question, to ask "How should behavioral scientists be like individual perceivers?"

Whatever its scientific implications, the attributional analysis of blame is more than a summary of philosophical arguments. It is a detailed description of a social process inherent in much of everyday life. To recall examples from Chapter 1, whether the event is a lover's quarrel, a failure of a mechanical system constructed and operated by people, or an action against the prevailing morality, the future social relations among the affected parties will be determined to no small degree by the way in which blame is assigned for the occurrence. The accusation, "It's *your* fault" and the claim "It isn't *my* fault" are virtual staples of human interaction. The assignment of blame is an essential ingredient of recovery from victimization, of psychological disorder and therapy, and of the maintenance or dissolution of friendship. Consequently, a thorough study of the process of blaming can lead to better understanding of a wide range of social behavior.

If as perceivers we pause before passing judgment on others, we may discover that some of the necessary elements for veridical blame are missing. Was the person I am about to accuse the sole cause of the negative event? Was that person's action intentional? Did the person really have the capacity to understand that the behavior was wrong? Is there a plausible justification for the action, or barring that, an acceptable excuse? Perhaps more importantly, is it possible that I have misconstrued any of these elements of the process? If, as potential objects of blame, we realize all of the conditions that must be met, then we can at the very least understand *why* our conduct is being regarded with disapproval. Moreover, if we truly believe we are being falsely accused, we can ask the perceiver to trace through the process a step at a time, so that the misunderstanding (if there is one) can be uncovered. If all that a formal theory of blame causes us to do is to talk to each other more carefully about a social process as important as blame, the theory will have served a valuable practical purpose.

What is the cause? Who is responsible? Who is to blame? These are the three fundamental questions with which this volume began. By examining each question in detail, a great deal was learned about the assignment of blame. The resulting theory of blame is in part descriptive of the judgments people make, in part prescriptive for the judgments they should make. Refining that theory and using it as the basis for study of errors that arise from fear, anger, or moral outrage are tasks that must be left for the future. The theory is a good beginning, but there is still much to be discovered about causality, responsibility, and blame.

References

Ajzen, I., & Fishbein, M. (1975). A Bayesian analysis of attribution processes. *Psychological Bulletin, 82*, 261–277.

Ajzen, I., & Fishbein, M. (1983). Relevance and availability in the attribution process. In J. Jaspars, F. D. Fincham, & M. Hewstone (Eds.), *Attribution theory and research: Conceptual, developmental, and social dimensions* (pp. 63–89). London: Academic.

Alston, W. P. (1967). Motives and motivation. In P. Edwards (Ed.), *Encyclopedia of philosophy* (Vol. 5, pp. 399–409). New York: Macmillan.

Anscombe, G. E. M. (1957). *Intention*. Oxford: Basil Blackwell.

Aristotle (1952). Nicomachean ethics (W. D. Ross, Trans.). In R. M. Hutchins (Ed.), *Great books of the western world* (Vol. 9, pp. 335–436). Chicago: Encyclopaedia Brittanica.

Austin, J. L. (1961). *Philosophical papers*. Oxford: Clarendon.

Bacon, F. (1952). Novum organum. In R. M. Hutchins (Ed.), *Great books of the western world* (Vol. 30, pp. 105–195). Chicago: Encyclopaedia Brittanica. (Original work published 1620)

Bardis, P. (1961). A religion scale. *Social Science, 36*, 120–123.

Beauchamp, T. L. (Ed.). (1974). *Philosophical problems of causation*. Encino, CA: Dickenson.

Beck, L. W. (1967). Once more unto the breach: Kant's answer to Hume, again. *Ratio, 9*, 33–37.

Bentham, J. (1879). *An introduction to the principles of morals and legislation*. Oxford: Clarendon. (Original work published 1789)

Berkeley, G. (1952). The principles of human knowledge. In R. M. Hutchins (Ed.), *Great books of the western world* (Vol. 35, pp. 401–444). Chicago: Encyclopaedia Brittanica. (Original work published 1710)

Berofsky, B. (Ed.). (1966). *Free will and determinism*. New York: Harper & Row.

Borgida, E., & Brekke, N. (1981). The base rate fallacy in attribution and prediction. In J. H. Harvey, W. Ickes, & R. F. Kidd (Eds.), *New directions in attribution research* (Vol. 3, pp. 63–95). Hillsdale, NJ: Erlbaum.

Bradley, F. H. (1927). *Ethical studies*. London: Clarendon.

Bradley, G. W. (1978). Self-serving biases in the attribution process: A reexamination of the fact or fiction question. *Journal of Personality and Social Psychology, 36*, 56–71.

Brand, M. (Ed.). (1976). *The nature of causation*. Urbana, IL: University of Illinois Press.

Brewer, M. B. (1977). An information-processing approach to attribution of responsibility. *Journal of Experimental Social Psychology, 13*, 58–69.

Brown, R. W., & Lenneberg, E. H. (1958). Studies in linguistic relativity. In E. E. Maccoby, T. M. Newcomb, & E. L. Hartley (Eds.), *Readings in social psychology* (3rd ed., pp. 9–18). New York: Holt, Rinehart, & Winston.

Bulman, R. J., & Wortman, C. B. (1977). Attributions of blame and coping in the "real world": Severe accident victims react to their lot. *Journal of Personality and Social Psychology, 35*, 351–363.

Bunge, M. (1959). *Causality*. Cambridge, MA: Harvard University Press.

Burger, J. M. (1981). Motivational biases in the attribution of responsibility for an accident: A meta-analysis of the defensive attribution hypothesis. *Psychological Bulletin, 90*, 496–512.

Buss, A. R. (1978). Causes and reasons in attribution theory: A conceptual critique. *Journal of Personality and Social Psychology, 36*, 1311–1321.

Campbell, C. A. (1957). *On selfhood and godhood*. London: Allen & Unwin.

Chaikin, A. L., & Darley, J. M., Jr. (1973). Victim or perpetrator: Defensive attribution and the need for order and justice. *Journal of Personality and Social Psychology, 25*, 268–275.

Collingwood, R. G. (1940). *An essay on metaphysics*. Oxford: Clarendon.

Collins, B. E. (1974). Four components of the Rotter Internal–External Scale: Belief in a difficult world, a just world, a predictable world, and a politically responsive world. *Journal of Personality and Social Psychology, 29*, 381–391.

Cook, T. D., & Campbell, D. T. (1979). *Quasi-experimentation: Design and analysis issues for field settings*. Chicago: Rand McNally.

Danto, A. (1963). What we can do. *The Journal of Philosophy, 60*, 685–700.

Darley, J. M., Klosson, E. C., & Zanna, M. P. (1978). Intentions and their contexts in the moral judgments of children and adults. *Child Development, 49*, 66–74.

Darley, J. M., & Shaver, K. G. (1983). *Psychology and law: An analysis of assumptions*. Unpublished manuscript, Princeton University, Princeton NJ.

Davidson, D. (1963). Actions, reasons, and causes. *The Journal of Philosophy, 60*, 685–700.

Davis, M. S., & Shaver, K. G. (1982, April). *Justice motives in attributions for an earthquake: Whose fault is it?* Paper presented at the meeting of the Eastern Psychological Association, Baltimore.

Descartes, R. (1952). Objections against the meditations, and replies (Elizabeth S. Haldane & G. R. T. Ross, Trans.). In R. M. Hutchins (Ed.), *Great books of the western world* (Vol. 31, pp. 104–203). Chicago: Encyclopaedia Brittanica. (Original work published 1641)

Ducasse, C. J. (1969). *Causation and the types of necessity*. New York: Dover.

Durham v. United States, 214 F.2d 862 (D.C. Cir. 1954).

Elig, T. W., & Frieze, I. H. (1975). Measuring causal attributions for success and failure. *Journal of Personality and Social Psychology, 37*, 621–634.

Fauconnet, P. (1920). *La responsibilité* [Responsibility]. Paris: Alcan.

Feinberg, J. (1980). Punishment. In J. Feinberg & H. Gross (Eds.), *Philosophy of law* (2nd ed., pp. 514–522). Belmont, CA: Wadsworth.

Feinberg, J. (Ed.). (1981). *Reason and responsibility* (5th ed.). Belmont, CA: Wadsworth.

Feller, W. (1968). *An introduction to probability theory and its applications* (3rd ed.). New York: Wiley.

Fincham, F., & Jaspars, J. (1979). Attribution of responsibility to the self and other in children and adults. *Journal of Personality and Social Psychology, 37*, 1589–1602.

Fincham, F. D., & Jaspars, J. M. (1980). Attribution of responsibility: From man the scientist to man as lawyer. In L. Berkowitz (Ed.), *Advances in experimental social psychology* (Vol. 13, pp. 81–138). New York: Academic.

Fischhoff, B. (1976). Attribution theory and judgment under uncertainty. In J. H. Harvey, W. J. Ickes, & R. F. Kidd (Eds.), *New directions in attribution research* (Vol. 1, pp. 421–452). Hillsdale, NJ: Erlbaum.

Fishbein, M., & Ajzen, I. (1973). Attribution of responsibility: A theoretical note. *Journal of Experimental Social Psychology, 9*, 148–153.

Freud, S. (1952). Beyond the pleasure principle (C. J. M. Hubback, Trans.). In R. M. Hutchins (Ed.), *Great books of the western world* (Vol. 54, pp. 639–663). Chicago: Encyclopaedia Brittanica. (Original work published 1920)

Goffman, E. (1959). *The presentation of self in everyday life*. Garden City, NY: Doubleday.

Goldman, A. I. (1970). *A theory of human action*. Englewood Cliffs, NJ: Prentice-Hall.

Greenberg, J., Pyszczynski, T., & Solomon, S. (1982). The self-serving attributional bias: Beyond self-presentation. *Journal of Experimental Social Psychology, 18*, 56–67.

Guttman, L. A. (1944). A basis for scaling qualitative data. *American Sociological Review, 9*, 139–150.

Hadfield (The trial of), 27 Howell's State Trials 885 (1800).

Hamilton, V. L. (1978). Who is responsible? Toward a *social* psychology of responsibility attribution. *Social Psychology, 41*, 316–328.

Hamilton, V. L. (1980). Intuitive psychologist or intuitive lawyer? Alternative models of the attribution process. *Journal of Personality and Social Psychology, 39*, 767–772.

Hancock, R. (1967). History of metaphysics. In P. Edwards (Ed.), *Encyclopedia of philosophy* (Vol. 5, pp. 289–300). New York: Macmillan.

Hart, H. L. A. (1968). *Punishment and responsibility*. New York: Oxford University Press.

Hart, H. L. A., & Honoré, A. M. (1959). *Causation in the law*. Oxford: Oxford University Press.

Harvey, J. H., & Tucker, J. A. (1979). On problems with the cause–reason distinction in attribution theory. *Journal of Personality and Social Psychology, 37*, 1441–1446.

Heider, F. (1944). Social perception and phenomenal causality. *Psychological Review, 51*, 358–374.

Heider, F. (1958). *The psychology of interpersonal relations*. New York: Wiley.

Holmes, O. W., Jr. (1881). *The common law*. Boston: Little, Brown.

Holton, G. (1973). *Thematic origins of scientific revolutions*. Cambridge, MA: Harvard University Press.

Hospers, J. (1950). Meaning and free will. *Philosophy and Phenomenological Research, 10*, 313–330.

Hume, D. (1952). Enquiry concerning human understanding. In R. M. Hutchins (Ed.), *Great books of the western world* (Vol. 35, pp. 449–509). Chicago: Encyclopaedia Brittanica. (Original work published 1748)

Jaspars, J., Hewstone, M., & Fincham, F. D. (1983). Attribution theory and research: The state of the art. In J. Jaspars, F. D. Fincham, & M. Hewstone (Eds.), *Attribution theory and research: Conceptual, developmental and social dimensions* (pp. 3–36). London: Academic.

Jones, E. E. (1978). A conversation with Edward E. Jones and Harold H. Kelley. In J. H. Harvey, W. Ickes, & R. F. Kidd (Eds.), *New directions in attribution research* (Vol. 2, pp. 371–388). Hillsdale, NJ: Erlbaum.

Jones, E. E., & Davis, K. E. (1965). From acts to dispositions: The attribution process in person perception. In L. Berkowitz (Ed.), *Advances in experimental social psychology* (Vol. 2, pp. 219–266). New York: Academic.

Jones, E. E., & McGillis, D. (1976). Correspondent inferences and the attribution cube: A comparative reappraisal. In J. H. Harvey, W. J. Ickes, & R. F. Kidd (Eds.), *New directions in attribution research* (Vol. 1, pp. 389–420). Hillsdale, NJ: Erlbaum.

Jones, E. E., & Nisbett, R. E. (1971). *The actor and the observer: Divergent perceptions of the causes of behavior.* Morristown, NJ: General Learning Press.

Kahneman, D., & Tversky, A. (1973). On the psychology of prediction. *Psychological Review, 80,* 237–251.

Kant, I. (1952). The critique of pure reason. (J. M. D. Meiklejohn, Trans.). In R. M. Hutchins (Ed.), *Great books of the western world* (Vol. 42, pp. 1–250). Chicago: Encyclopaedia Brittanica. (Original work published 1781)

Kantorowicz, H. (1958). *The definition of law.* Cambridge: Cambridge University Press.

Kelley, H. H. (1967). Attribution theory in social psychology. In D. Levine (Ed.), *Nebraska symposium on motivation 1967* (pp. 192–238). Lincoln, NE: University of Nebraska Press.

Kelley, H. H. (1972). Causal schemata and the attribution process. In E. E. Jones, D. E. Kanouse, H. H. Kelley, R. E. Nisbett, S. Valins, & B. Weiner (Eds.), *Attribution: Perceiving the causes of behavior* (pp. 151–174). Morristown, NJ: General Learning Press.

Kelley, H. H. (1973). The processes of causal attribution. *American Psychologist, 28,* 107–128.

Kelley, H. H., & Michela, J. L. (1980). Attribution theory and research. *Annual Review of Psychology, 31,* 457–501.

Kruglanski, A. W. (1979). Causal explanation, teleological explanation: On radical particularism in attribution theory. *Journal of Personality and Social Psychology, 37,* 1447–1457.

Kruglanski, A. W., Hamel, I. Z., Maides, S. A., & Schwartz, J. M. (1978). Attribution theory as a case of lay epistemology. In J. H. Harvey, W. Ickes, & R. F. Kidd (Eds.), *New directions in attribution research* (Vol. 2, pp. 299–333). Hillsdale, NJ: Erlbaum.

Kruskal, J. B., Young, F. W., & Seery, J. B. (1973). *How to use KYST, a very flexible program to do multidimensional scaling and unfolding.* Murray Hill, NJ: Bell Laboratories.

Kruskal, J. B. & Wish, M. (1978). *Multidimensional scaling.* Beverly Hills, CA: Sage.

Kuhn, T. S. (1962). *The structure of scientific revolutions.* Chicago: University of Chicago Press.

Latané, B., & Darley, J. M., Jr. (1970). *The unresponsive bystander: Why doesn't he help?* New York: Appleton-Century-Crofts.

Lerner, M. J., & Matthews, G. (1967). Reactions to suffering of others under conditions of indirect responsibility. *Journal of Personality and Social Psychology, 5,* 319–325.

Lerner, M. J., & Miller, D. T. (1978). Just world research and the attribution process: Looking back and ahead. *Psychological Bulletin, 85,* 1030–1051.

Lloyd-Bostock, S. (1983). Attributions of cause and responsibility as social phenomena. In J. Jaspars, F. D. Fincham, & M. Hewstone (Eds.), *Attribution theory and research: Conceptual, developmental and social dimensions* (pp. 261–289). London: Academic.

Locke, D., & Pennington, D. (1982). Reasons and other causes: Their role in attribution processes. *Journal of Personality and Social Psychology, 42,* 212–223.

Mackie, J. L. (1965). Causes and conditions. *American Philosophical Quarterly, 2,* 245–264.

Maselli, M. D., & Altrocchi, J. (1969). Attribution of intent. *Psychological Bulletin, 71,* 445–454.

Mayr, E. (1965). Cause and effect in biology. In D. Lerner (Ed.), *Cause and effect* (pp. 33–50). New York: Free Press.

McArthur, L. A. (1972). The how and the what of why: Some determinants and consequences of causal attribution. *Journal of Personality and Social Psychology, 22*, 171–193.

Melden, A. I. (1961). *Free action*. London: Routledge & Kegan Paul.

Michotte, A. (1963). *The perception of causality* (T. R. Miles & E. Miles, Trans.). New York: Basic Books. (Original work published 1946)

Milgram, S. (1963). Behavioral study of obedience. *Journal of Abnormal and Social Psychology, 67*, 371–378.

Mill, J. S. (1888). *A system of logic*. New York: Harper & Row.

Mill, J. S. (1907). *Utilitarianism* (15th ed.). London: Longmans, Green. (Original work published 1861)

Miller, D. T., & Ross, M. (1975). Self-serving biases in the attribution of causality: Fact or fiction? *Psychological Bulletin, 82*, 213–225.

Miller, F. D., Smith, E. R., & Uleman, J. (1981). Measurement and interpretation of situational and dispositional attributions. *Journal of Experimental Social Psychology, 17*, 80–95.

M'Naghten (The trial of), Vol. VII, English Reports 718 (1843).

Nagel, E. (1965). Types of causal explanation in science. In D. Lerner (Ed.), *Cause and effect* (pp. 11–32). New York: Free Press.

Newtson, D. (1976). Foundations of attribution: The perception of ongoing behavior. In J. H. Harvey, W. J. Ickes, & R. F. Kidd (Eds.), *New directions in attribution research* (Vol. 1, pp. 223–247). Hillsdale, NJ: Erlbaum.

Nisbett, R. E., & Borgida, E. (1975). Attribution and the psychology of prediction. *Journal of Personality and Social Psychology, 32*, 932–943.

Nisbett, R. E., & Ross, L. (1980). *Human inference: Strategies and shortcomings of social judgment*. Englewood Cliffs, NJ: Prentice-Hall.

Nisbett, R. E., & Wilson, T. D. (1977). Telling more than we can know: Verbal reports on mental processes. *Psychological Review, 84*, 231–259.

Pargament, K. L., Steele, R. E., & Tyler, R. B. (1979). Religious participation, religious motivation, and individual psychosocial competence. *Journal for the Scientific Study of Religion, 18*, 412–419.

Peters, R. S. (1958). *The concept of motivation*. London: Routledge & Kegan Paul.

Piaget, J. (1932). *The moral judgment of the child*. London: Paul, Trench, Tribner.

Plato. (1952). Dialogues (B. Jowett, Trans.). In R. M. Hutchins (Ed.), *Great books of the western world* (Vol. 7, pp. 1–294). Chicago: Encyclopaedia Brittanica.

Popper, K. R. (1959). *The logic of scientific discovery*. New York: Harper and Row.

President's Commission on Law Enforcement and Administration of Justice. (1967). *The challenge of crime in a free society*. Washington, DC: U.S. Government Printing Office.

Reid, T. (1863a). Letters to Dr. James Gregory. In W. Hamilton (Ed.), *The works of Thomas Reid, D. D.* (6th ed., Vol. 1, pp. 62–88). Edinburgh: Machlachlan & Stewart.

Reid, T. (1863b). Of the liberty of moral agents. In W. Hamilton (Ed.), *The works of Thomas Reid, D. D.* (6th ed., Vol. 2, pp. 599–636). Edinburgh: Machlachlan & Stewart.

Rescher, N. (1966). *Distributive justice: A constructive critique of the utilitarian theory of distribution*. Indianapolis: Bobbs-Merrill.

Rosenberg, S., & Sedlak, A. (1972). Structural representations of implicit personality theory. In L. Berkowitz (Ed.), *Advances in experimental social psychology* (Vol. 6, pp. 235–297). New York: Academic.

Ross, L. D. (1977). The intuitive psychologist and his shortcomings: Distortions in the attribution process. In L. Berkowitz (Ed.), *Advances in experimental social psychology* (Vol. 10, pp. 173–220). New York: Academic.

Rotter, J. B. (1966). Generalized expectancies for internal versus external locus of control of reinforcement. *Psychological Monographs, 80*, 1–28.

Russell, B. (1925). *Mysticism and logic and other essays*. London: Longmans, Green.

Russell, B. (1945). *A history of western philosophy*. New York: Simon & Schuster.

Ryan, W. (1976). *Blaming the victim*. New York: Vintage.

Ryle, G. (1949). *The concept of mind*. London: Hutchinson.

Schopler, J., & Layton, B. D. (1972). *Attribution of interpersonal power and influence*. Morristown, NJ: General Learning Press.

Scriven, M. (1964). The structure of science. *Review of Metaphysics, 27*, 403–424.

Shaver, K. G. (1970). Defensive attribution: Effects of severity and relevance on the responsibility assigned for an accident. *Journal of Personality and Social Psychology, 14*, 101–113.

Shaver, K. G. (1973). *Intentional ambiguity in the attribution of responsibility: A reply to Fishbein and Ajzen*. Unpublished manuscript, College of William and Mary.

Shaver, K. G. (1975). *An introduction to attribution processes*. Cambridge, MA: Winthrop.

Shaver, K. G. (1979, August). Attribution theory and the explanation of religious experience. In M. J. Meadow (Chair), *Applications of general psychological theory to the study of religion*. Symposium conducted at the meeting of the American Psychological Association, New York.

Shaver, K. G. (1981). Back to basics: On the role of theory in the attribution of causality. In J. H. Harvey, W. Ickes, & R. F. Kidd (Eds.), *New directions in attribution research* (Vol. 3, pp. 331–358). Hillsdale, NJ: Erlbaum.

Shaver, K. G., Null, C. H., & Huff, C. W. (1982, October). *Multidimensional scaling of responsibility-related words*. Paper presented at the meeting of the Psychonomic Society, Minneapolis, MN.

Shaver, K. G., Payne, M. R., Bloch, R. M., Burch, M. C., Davis, M. S., & Shean, G. D. (1984). Logic in distortion: Attributions of causality and responsibility among schizophrenics. *Journal of Social and Clinical Psychology, 2*, 193–214.

Shaver, K. G., Turnbull, A. A., & Sterling, M. P. (1973). Defensive attribution: The effects of occupational danger and locus of control; perceiver sex and self-esteem. *Journal Supplement Abstract Service Catalog of Selected Documents in Psychology, 3*, 48.

Shaw, M. E., Briscoe, M. E., & Garcia-Esteve, J. (1968). A cross-cultural study of attribution of responsibility. *International Journal of Psychology, 3*, 51–60.

Shaw, M. E., & Schneider, F. W. (1969). Negro–white differences in attribution of responsibility as a function of age. *Psychonomic Science, 16*, 289–291.

Shaw, M. E., & Sulzer, J. L. (1964). An empirical test of Heider's levels in attribution of responsibility. *Journal of Abnormal and Social Psychology, 69*, 39–46.

Shultz, T. R., & Schleifer, M. (1983). Towards a refinement of attribution concepts. In J. Jaspars, F. D. Fincham, & M. Hewstone (Eds.), *Attribution theory and research: Conceptual, developmental and social dimensions* (pp. 37–62). London: Academic.

Shultz, T. R., Schleifer, M., & Altman, I. (1981). Judgments of causation, responsibility, and punishment in cases of harm-doing. *Canadian Journal of Behavioural Science, 13*, 238–253.

Skinner, B. F. (1953). *Science and human behavior*. New York: Macmillan.

Slocumb, F. G., Forsyth, D. R., & Shaver, K. G. (1983, April). *Superphysical causality: A neglected attributional category*. Paper presented at the meeting of the Eastern Psychological Association, Philadelphia.

Smith, E. R., Miller, F. D. (1978). Limits on perception of cognitive processes: A reply to Nisbett and Wilson. *Psychological Review, 85*, 355–362.

Smith, M. C. (1981). *Gorky park*. New York: Random House.

Solomon, S. (1978). Measuring dispositional and situational attributions. *Personality and Social Psychology Bulletin, 4*, 589–594.

Spinoza, B. (1952). Ethics. (W. H. White, Trans., rev. by A. H. Stirling). In R. M. Hutchins (Ed.), *Great books of the western world* (Vol. 31, pp. 355–463). Chicago: Encyclopaedia Brittanica. (Original work published 1677)

Stace, W. T. (1952). *Religion and the modern mind*. Philadelphia: Lippincott.

Steiner, I. (1970). Perceived freedom. In L. Berkowitz (Ed.), *Advances in experimental social psychology* (Vol. 5, pp. 187–249). New York: Academic.

Suchting, W. A. (1967). Kant's second analogy of experience. *Kant-Studien, 58*, 355–369.

Sulzer, J. L. (1971, July). *Heider's "Levels model" of responsibility attribution*. Paper presented at the Symposium on Attribution of Responsibility Research, Williamsburg,VA.

Szasz, T. S. (1974). *The myth of mental illness*. New York: Harper & Row.

Takane, Y., Young, F. W., & deLeeuw, J. (1977). Nonmetric individual differences multidimensional scaling: An alternating least squares method with optimal scaling features. *Psychometrika, 42*, 7–67.

Tapp, J. L., & Kohlberg, L. (1971). Developing senses of law and legal justice. *Journal of Social Issues, 27*, 65–91.

Tetlock, P. E., & Levi, A. (1982). Attribution bias: On the inconclusiveness of the cognition–motivation debate. *Journal of Experimental Social Psychology, 18*, 68–88.

Thornton, B. (1984). Defensive attribution of responsibility: Evidence for an arousal-based motivational bias. *Journal of Personality and Social Psychology, 46*, 721–734.

Tyler, T. R., & Devinitz, V. (1981). Self-serving bias in the attribution of responsibility: Cognitive versus motivational explanations. *Journal of Experimental Social Psychology, 17*, 408–416.

United States v. Brawner, 471 F.2d 969 (D.C. Cir. 1972).

Vallacher, R. R., & Wegner, D. M. (in press). *A theory of action identification*. Hillsdale, NJ: Erlbaum.

Wallace, W. A. (1972). *Causality and scientific explanation: Vol. 1. Medieval and early classical science*. Ann Arbor, MI: University of Michigan Press.

Wallace, W. A. (1974). *Causality and scientific explanation: Vol. 2. Classical and contemporary science*. Ann Arbor, MI: University of Michigan Press.

Walster, E. (1966). Assignment of responsibility for an accident. *Journal of Personality and Social Psychology, 3*, 73–79.

Weary, G., & Arkin, R. M. (1981). Attributional self-presentation. In J. H. Harvey, W. Ickes, & R. F. Kidd (Eds.), *New directions in attribution research* (Vol. 3, pp. 223–246). Hillsdale, NJ: Erlbaum.

Wegner, D. M., Vallacher, R. R., Macomber, G., Wood, R., & Arps, K. (1984). The emergence of action. *Journal of Personality and Social Psychology, 46*, 269–279.

Whorf, B. L. (1958). Science and linguistics. In E. E. Maccoby, T. M. Newcomb, & E. L. Hartley (Eds.), *Readings in social psychology* (3rd ed., pp. 1–9). New York: Holt, Rinehart, & Winston.

Williams, G. L. (1953). *Criminal law: The general part*. London: Stevens & Sons.

Winch, P. (1958). *The idea of a social science*. London: Routledge & Kegan Paul.

Yerkes, R. M., & Dodson, J. D. (1908). The relation of strength of stimulus to rapidity of habit-formation. *Journal of Comparative Neurology and Psychology, 18*, 459–482.

Author Index

Ajzen, I., 42, 90, 91, 93, 94, 117, 118,
    130, 131, 132, 138, 143, 177, 178
Alston, W.P., 128, 177
Altman, I., 162, 182
Altrocchi, J., 116, 180
Anscombe, G.E.M., 41, 42, 44, 80, 115,
    116, 119, 120, 122, 123, 126, 127,
    177
Aristotle, 9, 12, 17, 25, 27, 36, 80, 126,
    177
Arkin, R.M., 42, 130, 183
Arps, K., 44, 183
Austin, J.L., 66, 79, 82, 85, 143, 163,
    177

Bacon, F., 50, 177
Bardis, P., 139, 140, 141, 177
Beauchamp, T.L., 22, 24, 177
Beck, L.W., 21, 177
Bentham, J., 72, 162, 177
Berkeley, G., 17, 26, 43, 177
Berofsky, B., 74, 177
Borgida, E., 42, 177, 181
Bradley, F.H., 67, 80, 85, 109, 177
Bradley, G.W., 130, 177
Brand, M., 12, 18, 30, 177
Brawner, A.W., 3, 183
Brekke, N., 42, 177

Brewer, M.B., 42, 90, 91, 92, 93, 100,
    129, 130, 132, 135, 143, 178
Briscoe, M.E., 93, 182
Brown, R.W., 155, 178
Bulman, R.J., 139, 178
Bunge, M., 15, 16, 178
Burger, J. M., 135, 178
Buss, A.R., 126, 127, 128, 129, 178

Campbell, C.A., 77, 78, 80, 81, 123, 178
Campbell, D.T., 16, 158, 178
Chaikin, A.L., 135, 178
Collingwood, R.G., 26, 27, 28, 29, 30,
    31, 32, 41, 50, 122, 171, 178
Collins, B.E., 140, 178
Cook, T.D., 16, 158, 178

Danto, A., 41, 44, 120, 178
Darley, J.M., 61, 70, 135, 171, 178, 180
Davidson, D., 123, 178
Davis, K.E., 7, 88, 96, 108, 116, 133,
    174, 179
Davis, M.S., 134, 178
deLeeuw, J., 145, 183
Descartes, R., 17, 26, 178
Devinitz, V., 135, 183
Dodson, J.D., 95, 183

Ducasse, C.J., 18, 20, 21, 22, 29, 32, 50, 178
Durham, M., 3, 178

Elig, T.W., 53, 178

Fauconnet, P., 87, 178
Feinberg, J., 70, 73, 74, 77, 178
Feller, W., 117, 178
Fincham, F.D., 53, 70, 90, 91, 92, 94, 103, 105, 138, 163, 178, 179
Fischhoff, B., 130, 179
Fishbein, M., 40, 90, 91, 93, 94, 117, 118, 130, 131, 132, 138, 143, 179
Forsyth, D.R., 138, 182
Freud, S., 13, 64, 75, 179
Frieze, I.H., 53, 178

Garcia-Esteve, J., 93, 182
Goffman, E., 165, 179
Goldman, A.I., 41, 44, 57, 119, 120, 121, 122, 123, 124, 125, 126, 179
Greenberg, J., 130, 179
Guttman, L.A., 90, 95, 103, 179

Hadfield, J., 3, 179
Hamel, I.Z., 4, 180
Hamilton, V.L., 99, 104, 107, 144, 174, 179
Hancock, R., 24, 179
Hart, H.L.A., 33, 64, 65, 66, 67, 68, 70, 85, 87, 99, 103, 111, 143, 159, 163, 171, 179
Harvey, J.H., 126, 128, 179
Heider, F., 6, 7, 8, 26, 36, 37, 50, 52, 81, 88, 89, 90, 91, 92, 93, 94, 95, 96, 99, 103, 104, 105, 106, 108, 109, 110, 116, 125, 126, 127, 128, 129, 132, 138, 143, 146, 155, 158, 179
Hewstone, M., 53, 179
Holmes, O.W., Jr., 8, 67, 68, 179
Holton, G., 14, 15, 157, 158, 179
Honoré, A.M., 33, 70, 99, 163, 179
Hospers, J., 75, 179

Huff, C.W., 85, 138, 182
Hume, D., 17, 18, 19, 20, 21, 22, 23, 24, 25, 28, 32, 36, 43, 76, 77, 179

Jaspars, J., 53, 70, 90, 91, 92, 94, 103, 105, 138, 163, 178, 179
Jones, E.E., 7, 88, 96, 97, 98, 99, 108, 109, 116, 128, 133, 138, 174, 179, 180

Kahneman, D., 130, 180
Kant, I., 21, 22, 23, 24, 180
Kantorowicz, H., 67, 180
Kelley, H.H., 7, 8, 16, 19, 50, 52, 53, 54, 55, 56, 57, 58, 61, 99, 100, 103, 104, 108, 174, 180
Klosson, E.C., 70, 178
Kohlberg, L., 73, 183
Kruglanski, A.W., 4, 126, 127, 128, 129, 180
Kruskal, J.B., 145, 147, 180
Kuhn, T.S., 5, 13, 14, 180

Latané, B., 61, 180
Layton, B.D., 91, 182
Lenneberg, E.H., 155, 178
Lerner, M.J., 133, 134, 180
Levi, A., 135, 183
Lloyd-Bostock, S., 170, 180
Locke, D., 127, 128, 129, 138, 180

Mackie, J.L., 33, 47, 48, 49, 50, 180
Macomber, G., 44, 183
Maides, S.A., 4, 180
Maselli, M.D., 116, 180
Matthews, G., 133, 180
Mayr, E., 16, 180
McArthur, L.A., 53, 181
McGillis, D., 7, 88, 96, 97, 98, 99, 108, 116, 133, 138, 174, 179
Melden, A.I., 79, 123, 126, 181
Michela, J.L., 53, 180
Michotte, A., 5, 180
Milgram, S., 110, 111, 181

Mill, J.S., 8, 28, 29, 30, 31, 32, 46, 49, 50, 51, 52, 56, 72, 73, 181
Miller, D.T., 42, 129, 132, 133, 134, 181
Miller, F.D., 42, 138, 181, 182
M'Naghten, 3, 181

Nagel, E., 33, 181
Newtson, D., 37, 40, 181
Nisbett, R.E., 42, 109, 130, 180, 181
Null, C.H., 85, 138, 182

Pargament, K.L., 142, 181
Pennington, D., 127, 128, 129, 138, 180
Peters, R.S., 123, 126, 181
Piaget, J., 89, 181
Plato, 9, 181
Popper, K.R., 50, 181
Pyszczynski, T., 130, 179

Reid, T., 25, 26, 28, 36, 77, 87, 122, 124, 181
Rescher, N., 72, 181
Rosenberg, S., 82, 181
Ross, L.D., 42, 109, 129, 130, 132, 181
Ross, M., 129, 130, 132, 181
Rotter, J.B., 139, 142, 182
Russell, B., 12, 13, 17, 32, 92, 182
Ryan, W., 2, 182
Ryle, G., 26, 70, 79, 80, 85, 123, 181

Schopler, J., 91, 182
Schleifer, M., 70, 71, 138, 143, 162, 163, 164, 182
Schneider, F.W., 93, 182
Schwartz, J.M., 4, 180
Scriven, M., 49, 182
Sedlak, A., 82, 181
Seery, J.B., 145, 180
Shaver, K.G., 46, 49, 52, 55, 57, 85, 90, 93, 94, 126, 133, 134, 135, 138, 139, 143, 155, 171, 174, 178, 182
Shaw, M.E., 93, 94, 182
Shultz, T.R., 70, 71, 138, 143, 162, 163, 164, 182
Skinner, B.F., 13, 64, 75, 79, 182

Slocumb, F.G., 138, 139, 142, 182
Smith, E.R., 42, 138, 181, 182
Smith, M.C., 1, 2, 182
Solomon, S., 130, 138, 179, 183
Spinoza, B., 75, 139, 183
Stace, W.T., 76, 183
Steele, R.E., 142, 181
Steiner, I., 116, 183
Sterling, M.P., 135, 182
Suchting, W.A., 22, 183
Sulzer, J.L., 88, 93, 94, 182, 183
Szasz, T.S., 2, 183

Takane, Y., 145, 183
Tapp, J.L., 73, 183
Tetlock, P.E., 135, 183
Thornton, B., 135, 136, 183
Tucker, J.A., 126, 128, 179
Turnbull, A.A., 135, 182
Tversky, A., 181, 180
Tyler, R.B., 142, 181
Tyler, T.R., 135, 183

Uleman, J., 138, 181

Vallacher, R.R., 43, 44, 121, 183

Wallace, W.A., 12, 13, 15, 17, 19, 20, 26, 32, 183
Walster, E.H., 134, 174, 183
Weary, G., 42, 130, 183
Wegner, D.M., 43, 44, 121, 183
Whorf, B.L., 155, 183
Williams, G.L., 67, 183
Wilson, T.D., 42, 181
Winch, P., 126, 183
Wish, M., 147, 180
Wood, R., 44, 183
Wortman, C.B., 139, 178

Yerkes, R.M., 95, 183
Young, F.W., 145, 180, 183

Zanna, M.P., 70, 178

Subject Index

Ability, 7, 108, 121, 122

Act individuation (*see* Acts, individuation of)

Action identification, 43–44, 59, 60, 102, 121, 161

Action plan, 121, 124, 126

Activity theory (*see* Causality, activity theory of)

Actor
  self-attribution, 129
  vs. observer, divergent attributions, 127, 128, 129

Acts
  basic, 41, 120, 121
  individuation of, 41, 121
  nonbasic, 41, 120, 121

Actus reus, 67, 68, 69

Agency, 26, 31, 33, 35, 86, 127, 162, 175

ALSCAL, 145, 147

Analysis of variance analogy for attribution, 52–53

Association (*see* Levels of responsibility)

Augmentation principle, 8, 54, 55, 56, 58, 60, 61, 104, 105, 167

Basic acts (*see* Acts, basic)

Bayes' theorem, 117–118

Behaviorism, 13, 32, 79, 175

Biases in attribution (*see* Errors in attribution)

Blame
  definition of, 160, 162, 172–173
  distinguished from responsibility, 67, 82, 146, 162, 163, 164, 165
  model for attribution of, 166
  of victims, 2, 3, 133, 134

Capacity responsibility, 65, 111, 112, 159, 171

Category-based expectancy (*see* Expectancy, category-based)

Causality
  activity theory of, 23–28, 30, 31, 32, 47, 77, 122, 127, 159
  in blame assignment, 168–170
  constant conjunction in, 18, 19, 20, 21, 22, 24, 28
  dimension of responsibility, 85, 101, 102–106, 134
  distinguished from responsibility, 63, 70–71, 87, 91, 92, 93, 132
  level of responsibility (*see* Levels of responsibility)
  model for attribution of, 59–61
  necessity theory of, 21, 22, 23, 28, 30, 31
  precondition for responsibility, 70–72

Causality (*cont.*)
  regularity theory of, 17–21, 28, 30, 31,
    127
  uniformity of nature principle of, 24, 25,
    26, 29, 31, 32, 175
Causal elements, 46–50, 54–58, 90, 124,
    128, 161, 162, 164
  nonredundant, 49
  redundant, 49, 55, 61
Causal subsets, 32–33, 45–50, 54–58, 59,
    60, 83, 95, 102, 124, 125, 128,
    158, 161, 168, 171, 173
Cause
  Aristotle's four kinds of, 9, 12, 17, 126
  compensatory, 54, 55, 56, 57, 58, 60
    logical problem with, 56–58
  definition of, 18, 30–33, 35, 45, 57,
    70–71, 105, 123
    by activity theory, 25
    by necessity theory, 22
    by regularity theory, 18
  historical sense of, 26–27
  multiple necessary, 47, 54, 56, 60
  multiple sufficient, 47, 54, 56, 60
  practical science sense of, 27–28
  reasons as, 9, 77, 122–129, 136
  relativity of, principle, 30, 41
  superphysical, 9, 139, 140, 141, 153
Coercion, 85, 89, 91, 92, 101, 109–111,
    134, 145, 149–151, 152, 153, 156,
    160
Cognitive heuristics, 42, 131–132, 160,
    167
Conditions
  antecedents of effects, 28–30, 32
  distinguished from causes, 46–50, 51
Consensus, 52, 53, 61
Consistency, 52, 53, 61, 99, 108
Constant conjunction of cause and effect,
    18, 19, 20, 21, 22, 24, 28
Correspondent inference theory, 7, 96–
    101, 108, 111, 116, 121, 128, 132,
    138, 174
  noncommon effects in, 7, 96, 98, 99,
    117
Could have done otherwise, principle, 76,
    77, 78, 79, 81, 85, 99, 117, 146,
    159

Covariation principle, 52, 53, 60, 61, 99,
    108, 128, 168

Defensive attribution, 133, 134–136, 167,
    173
Determinism, 64, 74–78, 139, 159, 175
  biological, 75
  dilemma of, 74–75, 122
  incompatibilism view of, 75
  libertarianism view of, 77
  reconciliationism view of, 76–77
Dimensions of responsibility, 84–86, 101–
    112, 143–153, 156, 161, 166, 167,
    168, 170–172
  appreciation of moral wrongfulness, 86,
    111–112, 134, 171–172
  causal, 85, 102–106, 134, 158, 170, 171
  coercion, 85, 109–111, 134, 145, 149–
    151, 152, 153
  intentionality, 85–86, 101, 106, 107–
    109, 134
  knowledge, 85, 101, 106–107, 109, 111
Discounting principle, 54, 55, 58, 60, 61,
    103, 104, 105, 167, 171
Distinctiveness, 52, 53, 61, 128

Effects of action, 96–99, 108, 120, 122
Empiricism, 17, 18, 20, 76
Environmental force, 38–39, 88, 89, 96,
    138
Equifinality, 36–38, 99, 108, 116, 121
Errors in attribution (*see* Biases in
    attribution)
  cognitive heuristics, 42, 131–132, 160
  fundamental attribution error, 110, 117,
    167
  motivationally based, 2, 3, 9, 118, 119,
    129–136, 167, 173
Event distribution, 40–45, 59, 60, 102,
    156, 160, 161
Excuses, 66, 73, 81–83, 111, 116, 160,
    162–165, 172
Expectancy
  category-based, 97, 98, 99, 100, 101,
    107, 108
  target-based, 97, 98, 99, 100, 101, 102,
    108

violation of, as cue to intentionality, 98, 100, 101, 116

Failure, attributions for, 129–130, 132
Fault
  behavioral, 133, 134, 135, 153
  characterological, 133, 134, 135, 153
Fine-grained manner of describing
  actions, 41, 69, 123, 124
  events, 40–41, 43, 57
Foreseeability (*see* Levels of responsibility)
Freedom (*see* Perceived freedom)
Free will, 5, 13, 74, 75, 76, 77, 81, 139
Fundamental attribution error (*see* Errors in attribution)

Identity level, 44, 59
Incompatibilism, 75, 78, 109, 122, 159
Insanity defense, 112, 171, 172
Intention, 7, 9, 26, 38, 39, 41, 42, 44, 62,
  67, 68, 80, 84, 91, 92, 96, 97,
  106, 110, 115–121, 123, 128, 144,
  160, 164
  definition of, 100, 113, 120, 121–122
  inference of, 39, 42, 81, 96, 97, 98, 99,
  108–109, 116, 118, 119, 120, 121
Intentional action, 36, 37, 123, 124, 125,
  129, 131, 133, 138, 146, 174
Intentionality
  as dimension of responsibility (*see* Dimensions of responsibility)
  as level of responsibility (*see* Levels of responsibility)
INUS condition, 48, 49, 60, 61, 83, 89,
  124, 161

Justifiability (*see* Levels of responsibility)
Justifications, 82–83, 162–165, 172
Just world, need to believe in, 3, 133, 167

Knowledge
  of consequences of action, 7, 80, 85,
  97, 98, 104, 108, 111, 121, 122
  as dimension of responsibility (*see* Dimensions of responsibility

KYST, 145, 147

Legal accountability, 63, 67, 68, 69
Legal responsibility, 73, 96, 106
  distinguished from moral responsibility,
  67–70
Levels of responsibility
  association, 88, 103
  causality, 88, 158
  foreseeability, 88–89, 104, 105, 107
  intentionality, 89, 90, 91, 93, 94, 95,
  106, 117, 158
  justifiability, 89, 90, 91, 93, 94, 95,
  109, 117
Likelihood ratio, 118–119
Local causality, 36–38, 108, 116
Locus of control scales, 139
Logical positivism, 32

Mens rea, 67, 68, 96
Mental disorder, and attributions of responsibility, 93–94
Method of Concomitant Variations, 51, 56
Method of Difference, 8, 50–56, 59, 60,
  61
Minimally sufficient causal subset, 32, 33,
  56, 57, 59, 60, 83, 95, 125, 128,
  158, 160, 161, 168, 171, 173
Moral responsibility, 70, 74, 85, 160, 163
  distinguished from legal responsibility,
  67–70
Motivation (*see also* Errors in attribution)
  as compared to cognition, 130–132
  influence on attributions, 2, 9, 118, 119,
  129–136
Multidimensional scaling, 119, 144, 145,
  146, 147, 148, 149, 150, 151, 152,
  153
Multiple causes
  augmentation principle, 8, 54, 55, 56,
  58, 60, 61, 104, 105, 167
  compensatory, 54, 55, 56, 57, 60
  discounting principle, 54, 55, 58, 60,
  61, 103, 104, 105, 167, 171
  discrete, 56–58 (*see also* Minimally sufficient causal subsets)
  necessary, 47, 60, 61

Multiple causes (*cont.*)
    sufficient, 47, 54, 56, 60

Naive psychology, 6–7, 9, 16, 26, 36, 88–
        89, 125, 143, 146–149, 153
    difficulties with, 37–38
Necessity theory (*see* Causality, necessity
        theory of)
Negligence, 104, 166
Nonbasic acts (*see* Acts, nonbasic)
Noncommon effects (*see* Correspondent in-
        ference theory)

Perceived freedom, 116–117
Personal causality, 36–39, 83, 128
Personal force, 38–39, 88, 89, 96, 138
Proposition space, 14, 157, 158
Psychological context view, 12–16, 31,
        156–159

Reasons as causes, 9, 77, 122–129, 136
Reconciliationism, 76–77, 78, 85, 109,
        122, 123, 159
Regularity theory (*see* Causality, regularity
        theory of)
Responsibility
    as answerability, 71, 72, 171
    capacity, 65, 111, 112, 159, 171
    defensive attribution of, 133, 134–136,
        167, 173
    definition of, 70, 84–86, 143
    dimensions of (*see* Dimensions of
        responsibility)
    as disputed social judgment, 159–162
    distinguished from blameworthiness, 67,
        82, 146

    distinguished from causality, 63, 70–71,
        87, 91–92, 93
    levels of (*see* Levels of responsibility)
    measurement of, 84–86, 90, 146
    role, 64–65, 160
    vicarious, 71, 103, 105, 146, 162
Retributivism, 72

Schemata, 8, 50, 54–59, 60, 61, 62, 99,
        111, 168 (*see also* Multiple causes)
Strict liability, 68, 104, 146
Success, attributions for, 129–130, 132

Target-based expectancy (*see* Expectancy,
        target-based)
Themata of scientific explanation, 14, 15,
        16, 26, 31, 74, 156–159

Utilitarianism, 72, 84

Veridicality in attribution (*see* Errors in
        attribution)
Vicarious responsibility (*see* Responsibil-
        ity, vicarious)
Vienna Circle, 32, 175
Voluntary
    as characteristic of action, 25, 64, 75,
        76, 78–81, 156
    as dimension of responsibility (*see* Di-
        mensions of responsibility)

Wants, 120, 121, 122, 123, 125, 126,
        128, 129
    occurrent, 121, 123
    standing, 121, 123

Springer Series in Social Psychology

Attention and Self-Regulation: A Control-Theory Approach to Human Behavior
Charles S. Carver/Michael F. Scheier

Gender and Nonverbal Behavior
Clara Mayo/Nancy M. Henley (Editors)

Personality, Roles, and Social Behavior
William Ickes/Eric S. Knowles (Editors)

Toward Transformation in Social Knowledge
Kenneth J. Gergen

The Ethics of Social Research: Surveys and Experiments
Joan E. Sieber (Editor)

The Ethics of Social Research: Fieldwork, Regulation, and Publication
Joan E. Sieber (Editor)

Anger and Aggression: An Essay on Emotion
James R. Averill

The Social Psychology of Creativity
Teresa M. Amabile

Sports Violence
Jeffrey H. Goldstein (Editor)

Nonverbal Behavior: A Functional Perspective
Miles L. Patterson

Basic Group Processes
Paul B. Paulus (Editor)

Attitudinal Judgment
J. Richard Eiser (Editor)

Social Psychology of Aggression: From Individual Behavior to Social Interaction
Amélie Mummendey (Editor)

Directions in Soviet Social Psychology
Lloyd H. Strickland (Editor)

Sociophysiology
William M. Waid (Editor)

Compatible and Incompatible Relationships
William Ickes (Editor)

Facet Theory: Approaches to Social Research
David Canter (Editor)

Action Control: From Cognition to Behavior
Julius Kuhl/Jürgen Beckmann (Editors)

Springer Series in Social Psychology

The Social Construction of the Person
Kenneth J. Gergen/Keith E. Davis (Editors)

Entrapment in Escalating Conflicts: A Social Psychological Analysis
Joel Brockner/Jeffrey Z. Rubin

The Attribution of Blame: Causality, Responsibility, and Blameworthiness
Kelly G. Shaver

Language and Social Situations
Joseph P. Forgas (Editor)

Power, Dominance, and Nonverbal Behavior
Steve L. Ellyson/John F. Dovidio (Editors)

Changing Conceptions of Crowd Mind and Behavior
Carl F. Graumann/Serge Moscovici (Editors)